CHEKHOV
The Evolution of his Art

cds ord 2·22·85

CHEKHOV
The Evolution of his Art

DONALD RAYFIELD

PAUL ELEK : LONDON

First published 1975 in Great Britain by
Elek Books Limited
54–58 Caledonian Road London N1 9RN

ISBN 0 236 31007 0

Made and printed in Great Britain by
Clarke, Doble & Brendon Ltd
Plymouth

Contents

Author's Note

Titles of Chekhov's works in English are, wherever possible, given in the version preferred by the *Oxford Chekhov*. Transliteration from Russian follows the W. K. Matthews system—the so-called 'British system'—except where confusion might arise. All translations are my own.

D.R.

I
Introduction

Another book on Chekhov for the English-speaking reader calls for explanation. My purpose is to look at Chekhov's work as an organic structure, to attempt to show the interaction of his background, his experience of life and his ideas with the poetics of his stories and plays—their themes, imagery, construction and philosophy, and thus to show the evolution of the artist. None of the critical studies and biographies available in English has set out to do this. There is a full biography, by E. J. Simmons, in which every important fact about Chekhov's life is fairly presented and interpreted; there are a number of meticulous studies of the mature plays, which amount to workshop manuals for producers and directors; there are surveys of Chekhov's stories, which give résumés of the plots and characters, an account of their reception by Chekhov's contemporaries, and a few insights *en passant*. When it is considered that Chekhov, with his understatement and irony, appeals perhaps more directly than any other Russian writer to the English reader, and that he has had an overwhelming influence on the English short story and drama, this lack of a complete view of his work is hard to explain.

Chekhov is a very complex and, in some senses, difficult writer. He carefully purged the text of his mature stories of anything didactic and his stories and plays are very often 'pre-stories' that lead up to the moment of crisis and clarity with which a more ordinary writer would begin. His voluminous correspondence with readers and fellow-writers is full of irony, reserve and downright mystification : it cannot easily be used as a guide to a correct interpretation of his art. For the Russian reader, Chekhov presents ideological difficulties. Unlike Tolstoy or Dostoyevsky, he does not commit himself to any particular stance, he does not give moral commandments to the reader, he bequeaths no mystical enlightenment to a darkling humanity. His reticence was—and is—strange, even offensive to a Russian audience. For the English reader, apart from the strangeness of the milieu, there has been the problem, until recently, of a paucity of good translations. The appearance of the *Oxford Chekhov* largely obviates linguistic barriers, and makes the need for an adequate interpretation all the more urgent.

The first stage in interpreting Chekhov is to bridge the gaps between the various Chekhovs that are brought out in any study of a particular aspect of his work. The most striking gap is that between Chekhov the dramatist, in particular the creator of *The Seagull, Uncle Vanya, Three Sisters* and *The Cherry Orchard*, and the Chekhov of the stories written in the 1890s, before and simultaneously with the major plays. Most critics of Chekhov's plays urge a reading based on one of three quite incompatible views of the dramatist's intentions. One view sees the plays as a requiem for the degenerate gentry, a prophecy of a new age of sanity and equality shortly to dawn. Another, more fashionable and sophisticated, takes the plays to be a statement of the absurdity of the human condition, in which there is no escape, no development, no reason. Thirdly, we are enjoined to look at the drama as ultimate realism—a minute recreation of what takes place in the pathology of human experience. Yet no one of these three Chekhovs—optimist, pessimist-decadent, or scientific impressionist—can be corroborated by the stories of the time, e.g. *My Life, The House with the Mezzanine, The Bishop*.

Chekhov was not a schizophrenic. The brave, muted optimism of the 'drop-out' Poloznev in *My Life*, the dissolution of all philosophies that we find in *The House with the Mezzanine*, and the extreme lyricism, as completely committed as Rimbaud's and Wordsworth's, of *The Bishop*—all this is as essentially Chekhovian as the off-stage noises, the speculation about life in two or three hundred years' time, and the tics of the characters in the plays. Nine-tenths of the perennial arguments on how to produce Chekhov's plays would be silenced for ever if only they were read together with the stories whose characters, situations, themes and techniques they continue.

A more general discrepancy lies between the image of Chekhov the man and Chekhov the artist. To a certain extent, every writer seems to contradict with his life what he says in his work; but Chekhov's life, with his close, unbroken relationship with his sister and his brothers, his strictly controlled sexuality, his affirmation of the future by planting trees, building libraries and schools, very disconcertingly belies the despairing agnostic whom we infer, only too naturally, from much of his work.

Chekhov's life was no façade. It had the vitality that only his foreknowledge of death could give. His estate at Melikhovo and his houses at Yalta, full of bustle and visitors, may be seen as attempts to create a positive world that would outweigh the emptiness and negation expressed in so much of his prose of the 1890s. Between the energy and common sense of Chekhov as his biographers know him and the intellectual deadlock that critics see in his work lies a wide gap indeed—but it is not unbridgeable.

Another of the conflicting elements of Chekhov that cannot be accounted for by the changing outlook of a rapidly maturing and ageing writer is that between the lyrical and the comic. It is not quite enough to explain the conflict away by saying that Chekhov began with a comic approach to human quirks of behaviour and only with an increasingly close focus became lyrical rather than satirical; the comic element is always there, even in the ghastly hell of *In the Gully*, where the curate, as tradition demands, is a glutton; and in Chekhov's last play, *The Cherry Orchard*, the subtitle and everything Chekhov said about it insists on the word *comedy*.

Finally, in Chekhov the artist and the scientist do not add up to a complete whole. Chekhov was not only an able doctor of medicine; he also had a professional interest in psychiatry, social medicine, sociology, zoology, horticulture and the philosophy of science. In much of his work it is even a little too obvious that he is making use of his professional knowledge. His scientific approach, especially in the late 1880s just before his fateful journey to Sakhalin, seems to rule out much of the compassion for the weak and the nostalgia for what is lost which his artistic intuition expresses. The artist tended to oust the scientist in his make-up, but the central body of his work (roughly between 1888 and 1895) forces us to reconcile the two.

This book, then, is intended as a synthesis. There is little original research in it : all the facts we are ever likely to have for a biography of Chekhov are now to hand; most of the textual problems of his stories have been clarified. The only important unpublished part of Chekhov's archives is the bulk of the seven thousand letters written to him, but there is no reason to think that the clue to his work lies in this correspondence, rather than in a meticulous and open-minded

reading of Chekhov's texts. Chekhov's letters play a peripheral role
in this book. Of the well over four thousand which survive,
comparatively few shed real light on his creative purposes and
methods. Brilliant though he was as a correspondent, he had a
chameleon-like capacity to adapt his tone to his addressee. Letters
to importunate women, to men of the theatre, to his kith and kin,
to writers of his own generation, to his publishers all have an element of protective mimicry. His letters can suggest and confirm, but
not prove, any line of approach to his work.

Least reliable of all sources are the memoirs of his contemporaries.
Many were written some years after meetings with him; many try
to recreate him in a revolutionary mould and themselves in a more
flattering light; very few, even as close to him as his widow Ol'ga
Knipper, had a real grasp of his personality. Behind the frankness,
the honesty and friendliness was a seemingly very firmly held reserve, which will always remain inviolate.

Close examination of Chekhov's texts calls for the techniques of
poetic analysis. Many of the typical features of prose narrative are
often absent, such as intrigue and dénouement, even though there
is a great deal of action; often the distinction between hero and
narrator is blurred. Other elements dominate the structure : a recurrent, variable image, for instance of clear and contaminated water;
or a senseless, half-conscious refrain uttered by one of the characters. Chekhov's sentences, especially in his landscapes or his interior monologues, have a rhythmic and intonational power just as
important to the final effect as his handling of plot (or anti-plot).

Often as instructive as the definitive text are the deletions and
alterations Chekhov made when preparing his stories for book publication; sometimes he deleted a passage out of sheer delicacy,
unwilling to impose an authorial interpretation on his reader; sometimes his own taste had altered. No other Russian writer made such
extensive and such significant revisions of his work, thus giving us
valuable insights into his 'creative laboratory'.

Also revealing is contemporary critical reaction, often showing
us the roots of our own misreading and misunderstanding, illustrat-
ing the *Zeitgeist* around Chekhov and the demands his readers made
on him; mostly, however, his critics have told us more of their own
philosophy of life and literature than of his. For critics of Chekhov's
times and of ours a major stumbling-block has always been a formulation of Chekhov's moral philosophy. The greater the willingness

to rank him as one of the world's greatest writers, the more deplorable is found the absence or inadequacy of any moral or spiritual directive in his work. A gamut of philosophies from Diogenes' to Schopenhauer's is propounded by characters in his work; some philosophies, humanist, romantic and Christian, are those of the narrators. But it would be as naïve as it would be impossible to extract a coherent body of maxims from Chekhov's statements about human life and our planet. Even if the narrator of a mature story is unnamed and self-effacing and the words 'I', 'me' do not occur, the narrator is not Chekhov, any more than the busybody narrators of Dostoyevsky's novels are Dostoyevsky. The narrator is an extension of the most complex and sympathetic characters of a story, endowed with Chekhov's own gifts of self-expression and formulation; but he or she is not Chekhov himself, and the descriptions in the narrative are not those of an all-seeing, all-foreseeing author, but of a narrator-character who is as subject to the laws of time and space as any other character in the story.

The difficulties of relating views expressed in the stories to those of Chekhov himself emerge in this passage from *The Lady with the Little Dog*, where the hero Gurov, finding his casual affair unexpectedly all-absorbing, takes Anna up into the mountains overlooking the Black Sea at Oreanda; the narrator's thought merges into the hero's:

and so [the sea] will roar, dully, indifferently, when we are no more. And in this continual indifference to the life and death of each of us is to be found the pledge of our eternal salvation, of the uninterrupted movement of life on earth and its endless perfection. Sitting next to a young woman who seemed so beautiful in the dawn light, Gurov, softened and charmed by the fairytale scene, the sea, the mountains, the wide sky, thought how good everything on earth was, if one went into it, everything except what we ourselves think and do, when we forget the higher purposes of life and our human dignity.

From the latter half of the last sentence, three different ideas, each with overtones expressed elsewhere in Chekhov, can be distilled. One—the perfect joy of life on earth; two—nature, marred only by human consciousness and action; three—a human ideal from which man has only lapsed and to which he will return. None of these ideas is definitive; like all the thoughts of Chekhov's heroes, each is tinged and limited by the objects and sensations that give rise to it. Gurov is sexually and emotionally vulnerable; he is overcome by the setting of a beauty spot, so famous as to be banal; his thoughts are those of the moment.

Even the first half of the passage, with its romantic idea of the sea as an element opposite, indifferent and yet analogous to man does not amount to a fundamental idea to which the rest of the passage is subordinated. Chekhov's description of the sea, which in the Russian has the crashing rhythm and the 'sh', 'kh' sounds of the waves themselves, is a response to an actual sight, giving the reader the eerie feeling of an ectoplasm, half Gurov, half the author, standing, looking at and overwhelmed by the same view. The response is poetic, exciting, true—but we cannot hold the author to it in the way that we hold Tolstoy, for instance, to his moral judgements about human responsibility.

Like some modern practitioners of linguistic analysis, Chekhov is not, perhaps, interested in metaphysical statements so much as in the chance stimulus and the words which make people formulate such statements. In some stories, notably *The House with the Mezzanine* and *The Duel*, Chekhov's characters expound conflicting philosophies: the point lies not in the viability of the philosophies themselves but in the forces that prompt characters to espouse them.

Similar problems arise when we try to distinguish between heroes and villains. To a certain extent, Chekhov's categories are aesthetic, not ethic; a complex, changing, responsive character is evidently far more attractive to him than a consistent monolith, who repeats the same actions and words. His criteria may be seen as those of a pathologist. Characters who are not diseased or in turmoil tend to bore him. Suffering-insufferable replaces good-bad. Whether this amounts to a morality is a question to be set out, if not to be answered.

The handle to Chekhov that is perhaps easiest to grasp lies in the theme of conservation. Throughout his work, but especially in the plays and the late stories, he sees human suffering as wastage of resources, and evil as destruction of the environment. Through the plays runs the symbol of chopped-down forests; through the stories the symbol of rivers polluted by brickworks or bone-processors. One of the most modern aspects of Chekhov is his feeling for the smallness and fragility of the earth, and to the idea of its conservation he subjugates all the old-fashioned, anthropocentric ethical systems of the past. In the plays, this fearful feeling comes out in the speeches of characters like Doctor Astrov; in the stories it is expressed in innumerable symbols that colour an apparently straightforward realistic narrative.

Any biography of Chekhov makes quite clear two elements of his make-up, which few critical studies admit to a discussion of his art. One is his irony; the other is his deference to the strong. Chekhov's irony is not the self-satisfied amusement of an author pulling his characters along on strings through a labyrinth; it is not the cynical resignation to fate of Greek tragedy; it is not just a manner that hints at gold reserves of knowledge to back the paper currency of talk. Chekhov's irony is much more modern, much closer to Samuel Beckett than to the great tradition of the European novel. What he knows and what his characters often ignore is that 'les choses sont contre nous'. His characters' statements not only get them nowhere, they are not even possible to complete, so insistent is the absurd importunacy of sand in the speaker's boots, the compulsion to fiddle with a sleeve, the banging of an iron rail outside the house. Not only the plays but also the stories are full of extraneous noises, physical tics and silences which give an ironic impotence to the sanest of rationalisations.

Chekhov's irony is tough and brutal, part of his hard core. So is his deference to strength. In real life, this is to be seen in his long friendship with Suvorin, the Beaverbrook or Hearst of Tsarist Russia; in his enthusiasm for Darwinism in the mid-1880s; in his admiration and emulation of the lone explorer of the Far East, Przhevalsky. In his work, this love of strength is attenuated, but it is undoubtedly there in the Nietzschean von Koren of *The Duel*, in the railway engineer of *My Life*, in Lopakhin of *The Cherry Orchard*. Chekhov by no means intended us to deplore these characters.

Like Tolstoy, whom he long worshipped as a philosopher and always as a man, Chekhov had an inborn distrust of abstractions, even of abstract words such as 'kindness', 'bravery' or 'purity', and an inborn admiration for concrete, animal directness. But unlike Tolstoy, he refrained from creating abstractions and philosophies of his own to replace those he had debunked. As he said in a letter, he lacked 'mystical experience'—and this is the source both of his greatness and of our difficulty in defining it. But the sense of irony and the tubercular love of vital, even if brutal, strength give us a key to his undogmatic, unordered idea of the world. Without the authority of mystical experience, he does not weigh us down with tablets from Mount Sinai; he gives us the means rather than the goal for existence.

By 1888, when Chekhov first began to receive consistent critical attention, his technique as a storywriter, and to a lesser degree as a playwright, had achieved the concision, the 'polyphonic' structure and the objectivity of all his best work. Technically, it is possible to divide his work into three periods. The first, up to 1886, is comparatively subjective : that is, we are aware of an author-narrator controlling events and characters. Between 1887 and 1896, the narrator is usually suppressed and a chief protagonist fills the stories not only with his personality, but also with his language, his attitudes and mannerisms. In the last period the narrator reappears, to set scenes, lament, reflect and enlarge, but always dependent on the protagonists, expressing only more effectively what they sense.

The biographical divisions are similar. By 1888 Chekhov was successful enough to write largely what he wanted to write. From this moment a series of traumas—the death of his brother Nikolay, the attacks from socially 'committed' critics, the terrible journey of 1890 across Siberia, the curious love-affair with Lika Mizinova—naturally opens up a number of tragic possibilities, realised through the major protagonists of his work. From 1893 to the writing of *The Seagull* in 1895 was a period of despondency in life and of determined experimentation in prose. It might be argued that the narrative technique of Chekhov's last stories mirrors his acceptance of fate and his scrupulous use of every remaining minute of time.

A unity of thematic resources and treatment, however, underlies Chekhov's evolution. For all the great variety of characters and settings, certain types and certain places recur throughout his work. The most noticeable character—participating or commenting—is an introverted doctor, whom Chekhov takes over from the traditional nineteenth-century portrayal of wisdom and sceptical foresight, and develops into a figure which is now an intermediary in the struggle of strong and weak, now the embodiment of man's struggle to find meaning in the cosmos. Less frequent, but also recurrent, is the schoolteacher, who demonstrates the corrupting force of decrepit institutions on a mind full of vapid idealism. The professor and the artist are likewise characte.. that exist outside any one story, and are incarnated at certain moments. The querulous, senile Professor Serebryakov of *Uncle Vanya* is only a degenerate form of the rough-hewn Faustian malcontent, the professor of *A*

Dreary Story: their frail but ruthless dependence on others, even their fear of thunderstorms, identify them.

The ecclesiastic characters form an even stronger chain; from the unintellectual father Kristofor of *Steppe* to the naïve theology student of *The Student* to *The Bishop* stretches an unbroken thread; all are men with an aura of enchantment, who can encompass sorrow and who exemplify a lost human innocence.

It is the women in Chekhov's work, however, who give it the greatest consistency. Although Chekhov enjoyed the company of women on all sorts of bases and although he was unencumbered by any bitterness or fears, he characterises them in a far more schematic way than men. Quite early in his work a division of women into two types is apparent: one strong, self-deluding and often repellent—such as Ariadna in the story of that name; the other more admirable and less predatory, passive and attractive. The division is very sharp in the two sisters of *The House with the Mezzanine*, or between Natasha and the 'three sisters', but it begins as early as the mid-1880s. On the few occasions that Chekhov's characterisations risk being caricatures, we find they are always of women. Not only occasional fits of misogyny but also the difficulty of showing total empathy with the other sex made Chekhov cast rather than forge women characters.

Chekhov's settings obviously reflect his own environment. All can be traced to places he knew well. But behind the variety of Moscow, country cottage, provincial town, country estate settings there lies a single purpose. Nearly all Chekhov's characters live in closed boxes, from which escape is not easy. They meet and conflict because they are unable to get away from each other, not because they want to discuss questions of life and death. The air of the closed box gives the plays their utterly convincing collisions of characters and their claustrophobia; but the stories use the same device to provoke clashes, for which other writers would use more elaborate settings.

The more mature the work, the more closely are both landscape and interior monologue rendered through the psychology of the characters. But many of Chekhov's techniques are established in early work. His landscapes, which aroused the admiration of his friend (and enemy) the painter Levitan, have a painter's quality, in that they are seen, not described. We feel an actual human retina and inner ear taking in sights and sounds, and the brain—at first of the author, then of the character—letting loose its irrational and imaginative responses. The prism of the senses in Chekhov's descriptions bends the perspectives and the priorities which conventional descriptions observe, giving his work a certain affinity with Impressionist painting. Furthermore, Chekhov presents nature description in terms of the psychology of the hero; though this sometimes gives his work a curious, outmoded Romantic quality of pathetic fallacy, his description of evening light, sea, storms lies at the heart of his world-outlook, in which human reflections and actions are only an ephemeral interruption of nature's continuum.

Whilst Chekhov's diagnosis of the human condition and his involvement with his narrative undergo development, the eye and the ear were his from the start. From early in his career he was a highly original prose-writer, and his qualities remained consistent. The condensation of whole scenes into one symbolic detail, the pregnant silences were learnt when he first started writing to the stringent requirements of the weekly humorous magazines, and he never lost his preference for primary impression over discourse.

Only in one aspect do Chekhov's eyes and ears seem to have failed him. He made several journeys, including his last anywhere, to Europe, and they leave only a surface mark in his work. A negative reaction would have made sense. Both Dostoyevsky and Tolstoy made an image of hell out of Western Europe. But Chekhov's values and prejudices as they appear in his letters to his brothers and to friends, such as Suvorin, are European to the core. They express an open fondness for the superficialities of European culture : polite formality, table manners, tolerance, empiricism, respect for science, moderation in all things, constitutionalism; they express a horror of 'Asiaticness' in all its forms, from the absence of lavatories to brutal officialdom, blind obedience and resistance to progress. Chekhov seems, at least in his terminology, as ardent a Westerner as Turgenev.

Chekhov's Europeanism was not a sham, nor only gratitude for his own progress from the status of a serf's grandson to that of a free man in command of his own destiny. For most Russians of his time, Europeanness meant, for better or for worse, having an *ad hoc*, easy-going but not strongly principled approach to life's problems. In this sense Chekhov was a European. On the other hand, the long division of Russian thinkers into Slavophiles, who believed Russia's future lay in its Christian and Imperial spirit and state, and

Westerners, who looked to Europe for institutions and ideas to compensate Russia for missing the Renaissance, had now virtually disappeared. In the 1880s and early 1890s Russia, though in many ways a cultural backwater, was politically, economically and philosophically very much part of Europe. International finance, the Franco-Russian alliance, the growth of heavy industry, the emergence of political parties all made the old arguments out of date. To be European was only common sense. Chekhov, when writing *Steppe*, wrote quite confidently that there would be no revolution in Russia. He died before the Russo-Japanese war had altered the political outlook, and he had no reason to doubt that Russia would go on acquiring the attributes and perquisites of a European polity.

Chekhov was handicapped and embarrassed in his Europeanism by his ignorance of foreign languages. He had a good grounding in German, but his French was never adequate to reading Maupassant or Zola in the original. Like Pushkin (with whom his art and personality have much in common), he was not an able linguist. Even his botanical and pharmaceutical Latin was faulty. On his journeys to France, Germany and Italy, his inability to make proper conversation isolated him effectively from any real involvement in the controversies and literary life of these countries. Apart from his passionate stand with Zola over the Dreyfus affair, he showed no more reaction than the average tourist. But the role played by European values and literature in his work is, on the other hand, not to be underestimated.

Chekhov's Europeanism is most apparent in his open-minded attitude to sex. He undoubtedly had a fastidious, even puritanical streak in his make-up : it shows in the earlier stories such as *Volodya*, or *An Attack* (of nerves), where the adolescent hero is violently disgusted by casual sexuality. He also went through periods of misogyny, which colours works such as *The Grasshopper*, *Ariadna* or *The Order of St Anne*. But a determined tolerance grows stronger and stronger, especially in the 1890s as he shakes off the hypnosis of Tolstoy, for whom woman was so often only a hindrance on the path to salvation.

For Chekhov as for other writers sexual love is the most important form of human involvement. Unlike Dostoyevsky and Tolstoy, he saw no need to incorporate the erotic into a scale of things in which Platonic love reigns supreme. In many of his later stories— *Ionych* or *The Lady with the Little Dog*—and in the plays, falling in love and acting on it amount to a brave self-fulfilment. Despite all the squalor of 'affairs'—hotel rooms and strewn underwear, which Chekhov found so distasteful, the commitment of one human being to another is one of the few ways in which the Chekhovian character can break out of his isolation and get round the uselessness of words for communication.

Chekhov came to accept without revulsion the animal in man, as had new trends in psychology, in which he was so interested. Here is one of the reasons for his modernity, for the appeal that his individualism still makes to us. His morality has an existentialist provisionality about it. He clearly believed human life to be an anomaly in a dead cosmos; his concept of man has no angelic pattern to live up to. Chekhov admires the human being who can make the most of his latencies, and this admiration explains his sympathy for self-made tycoons such as Suvorin, lone wolves like the explorer Przhevalsky, and naïve autodidacts like the young Gor'ky. In a meaningless world, each man overcomes the absurdity of the cosmos by expanding himself into a whole world. The innumerable remarks made by Chekhov and his characters about the oblivion which will swallow them up as soon as they die make all the clearer his ideal of living in the present, unchecked by habits of the past or fears of the future. The evil and depression that beset so much of his work can be equated with the dead weight of the past and the horror of the future. The desire to make the most of the present is not just a European hedonism; it is part of Chekhov's love of sense-impressions and dislike of ratiocination. It applies to the individual at a moment when a failure to act must imprison his life in the mould of his past, and it applies to humanity when failure to act must waste the beauty of the living earth.

2

The Moscow Weeklies

Given his modest origins, his difficult boyhood, and his intended career in medicine, Chekhov's metamorphosis into a writer seems a quirk of fate. But his inherited qualities and his early environment were not, in fact, a hindrance to his later development.

First of all, he was only two generations away from serfdom. We can see in the Chekhovs the *élan vital* which transformed them from serfs to gentry, echoed by Chekhov's own interest in the heroic and the outsider—whether Livingstone or Lopakhin—crashing through the social structure of his time. The relentless passion for work, the touches of Puritan ethic, above all, the knowledge that he was not born a *dvoryanin* (gentleman), helped Chekhov to develop to some extent outside the traditions of *dvoryanin* literature. The humiliations (for instance the difficulty he had in getting a passport as late as 1893[1]) were as stimulating as the advantages of being a low-born provincial.

Secondly, Chekhov's parents, so far as we can judge from their children's comments, both tended to melancholy and depression. They had good reason, for most of their life was spent in poverty, anxiety, bankruptcy and flight. The tyrannical, solitary pompousness of his father Pavel Ivanovich, and the whining temperament and helpless subjugation of his mother, Yevgeniya Yakovlevna, were inseparable from the remarkable genetic inheritance they left.

All five of their children were exceptional. Chekhov's elder brothers, Aleksandr (born 1855) and Nikolay (born 1858), appeared at an early age even more promising than Anton. Aleksandr was a remarkably versatile writer, albeit a hack, and a polyglot; Nikolay's early drawings and the few paintings he completed show a power and originality greater than anything Anton revealed in his first years. But Aleksandr and Nikolay were wrecked by their childhood. Both broke with their father, became alcoholics, and were entangled in common-law marriages which alienated them from their family and isolated them from the outside world. Aleksandr veered from satirical spleen to tearful sentimentality, while Nikolay sank into unbelievable idleness, to which drink, drugs and tuberculosis finally put an end when he was thirty-one. Both brothers played crucial parts in Anton Chekhov's development: they were antagonists, collocutors, patients and, above all, dreadful warnings of what talent, ungoverned by will-power, could degenerate into. Chekhov had to win moral primacy over them; even though Aleksandr, who was to live till 1912, recovered sufficiently to write a book on alcoholism in 1897, he very early lost his role of elder brother to Anton, who exercised it with the ruthlessness, almost, of his father. The younger brothers, Ivan (born 1861, a year after Anton) and Mikhail (born 1865), became respectively an eminent pedagogue and a successful civil servant and short-story writer, but their outlook on life, their principles, and even Mikhail's stories[2] were wholly subservient to Anton's. Chekhov's sister Maria devoted her entire free time to him (including more than forty years after his death), protecting his privacy and providing the conditions needed for his work.

All the Chekhov children were as articulate as their parents were dour; all showed the talent for music or drawing that their father seems to have expressed in his love of church and secular music and ritual, but only Anton had the luck to be born late enough to escape the traumas that crippled the elder brothers, and early enough to escape the sheltered Moscow life that led the younger ones into more conventional careers.

The date of Anton Chekhov's birth, 1860, is important in that it ensured his isolation. The 1860s were nothing like so culturally fertile as the 1820s or 1880s; there was almost no movement or pleiad in which Chekhov could have grown up or competed. He was crippled by his awareness that he was born in an interregnum, between the age of Turgenev, Tolstoy and Dostoyevsky and that of greatness still to come.

The place of his birth is even more significant. Taganrog, a port on the Sea of Azov, was not, in the 1870s, the provincial backwater that it might appear. When Chekhov revisited it in 1887, then a successful figure, Taganrog had decayed; his letters are full of wry deprecation of its squalor. But in his boyhood, it was in its heyday. It was not in fact a provincial town—with all the sleepy, spineless vacuity characteristic of the Russian provinces—so much as a colonial town. An entrepôt for the wheat trade, it had a brash, rich colonial class of Greeks and Italians, and its Russian inhabitants were economically, if not politically, colonials, with all the vibrancy, the resentments and tensions of the colonised. It had a good *gimnaziya* (grammar school) which left its mark on Chekhov for life, and it had theatres.

With Chekhov, like Shakespeare, the wonder is he knew so much. Certainly, he always apologised for his ignorance, and he portrayed schools as soulless totalitarian institutions, staffed by drudges and zombies. But Chekhov and many others of his year at the Taganrog *gimnaziya* made successful careers as lawyers and doctors. Chekhov left school, admittedly, with no knowledge of French, but with enough Latin to provide him with endless tags for his early stories, a command of German sufficient to read technical literature and Gerhart Hauptmann's plays (and, in the end, to speak his dying words), as well as a conventional knowledge of the classics of nineteenth-century Russian literature. Latin tags and repeated quotations from Pushkin might suggest that he and his fellow-pupils were taught like parrots, but Chekhov left Taganrog academically equipped as much for literature as for medicine.

Just as the theme of the school in Chekhov's stories can be traced back to his unpleasant experience in Taganrog, so his involvement, half love-affair, half feud, with the theatre dates from his boyhood there. While he was at school no fewer than 342 different titles appeared in the repertoire of the theatre in Taganrog.[3] Much of this was farce, but apart from trivia and the limited number of Russian classic plays, Chekhov must have encountered Shakespeare's tragedies and a whole range of European drama from Sheridan's *School for Scandal* to Victor Hugo's *Angelo*. With its wealthy Italian merchants, Taganrog was also a centre for Italian opera, and by all accounts, Chekhov was an enthusiastic theatregoer. The influence that this repertoire had on him was not less important for being negative. He reacted in his first letters and parodies against the spectacular histrionics of Hugo's drama or Italian opera; he had to gain an expert familiarity with the technique of farce before he could himself use it in a new way in his own comedies. Only Shakespeare's plays, and especially *Hamlet*, influenced him as directly as they influenced most Russian writers : the quotations and situations of *The Seagull* are only the culmination of a hundred references to *Hamlet*.

More important than the repertoire of Taganrog's theatres were the personalities and techniques. Chekhov was at once struck by the disparity between the pretensions of drama and the myopic outlook of the repertory actors and theatre management of the day. The financial disasters, the conceit and the waywardness of theatre people are among the most frequent topics of his early stories; they constitute the *idée fixe* behind his own drama, which was to undermine the authority of the actors by reasserting the dominance of author and director.

School and theatre were not the only Taganrog experiences to shape Chekhov's later work. Perhaps the most positive effect came from his experience as a chorister. He and his brothers were forced by their father to devote any spare time not only to helping in the failing family shop, but also to singing in church. Onerous though this duty was, it gave Chekhov a lifelong love for the clergy, the language and the ritual of the church. Early works such as *The Choristers* of February 1884 or a very late work such as the masterpiece *The Bishop* bring out the musicality and the wholeness of religious life which for the agnostic Chekhov was as beautiful and uncontaminated as nature.[4]

Taganrog's geography is the geography of many of Chekhov's fictional towns. The passage from the town centre to the countryside through the awful ring of buildings formed by the prison, the bone-factory and the cemetery is reiterated in his prose with symbolic connotations, and his poetry of escape into the country dates back to his journeys on foot to visit his country cousins. Taganrog was a port too, and without it there might never have been the seascapes and the sea-sounds that permeate so much of Chekhov's work : the sea symbolises eternity in *The Duel*, the peace of death in *Gusev*, forces of temptation in *The Lady with the Little Dog*. The echoes of Jack London in Chekhov, and the love of exploration, surely spring from a childhood spent in a sea-port.

Much of Chekhov's boyhood must have been miserable : enslavement to school, shop and church was one factor, sickness another. His love of life is characteristic of a man of fragile health. Nervous twitching while trying to sleep, chronic colitis and piles after childhood peritonitis were the prelude to a life spent fighting tuberculosis and depression. Added to this was the terrible anxiety of the family's last two years in Taganrog, before his parents fled to Moscow in 1876. His father's bankruptcy, the sale of the family house to a friend who got it by a trick and who for three years let Anton stay on as a lodger, a schoolboy paying his way by tutoring—this dismal financial story brought out in Chekhov a formidable toughness which is the foundation of his morality. All his life he fought, politely, even unconsciously, to preserve his independence and never to rely on another human being. He developed a reserve and a cold, hard centre which his elder brothers lacked and which carried him undamaged through many desolate periods.

As late as 1891 Chekhov still thought of medicine as his legitimate 'wife' and literature as a domineering mistress. The choice of medicine was simply the sensible choice of a Russian who was not a *dvoryanin* and who wanted a secure profession. The openings for Chekhov and his fellow-students were in medicine or law; and medicine in Russia was only just beginning to accept Russians as well as Germans, while the law had been possible as a career only since Alexander II had introduced the new European legal system in the 1860s. Chekhov had arranged to go to Zurich to study medicine, but because of his duty to help support his family, in 1879 he registered as a medical student in Moscow University, on a stipendium of twenty-five rubles a month from Taganrog.

Up to this point, his interest in literature had been limited to what the school syllabus and his brother Aleksandr had brought to his attention. Apart from *Hamlet, Don Quixote* and Turgenev (who was for Chekhov the ultimate 'good writer'), his tastes were for scientific reading. The geographer Humboldt's *Cosmos* which he read in 1876, or Goncharov's travelogue *The Frigate Pallada*, are the reading-matter of a future medical practitioner, rather than that of an artist.

Chekhov's early writing was not literature. At Aleksandr's suggestion he became a contributor to the Moscow weekly humorous magazines for five kopecks a line. The author of these pieces had to adapt his work to his market: he had to be concise for the editor, conventional for the censor, and light for the reader. There was no room for experimentation, ideas or self-expression: it was a disciplined school of writing that would have destroyed most writers, but Chekhov's sixty-odd contributions made between 1880 and 1882 show remarkable anticipations of his later literary work.

The journals for which he wrote up to and including 1883 were *Strekoza* (*Dragonfly*), *Budil'nik* (*Alarm-clock*), *Zritel'* (*Spectator*), *Moskva* (*Moscow*) (a daily paper), *Svet i Teni* (*Chiaroscuro*) and

Mirskoy Tolk (Talk of the World). As their titles suggest, they were
modelled on French and English humorous and political periodicals,
and aimed at the new generation of literates, the product of almost
universal urban primary education. But they could not match their
models: their audience was too unsophisticated and their censorship too severe. They were more like English periodicals such as
Reveille, Titbits or *Popular Science Siftings*. They were rigorously
topical, and the opening of a theatre or the hunting season, main
holidays, anniversaries, train crashes, visiting personalities all had to
appear in stories at the appropriate time. Slight but definite erotic
piquancy and satire aimed at the lower echelons of the official and
commercial hierarchies were essential, and although many of the
editors—notably Pushkarev, who edited *Svet i Teni* and *Mirskoy
Tolk*—would have liked to educate their readers and encouraged
the mention of European novelists and European politics, their
papers were financially so vulnerable that to risk alienating both
readers and censors was out of the question.

Chekhov, however, at once came to terms with the censors. If
his work at this time is almost cynically apolitical, it is not because
of indifference, but because of common sense. There is unpublished
material to show that he was as radical as anyone has a right to expect, but when writing for five kopecks a line, you do not risk being
unpublishable. Tsarist censorship was stricter in Moscow (as a
provincial city) than in Petersburg, and stricter on publications
aimed at the mass market than on those meant for the intelligentsia.
Every item in the Moscow weeklies was subject to precensorship,
and careless editing could result in a missed issue or a banned magazine. But the system was not inflexible. There was a committee of
appeal, some argument was allowed, and the author could always
copy out a banned piece, retitle it, and send it to another magazine :
Chekhov's casualness about titles may well be due to his retitling
of censored works for resubmission. But in many ways, the literary
field of the early 1880s was degenerate. *Budil'nik* had in the 1870s
been a bright political satirical Petersburg weekly, but especially
after the assassination of Alexander II in 1881, the lively discussion
of the 1860s and 1870s became impossible.

In 1880 Chekhov published about a dozen pieces in *Strekoza*.
Only retrospect makes them interesting, and perhaps the most telling
pieces are the parodies. A gift for mimicry and parody on a
Gogolian scale was one of the earliest signs of Chekhov's literary

genius and it tells us what attracted him and what he rejected. Parody is also important in his late work, whether it is the parody of stoic philosophy in *Ward No. 6*, or of symbolism in Konstantin's playlet in *The Seagull*, or of revolutionary youth in *The Cherry Orchard*. The parodies are curiously ambivalent; they begin by mocking but linger just long enough to show fascination, and those of 1880 point the way for Chekhov's reworking of the clichés at which he laughs.

Take for instance 'What do we find most often in novels, tales, etc. ?'

A count, a countess with traces of former beauty, a neighbouring baron, a liberal writer, an impoverished gentleman, a foreign musician, dim servants, nurses, governesses, a German manager, an esquire with an American inheritance. Ugly but nice, attractive characters. A hero saving the heorine from a mad horse, strong in spirit and able at any suitable moment to show the power of his fists.

The heavenly heights, the unfathomable distance . . . incomprehensible, in a word : nature ! ! ! . . .

A doctor with a worried face, giving hopes for a crisis : often has a stick with carved handle and a bald patch. If you have a doctor, you have rheumatism from just labours, migraine, brain inflammation, looking after a wounded man at a duel and the inevitable advice to take the waters.

A servant who has served the old masters, ready to go to hell and back for his masters. A remarkable wit.

A dog that does all but talk, a parrot and a nightingale.

A country house near Moscow and a mortgaged estate in the south. Electricity mostly quite out of place.

A morocco leather briefcase, Chinese porcelain, an English saddle, a revolver that never misfires, an order of merit in the buttonhole, pineapples, champagne, truffles and oysters.

Unsuspected overhearing as the cause of great discoveries.

A countless number of interjections and attempts to throw in a technical term.

Subtle hints at rather crude circumstances.

Very often the absence of an end.

Seven deadly sins in the beginning and marriage at the end.

The end.

This is a clever formula for the boulevard novel so popular in Russia and France at the time, but some of the ingredients are strikingly like those the mature Chekhov : the dog and electricity

of *Ionych*, the importance of the doctor-arbiter, the characters of
the later plays, the old servant Firs, the worship of nature, the
mortgaged estate in the south, the revolver, the technical terms.
There is more than irony here. Chekhov tended to parody as a
means of self-defence, to stop himself being involved, yet it is only
the mechanisation of the boulevard novel which he is attacking:
many of its elements are to be as fundamental to his work as they
were to the imitators of Turgenev and Paul Bourget.

Another kind of parody is more direct. *Tysyacha odna strast'* (*A
Thousand and One Passions*) is a condensation of an imaginary
Victor Hugo novel so violent as to collapse the romantic novel into
a surrealist joke. Hugo was several times subjected to Chekhov's
mockery; when he attempted the same tricks with Jules Verne, the
editor rejected the skit. Chekhov seldom wrote of important people
or world-shattering events: he always associated the heroic genre
with the egocentric author, and the heroic gesture with the idiotic,
and his Hugo novel-in-miniature has as its climax: 'A powerful
man, hurling his enemy down the crater of a volcano because of a
beautiful woman's eyes, is a magnificent, grandiose and edifying
picture! All it needed was lava!' Chekhov learnt to avoid 'magnificent, grandiose and edifying pictures'.

Strekoza was slow in paying and obtusely insulting in its comments on Chekhov's work. He did not appear in print again until
summer 1881; the dozen pieces of 1881 nearly appeared in *Zritel'*,
which was in fact edited by the three senior Chekhov brothers. It
had a short and interrupted life, but, illustrated by Nikolay, managed by Aleksandr, and fed material by Anton, it was at least
congenial. By now, Chekhov had settled on a pseudonym to which
he was to cling: Antosha Chekhonte, a name whose Greek sound
must have taken him back to his schooldays in the chaotic and
corrupt Greek primary school at Taganrog.

Much of the humour in the work of 1881 is immature; Chekhov
gives to his characters the names of relatives and schoolfriends. Some
of the pieces are only miscellanies of jokes, but in them are the
seeds of more substantial Chekhovian situations. There is an in-
formal trial by a gendarme whose brutal accusations have the obsessive quality of the later *NCO Prishibeyev*; the vaudeville jokes about
the bridegroom cheated of his dowry are later to become full-blown
dramas. *Temperamenty* (*Temperaments*), a sketch of the traditional
temperaments (sanguine, choleric, etc.), does in fact set out a

synopsis of later Chekhovian types, even though the medieval classi-
fication by humours was to be replaced by such modern terms as
'psychopath' and 'neurasthenic'.

The most important of these pieces are the reviews of the great
French actress Sarah Bernhardt, who played in Moscow at the
opening of the 1881–2 season. Chekhov shows an original reaction
to her acting, admiring its virtuosity but deploring its stylisation and
artificiality. Here is something of the low-class journalist determined
not to be impressed, but also something of the future dramatist who
is to change the theatre as Russia knew it. Comments, whether
critical : 'Her tears, her dying convulsions, all her acting is nothing
but an irreproachably and cleverly learnt lesson', or speculative :
'There is not a trifle in her parts, big or little, which hasn't gone
a hundred times through the purgatory of labour . . . If we were as
industrious as she is, what would we not write . . .'—all anticipate
the ideas of Stanislavsky. Chekhov's involvement with the Moscow
theatre had already begun : he was a theatregoer and critic, and he
had already met such figures of the theatrical future as Vladimir
Nemirovich-Danchenko; he may well have begun his first play
(which we now know as *Platonov*).

In 1882, writing gave him more than a casual supplementary
income. Nearly forty items were published and his stipendium must
have been doubled. His three most substantial works are attempts
at novels compressed into extended short stories. They did not
help Chekhov's reputation as a reliable, pithy and entertaining hack;
they are not even interesting in the way that he intended them to
be, but they do foreshadow his mature technique of reducing a
novel's material to a handful of crucial episodes, and they already
show the moral ambivalence—half-puritanical, half-permissive—of
his attitude towards dissipation, moral or otherwise. Their weaknesses were never fully overcome, but Chekhov learnt later not to
fill his stories and plays with aristocrats, Petersburg *beau monde*,
foreigners and other characters of whom he had no direct experience.

The first story is *Barynya* (*The Lady*), a melodrama about a
separated woman of the Balzacian age who takes her reluctant groom
for a lover. The groom's peasant family encourage the affair, and
the story ends when the groom kills his unfortunate wife and leaves
the 'lady' to fall back on her Polish manager as a lover. The stereo-
typed villainous Pole,[5] the dramatic crisis of the murder, the wise

Balzacian asides of an author aghast at the wickedness of his characters are embarrassingly naïve.

The same cat-like, thoughtlessly cruel female appears as the chief character of *Zhivoy tovar* (*Livestock*), but here a healthy streak of cynicism makes the story's improbability forgivable and its moral acceptable. Liza, the heroine, is caught by her husband, Bugrov, with her rich lover Grokhol'sky.[6] Grokhol'sky, to atone for his guilt, buys her from her husband for half his possessions. The husband with his new-found wealth sets up house next to Grokhol'sky and Liza, and he now appears more interesting and attractive to her. The story ends with a gruesome *ménage à trois*; the husband has been given Grokhol'sky's country estate on which he keeps a now fat, seal-like (not cat-like) Liza, and on which Grokhol'sky has become an unpaid servant. Superficial though the story is, with its perfunctory descriptions of nature and its omniscient narrator shaking his head at the end, it establishes in Chekhov's work the opposition of predatory female and immobilised male prey which is typical of his mature work.

The third story is *Tsvety zapozdalyye* (*Tardy Flowers*). The 'flowers' are two scions of the aristocracy in decline. Yegorushka is stupid and drinks, while his sister Marusya falls helplessly in love and dies of tuberculosis. The most important character, however, is Doctor Toporkov. Once a serf of the princely family he now treats, he has become a society doctor, who prescribes for Yegorushka's liver and Marusya's chest; Marusya falls in love with him, but, interested only in a dowry, he marries a plebeian merchant's daughter. Marusya, in a scene of unbearable staginess, declares her love, softens Toporkov's heart so that he takes her away to die in the South of France and, on his return, adopts Yegorushka to remind him of Marusya's profile. So much for the 'tardy flowers'. Chekhov was never at ease with aristocratic characters or great passions, but the story is the first of many to have a doctor as its hero (or anti-hero), a dour foil to his irresponsible patients, a man of bitter experience among people with none. Inevitably, the reader will see autobiographical traits in these doctors, and to a certain extent he will be right. They are often outsiders, provincials, if not always latter-day saints. Moreover, *Tardy Flowers* sets the pattern of stories such as *Ionych* (written some seventeen years later) in which the instinct for money and survival gradually kills the human responses in the struggling young doctor; Ionych makes the same mistake of ignoring love until it is too late. The difference between *Tardy Flowers* and *Ionych* is chiefly that between the work of a hack and that of a genius.

These imperfect works are rare examples in early Chekhov of freely chosen theme and style. Most of the work of 1882, and of the next four years, had to conform more closely to the policies of editors who liked to recognise the genre of a story easily. Parody was much liked; from fashionable authors, *Strekoza* and *Budil'nik* preferred pastiche. There is a faint liberalism in the parodies of *Novoye Vremya*, the conservative Petersburg newspaper to which Chekhov was later to owe so much, and a distinct philistinism in the parodies of romantic or philosophical prose. But adventure stories, such as those of Jules Verne or the Hungarian, Jokai, were taken more seriously, and such imitations as Chekhov's eighty-page *Nenuzhnaya pobeda* (*Unnecessary Victory*) of 1882 were written more in tribute than in mockery.

Some significance can be found in many of the 'local colour' pieces, all sketch and no plot, of 1882. They are pictures of market day, the opening of the hunting season, portraits of village medical assistants, provincial theatrical people. They are preparatory studies for later work, but the bulk of the work of 1882 is in itself worthless : farces, vaudeville sketches, sentimental tales, civil service jokes mine an almost exhausted literary seam. These pieces attracted the notice of the editor Leykin, and led to several years' regular work for the Petersburg *Oskolki* (*Fragments*), but they did little to advance Chekhov's talent, and when he was compiling his collected works at the turn of the century, he did not include any of the pieces written before 1883. Nor did any appear in his first successful collection, *Pyostryye rasskazy* (*Motley Stories*) of 1886, although six stories about the theatre had been reprinted in 1884 under the title *Melpomene's Fairytales*. The provincial theatre was almost the only theme favoured by both Chekhov and his editors; the farces and sketches of the sad world of acting, slight in themselves, are thematically closer to the mature Chekhov than anything else in the early 1880s. The disparity between the theatrical calling and the degradation of the called is to haunt Chekhov whenever he touches on it, in *A Dreary Story* or *The Seagull* no less than in these early works. Theatrical circles were his first source of live human material; his fellow-journalists, hacks and aspiring writers, his brother Nikolay,

his first friends such as Levitan, were *habitués* of the Moscow
theatres, and Chekhov's attitudes to writing, to art, to women, to
the public, to European drama, all have the bitter-sweet, disillusioned
intoxication of his first backstage contacts.

3
From Fragments to a Novel

In some accounts of Chekhov's career, Nikolay Aleksandrovich Leykin enters like a fairy godmother, buying some two hundred and
seventy stories and articles at eight kopecks a line, giving security,
an opening into Petersburg literary circles, guidance and friendship.
Leykin was himself a highly productive and facile writer and he was
both jealous and condescending towards Chekhov : his role was not
entirely that of a benefactor. He substantially delayed Chekhov's
entry into serious literature and he instilled in him a sense of
mediocrity and obligation that he could never wholly lose. The Grub
Street mentality of Leykin was poisonous : one of Chekhov's sketches
of 1884, *Marya Ivanovna*, shows it. It is a ludicrous self-parody. A
man makes a declaration of love to a fine lady, gets no reply, takes
off his boots and lies down. The lady turns out to be a picture. The
narrative is vestigial; most of the sketch shows an imaginary reader
complaining at the rubbish printed, while the author justifies himself. The justifications read like a *cri de coeur* :

None of us professional writers are dilettanti, we're all genuine literary
journeymen . . . all people like you . . . we have the same nerves, the
same guts . . . we have many more griefs than joys . . . But if we
were to obey your command 'don't write', if we gave in to boredom,
tiredness or fever, you might as well close down all current literature
. . . If rubbish like *Marya Ivanovna* gets printed, then evidently it's
because there is no better material . . . Sit down then, set out your
profound, resplendent thoughts and send them to some editor . . .
You'll get them back again.

Despite the sheer drudgery of frequently writing two pieces a
week and of conforming to the *Oskolki* style, Chekhov produced
about a dozen artistically satisfying pieces that were printed by Leykin in 1883 and 1884, years in which he virtually owned Chekhov.
Some of these pieces are well known, for Chekhov revised and re-

printed a few in his Collected Works (1899–1901), such as *Daughter of Albion* or *Fat Man and Thin Man*. But before we examine the work which he himself wished to retrieve from obscurity, it is worth looking at three pieces which were rejected for publication.

First, a political matter. Chekhov's apolitical stance is often deplored. It is remarkable that a student of Moscow University in the dark repressive period following the assassination of Alexander II in 1881 should not have made any protest, joined any movement, or spent any sleepless nights, when fellow-students were being hanged, jailed or deported, but Chekhov was supicious of any 'party line', any radical gestures; he hated the conformism of the non-conformist, and he had the common sense to appreciate that protest is futile. However, a satirical 'fairytale' (*skazka*)[1] of 1884, *Govorit' ili molchat'* (*To Talk or not to Talk*) shows a radical cynicism. Two friends are travelling by train; one is successful with women, the other not. The first tells the second that the secret of his success is that he keeps talking. The second follows his advice and talks to a stranger who sits down next to him and turns out to be a plain-clothes policeman. The second traveller disappears for two years. The 'fairytale' was rejected by the censor, who would allow criticism of uniformed police but not of security police, and Chekhov never again wasted his time on unpublishable satire.

Secondly, a full-blooded lyrical sketch of country life that anticipates the *trompe-l'oeil* imagery and passion for nature of *Steppe*. The piece *On ponyal* (*He Understood*) was too long for Leykin's *Oskolki*, and so Chekhov sent it in July 1883 to *Strekoza*, which rejected it with the comment 'almost devoid of humour and its simple plot does not correspond to its considerable length'. The plot is indeed simple: a poor peasant is caught poaching and taken to the office of the landowner, who is bewitched by the peasant's passion for hunting and lets him go. Apart from the cliché of a villainous Pole who is the estate manager, everything in the sketch is fresh and vivid. The sensation of sultry heat before a storm—so typical of the first acts of Chekhov's plays—the hunter's predatory alertness, the intimate knowledge of every tree and bird in the woods, the inarticulate confrontation of peasant and landowner, the final liberation of the peasant and of a wasp trapped in the same room, the self-effacement of the narrator—all make the sketch the most substantial and mature of Chekhov's hundred and more pieces of 1883. He finally placed it with *Priroda i Okhota* (*Nature and Field*

Sports), which paid him with a year's free subscription. It was one of the few pieces signed with Chekhov's real name.

The third rejection is a parody of Jules Verne, of his crude action-plots, the poor translations into Russian and the Anglomania and monumental vulgarity of his ideas. Leykin wrote to say that *Letuchiye ostrova* (*Flying Islands*) was too long; he rejected it instead of shortening it, and suggested that Chekhov should use his talents for parodies of Russian authors, Leskov among others. It is typical of Leykin to prefer a parody of a great writer, Leskov— Russia's Trollope and Thomas Hardy in one—to a parody of one of the three French writers most popular among his readers—Jules Verne, Emile Zola, and Gaboriau, but science fiction, sociological revelations and detective stories were sacred, and Leykin got what he wanted. In 1883 he printed some seventy pieces by Chekhov; usually the longer item each week was signed 'Antosha Chekhonte', and any smaller items 'The Man without a Spleen'. In 1884, when Chekhov was taking his final examinations in medicine, Leykin had some fifty items from him. In addition, from summer 1883 until autumn 1885, Chekhov was saddled with a weekly satirical diary, *Fragments of Moscow Life*, which was to reassure *Oskolki*'s Petersburg readers that Moscow was every bit as backward and scandalous as they thought. The fiction, however, had to follow the course of the seasons. Ghosts and annual official visits of respect began the year; then came Shrove Tuesday, Easter, the opening of the *dacha* season and the migration to the outer suburbs and the countryside; fishing began in June, and the shooting season opened on the twenty-ninth; leaves fell and the theatre season opened in October. Then came the first ice and the first snow, school holidays and Christmas. All these dictated the week's topics. Drudgery though this was, it gave Chekhov a unique accuracy in his descriptions of nature. The mature stories and the plays have an unerring exactitude[2] in the order in which the trees open their leaves, the times of dawn and dusk, the farming and sporting calendars, which stems from the demands made by the *Oskolki* readers' calendar. Long after Chekhov liberated himself from Leykin, he tended to describe the season during which the story was actually being written.

Apart from the year's schedule, contemporary events had to be reflected in Chekhov's early work. The most important, from the point of view also of his later work, was a major railway crash at Kukuyevka on the Moscow-Kursk line in summer 1882. It is men-

B

tioned specifically a score of times, the last being as late as 1886; the casualties were enormous, no one was compensated, the railway directors got off scot-free, and for Chekhov railways became symbols of ruthless modernity—for good, as in *Lights* of 1888, or for evil as in *My Life* of 1898—but in the early work Kukuyevka provided little more than a spiteful humorous aside whenever a story had a railway setting. Other events were the death of Turgenev in 1883, the trial of a fraudulent bank director, Rykov, and corruption in the Taganrog customs.

The death of Turgenev in August aroused feelings in Chekhov stronger than the *Oskolki* reader wished to share. A month afterwards a short sketch *V landau* (*In the Landau*) has a baron talking to three girls about Turgenev. The baron's opinions have the same philistine gallomania as those of the reading public of the day : 'I don't like reading nature descriptions.' He prefers Jean Richepain; two of the girls approve, but the country cousin can't bear it any longer and, with tears in her eyes, begs him to be quiet.[3] Leykin cut the story short. We do not know how it ended.

The Moscow papers were full of reports of the Rykov trial and the Taganrog customs affair. The latter was particularly interesting to Chekhov, as Aleksandr had taken a job in the Taganrog customs. The permanent effect on Chekhov's work was a tendency to see all financial dealings and the workings of capitalism as murky, anti-social conspiracies.

Thus, reacting to the topics of the day, Chekhov created values for himself. All his life Turgenev was to be an absolute measure of pure, disinterested art; the railways and the banks were symbols of inexorable forces breaking up the remnants of the old world.

Oskolki liked not only seasonability and topicality, but also a small number of easily recognised genres. One of the most common is the story of the half-pathetic, half-humorous *chinovnik* (clerk or civil servant). It is a type that goes back to Gogol's *The Overcoat*; hundreds of subsequent stories were modelled on that author's subhuman Akakiy Akakyevich and depiction of the tyranny of rank and routine. Almost a fifth of Chekhov's output in 1883 and 1884 was in this genre, a form of satire so well established that the censorship rarely tried to restrict it. Like the *chinovnik* heroes of Gogol', Dostoyevsky and Saltykov-Shchedrin, Chekhov's clerks have their little moments of love, liberalism and protest which die down almost as soon as they flare up, put out by their fear for their careers, their respect for authority and their distrust of outsiders. The *chinovnik* humbly waits outside while his superiors sleep with his wife and his dinner gets cold (*Na gvozde—On the Nail*, February 1883). At a Shrove Tuesday party he poses or crows like a cock for his boss in the hope of promotion (*Torzhestvo pobeditelya – The Victor's Triumph*, a story for Shrove Tuesday 1883). So strong is the hierarchy that even the boss's cat can caterwaul all night and mate the she-cats with impunity (*Kot—The Tomcat*, May 1883). A clerk dies of anxiety when he sneezes over a high-ranking official who can't be bothered with his apologies (*Smert' chinovnika—The Death of a Clerk*, July 1883). A thin man's joy at recognising his old friend in a fat man evaporates into sycophantic fear when he finds the fat man is higher in rank than himself. (*Tolstyy i tonkiy)—Fat Man and Thin Man*, October 1883). The genre was so well developed that there was little Chekhov could add to it. The best of his attempts was a story called *Noli me tangere* of October 1884, re-titled *Maska (The Mask)* in his Collected Works. Its effectiveness can be judged by the fact that Tolstoy listed it as one of his favourite Chekhov stories, and that the Ministry of Popular Enlightenment banned it from village and school libraries in 1905. At a masked ball a man tries to clear a room for an orgy with some prostitutes. Indignant officials, the town's intelligentsia, stop him, but no sooner has a police official compiled a record of the scandal than the man removes his mask and is revealed as the local millionaire. The police official leaves him to his orgy and the repentant *chinovniki* fawn on him and see him home when he has finished.

One *chinovnik* sketch, *Ekzamen na chin (An Examination for Promotion)*, in which a postman is nonplussed by a geography examination, was drawn from life in the town of Voskresensk, where Chekhov first practised medicine in the summer of 1884. But nearly all these sketches are stereotypes of the 'schoolmaster story', a closely allied genre, that shows a personal touch. All Chekhov's treatment of schoolteaching is coloured by his vision of the humiliated Russian schoolteacher as just another variety of *chinovnik*. He is portrayed at the same rank-ridden parties as the officials, suffering additionally from his puritanism, his love of beating, and his burden of irrelevant and useless knowledge. In *Kleveta (Slander*, December 1883) the schoolteacher is tortured by a rumour that he has been kissing the kitchenmaid; in *Repetitor (The Coach*, February 1884) he is humiliated by his pupil's father, who solves with an abacus a problem with which the teacher's algebra is too weak to cope. Chekhov was to write no more *chinovnik* stories, once he no longer had to, but the schoolteacher was to remain for him the epitome of repressed humanity.[4]

The genre that was in greatest demand was, however, the imitation of the modern French novel. The 1880s saw in Russia a heightened interest in the erotic, the detective, the high-society and the sociological novel. Zola's sensational *Nana*, about a courtesan worn out in her teens, was in fact published in Russian before it was published in French, and Chekhov's schoolboyish sketch, *My Nana*, of May 1883, is only one of his tributes to the vogue. He did not always write badly when he had to provide erotic piquancy : his first stories for *Novoye Vremya* in 1886 are none the worse for pandering to the reader's desire for sensationalism. But when he imitated the 'boulevard' novel with its dramas of high society, the effect is embarrassing. Stories such as *Barynya-Geroinya* (*The Lady Heroine*), with a gallant woman observing all the social niceties while she is inwardly tortured by the discovery of her husband's infidelities, are awkward renderings of the themes of Paul Bourget or du Boisgobey.

Periodically the reader of *Oskolki* or *Budil'nik* enjoyed having his social conscience wrung by pieces in the style of the death of Little Nell. These appeals to sentiment were as facile as the appeals to lubricity. But in Russia, particularly, there was an insatiable demand for literature of commiseration, a demand that Chekhov could not always resist, even when he was free to do so. In 1884, nicely timed for December, came *Ustritsy* (*Oysters*), the first of a number of stories about children, starving and oppressed, a first-person account of a starving child taken, for a joke, into a restaurant and fed ten rubles' worth of oysters. The details are convincing; the child's mingled revulsion and hunger are well described, but the story has the same touch of the spurious that vitiates many of Chekhov's stories of children and animals. The author has sensed the fashion for shedding tears and is assiduously pandering to it.

The most effective of Chekhov's tributes to contemporary taste, however, were his parodies and imitations of detective novels, in particular those of Gaboriau, who was the Georges Simenon of his day. His work was read all over Europe, and in Russia he was serialised in the Petersburg newspapers; Russian imitators, helped by the superficial similarities of the French and Russian criminal-investigation systems, were legion. Part of the popularity of the detective novel can be explained by the expansion of the railways, for a special sort of book was needed to while away the long, smooth journeys; by 1880, the majority of Russian bookshops were in fact station bookstalls.

> Ah, friend, how many and many a while
> They've made the slow time fleetly flow,
> And solaced pain and charmed exile,
> Boisgobey and Gaboriau.

Gaboriau's best invention was his detective, Lecoq, who employed a monumental intelligence and pure Gallic logic to unravel the most bizarre and complex mysteries. His most brilliant follower was undoubtedly Chekhov, whose first exercise in the genre is a parody, but one that shows a fully developed technique. *Shvedskaya spichka* (*The Safety Match*) has a young investigator, named Dyukovsky, who by sheer deduction traces the murderer from a dropped safety match. As tradition demands, he has to fight the scepticism and inertia of his superiors, but Chekhov's original touch is that, on going to arrest the murderer, the detective finds the victim alive and unharmed. A Russian Lecoq is nipped in the bud. Chekhov was proud enough of his detective story to sign it with his real name and to reprint it with only slight changes in his Collected Works.

The cult of Gaboriau led Chekhov almost flippantly into a novel-length parody. But despite his intentions, his first and only novel, *Drama na okhote* (*Drama at a Shooting Party*), grew into something more, and it is so important in its new techniques that discussion of it must be postponed to the end of this chapter.

Most of the early work can be classified roughly as *chinovnik*, pastiche French novel, seasonal sketch, vaudeville satire on love and marriage, professional stories centring around a doctor or an investigating magistrate, and stories of the degeneration of actors or impoverished landed gentry. The seasonal sketches, often without any plot at all, are the least ephemeral. A description of the bird market,[5] as *V Moskve na trubnoy ploshchadi* (*In Moscow on Trubnaya Square*), has personal involvement, as have childhood memories in *Pevchiye* (*The Choristers*). The lyrical element in these sketches keeps them fresh, so that the bird market is later re-used in *My Life* of 1896, while church music is to become one of the most potent

lyrical themes in Chekhov's clerical stories. The vaudeville satire and
associated jokes, however, make up the bulk of his early work.

The stories written round professional characters are more significant. They are some of the first middle-class stories in Russia, and
it is this newly hatched class, living on professional fees, not tied to
the soil, the state or the fight against it, which is to provide many
of Chekhov's heroes.[6] He had already established the character of
the doctor as gauche, puritanical and struggling; the lawyer, whom
he could model on many of his school and university friends, is
contrasted as a sophisticate who is hardened to human suffering and
is as hedonistic as the doctor is altruistic. In his late stories, such
as *On Official Business* (1899), when the figure of the doctor has
become more cynical, the position is reversed and the doctor con-
demns while the lawyer condones the sufferer. But the opposition
of doctor and lawyer remains, and it begins very early in Chekhov's work. A typical example, half-farcical, half-serious, is *Per-
petuum Mobile* (March 1884). Investigating magistrate and doctor
are going to carry out a post-mortem and inquest. They stop for
the night at a private house, where their host's daughter gives the
doctor a thinly veiled invitation to sleep with her. The doctor
refuses to take the opportunity and the lawyer, indignant with him
for his primness, tries to take his place. In the ensuing row doctor
and lawyer leave and the post-mortem is called off. The magistrate
and doctor not only show two poles of the middle classes; they also
lead us through the courts and through sickness to a vision of suffering humanity. Already some of the early stories show the incomprehension of court proceedings by the peasant victim and the impotence of medicine before mental suffering.

But most of Chekhov's portraits of suffering are sketches of
degeneracy. That of the actor was one of the first he had attempted.
Tragik (The Tragedy-actor) of early 1883, published at the opening of the theatre season in October, has a farcical plot involving
the tragedy-actor eloping with a rich man's daughter and beating
her when her father fails to send them money. The miserable in-
security and the cruel nomadic life of the actor anticipate the fate
of Katya in *A Dreary Story* or of Nina in *The Seagull*. It is one
of Chekhov's most constant themes.

Chekhov is pervasively thought of as a painter of the landed
gentry in its decline. The effete Ranevskaya household should not,
however, be assumed to be typical. Chekhov did not usually take a

sociological approach. The early stories about the gentleman *barin* reduced to penury and alcoholism must be seen as a continuation of a tradition of characterisation developed by Turgenev and Saltykov-Shchedrin. The best early example is *Osenyu (In Autumn,* 1883). In a remote inn a man keeps begging the innkeeper for more vodka and finally pawns his medallion. He turns out to be an unhappy landowner whose wife has run away with a lawyer. The innkeeper is so much moved by the story that he returns the medallion and gives the man more vodka. The sketch of a rainy autumn is better than the plot, but Chekhov thought well enough of the story to dramatise it as *Na bol'shoy doroge (On the Highway).* Clearly the censor felt the dramatised version (which has the runaway wife sheltering in the same inn) to be a libel on the landed gentry, for he wrote, 'This gloomy and filthy play cannot, in my opinion, be authorised for performance. Dramatic censor, Kaiser von Nilkheim.' Chekhov indeed did produce a number of minor classics in this 'superfluous man' genre, such as *Na puti (On the Way,* 1886), but it is peripheral to his main work. He rarely wrote about a class.

The chief interest of Chekhov's early pieces lies in their germs of later work. Nearly as important is the verbal material he is later to exploit. When he revised his early work for reprinting, the main changes were stylistic. He cut out the slang, the university student's Latin and German tags, the Gallicisms and the repetitions. The most popular of his early pieces do not have the journalistic tang of his *Oskolki* period—most of them were radically rewritten in 1889 and 1900—but even in those which Chekhov excluded from his Collected Works, had been unable to trace or had not retouched, one is struck by the anticipation of innumerable phrases and remarks in his late work.[7] Terms such as 'psychopath', 'psychiatry' and 'neurasthenic' are innovations of the early 1880s which Chekhov was to go on using. Topics like deforestation occur casually in stories such as *Naivny leshiy (The Naïve Wood-demon,* 1884); only later are they to become major themes. In Chekhov's journalism, especially the diary *Fragments of Moscow Life,* there are still more anticipations, the most important being the ironic enquiry about the life to come in two or three hundred years' time which is so frequent and so misunderstood in Chekhov's last work. It starts with remarks in 1884, such as 'when (in a hundred or so years' time) there will be no beggars on our planet', and is repeated throughout the 1880s and 1890s. The interest in Darwinism, the outrage at the decline of the Pushkin theatre into a *café chantant*, the feud that Chekhov conducted against the Moscow Zoo all begin in the *Fragments of Moscow Life.*

It must be remembered that in 1883 and 1884 Chekhov seemed more likely to become a professor of medicine than a man of letters. In April 1883 he sketched out a plan for a Master's dissertation on the History of Sexual Dominance; the argument was that the higher the mammal, the more equal were the sexes; the male is superior because his is the creative sex. As a subject this is more promising for a novelist than for a scientist, and Chekhov admitted that he had only deductive reasoning to back it, but it is worth recalling when we look at his view of the roles of the sexes. By 1883 he had read Sacher-Masoch as well as Spencer; only later was psychology to contribute anything to his writing. In September 1884, he naïvely asked Leykin to find him a post as a doctor in Petersburg through Botkin, the great professor of medicine. Perhaps the decisive moment was a drunken meeting with Leskov, when the latter came to Moscow in the summer of 1883. A bond was established. The conversation, according to Chekhov's letter to Aleksandr, ran : 'Leskov : "Do you know who I am ?"—"A mystic"—"You'll die before your brother. I shall anoint you with oil, as Samuel did David." ' The prophecy of death is uncanny, and is an indication of Leskov's mysticism, generally ignored at that time, but embodied by Chekhov in his more Leskovian works. Stories such as *The Choristers* of 1884 and the clerical tales of 1886 and 1888 distil the feeling for clerical life to be found in Leskov's *Sealed Angel* or *Enchanted Wanderer*,[8] and although Chekhov was to see Leskov only twice more, in 1888 and 1895, the anointing was a real consecration.

Of the work of 1883 and 1884 less than a quarter appears in the Collected Works, and the pieces chosen were included because Chekhov could trace them, because he felt they were of merit, or, perhaps, because they were characteristic of the period. Some were retitled and revised out of all recognition. Undoubtedly, objective considerations of merit were strongest, but none of the more sensational stories were reprinted, despite their qualities. Well-rounded tales like *The Choristers*, *Fat Man and Thin Man* and the famous *Doch' Al'biona* (*Daughter of Albion*), in which an English governess is quite unmoved when her Russian employer strips naked in front of her to free his fishing-line, had preference. Of the more ambitious pieces, only a Turgenevian story, *Pridanoye* (*The Dowry*), about a girl who spends her whole life making a trousseau for a fiancé who never materialises, full of genteel sadness and picturesque Russian detail, was kept. Chekhov underrated his parodies and disliked those works whose technique was outstripped by their ambition.

Of all Chekhov's works, his novel *Drama na okhote* (*Drama at a Shooting-Party*) was the most unlucky. It was serialised for nine months (from August 1884 to April 1885) in the Petersburg daily *Novosti Dnya* and was never reprinted during Chekhov's lifetime. It reflects almost everything he had ever read, from the *Sorrows of Young Werther* to *The Old Age of Lecoq*. It also contains embryonically almost everything he was to write. At the same time it is a detective story of unsurpassable ingenuity and, at certain points, a substantial psychological novel. The plot's ingenuity is in itself a dig at Gaboriau's elaborate construction and his insistence on the unpredictable but inevitable dénouement. The story is told in the first person 'from the notes of an investigating magistrate', as was usual, but there are a short introduction and epilogue which turn the whole narrative upside down. In the beginning we have what appears to be the editor of *Novosti Dnya* telling us how he came by the investigator's manuscript. At the end, the narrator calls for his payment and the editor points out that the solution is false and that the narrator himself is the murderer. Only then does the reader see the meaning of the investigator's dilatory incompetence in handling and solving the crime.

Kamyshev, the narrator, is a fully developed character. Of his two friends, Doctor Shchur, pure, naïve and generous, is a forerunner of Doctor Samoylenko in *The Duel*. The other is the dissolute Count, with whose decrepit affairs the novel is chiefly concerned. There is an autobiographical intensity in the opposing pull of the two friends on the narrator just as there is something of Chekhov's struggle with his elder brothers in the diatribes against the dehumanising effect of alcohol and loose living. The love interest is developed to a pitch that just fails to be absurd. Kamyshev is loved by Natasha, who in turn is loved by the doctor. Kamyshev, the Count and the Count's estate manager, Urbenin, all fall in love with the girl in red, Ol'ga, the forester's daughter. To escape her humdrum life, she marries the middle-aged Urbenin, falls in love with Kamyshev and tries to elope with him at the wedding feast; she soon ends up as the Count's mistress, amid several sensational orgies with the gypsies. Urbenin, destroyed by grief, becomes a tramp and vanishes. Then, at a shooting-party, the Count's Polish wife suddenly appears and Ol'ga, wandering off, is murdered. Kamyshev clumsily investigates, indicts Urbenin and secures his conviction; witnesses mysteriously disappear. That, until the editor of the manuscript intervenes, is all, except for an ironic twist at the end, reminiscent of the conclusion of *Livestock* of 1882 : Kamyshev keeps on the Count, now utterly degenerate, as a sort of trophy while he himself escapes unpunished.

Much of the detail is parody. The narrator murders his parrot in a scene that recalls the murder of the cat in Zola's *Thérèse Raquin*.[9] His servant reads Gaboriau; he himself is called Lecoq by the Count. Some of the nature description, such as the lake echoing the mood of the narrator, and episodes like the highly technical post-mortem report on the victim, are sheer padding. But there are touches that give a real strangeness to the novel. The Count's over-grown garden with its southern Russian flora is a very real evocation of decay, like the alleys of pines and lime-trees that fill Chekhov's late stories with suffocating aromas. The persistent animal imagery is not as cynically arbitrary as it might be. The tame hare in Ol'ga's house, when we first meet her as the simple 'girl in red', leads to a pattern of images of predators and prey—'a cat caught thieving', 'like a trapped mouse'—that culminates in Ol'ga's indifferently watching a bird's death-agonies before she herself is murdered at the shooting-party. Much of the highly melodramatic action is so vividly realised that it suspends disbelief as effectively as do Dostoyevsky's scandals. There is a scene of money being burnt very like that in *The Idiot*, and the monstrous wedding party and gypsy orgies owe a lot to *Crime and Punishment* and *The Brothers Karamazov*. The tension in the narrative builds up as we feel the pull of the degenerate Count overcoming the influence of the fastidious Doctor Shchur. There is a pessimism about human nature which gives the descriptions, at their best, the strange poetry of nature minus man that is so frequent in late Chekhov. In the portrayal of Ol'ga, predator and victim, we meet for the first time the misogynistic streak in Chekhov that develops in the very similar story *Ariadna* of 1895. The structure of the novel, beginning in May and ending in autumn, has the seasonal sequence of the late plays, the triumph of autumn over spring. Baroque in several senses of the word, *Drama at a Shooting-Party* deserves reappraisal, both for its own sake and for a better understanding of what Chekhov was later to write. At the very least, it was a major breakaway from Leykin's stranglehold. Chekhov had for the first time published something substantial in Petersburg, elsewhere than in *Oskolki*.

4

Into Literature—the 'Petersburg Newspaper'

Leykin realised that to keep Chekhov as a contributor he would have to loosen the reins. It was some time before relations grew at all acrimonious, but Chekhov's letters in 1884 and 1885 show a tactful impatience with Leykin's strictures. Finally, in April 1885 Leykin arranged with Khudekov, editor of the *Petersburg Newspaper* (*Peterburgskaya Gazeta*) to have Chekhov contribute a story every Monday, so as not to take readers away from *Oskolki*, which appeared on Saturdays. It is among the forty-three stories which Chekhov wrote for Khudekov's paper between April 1885 and February 1886 that there appear the first signs of an artist writing for himself rather than for his editor.

Freedom of choice in themes and treatment goes some way towards explaining the variety and originality of the stories of 1885, as up till then Chekhov could choose only between conforming to the preconceptions of the humorous weeklies and placing his work unpaid in *Priroda i Okhota*. But there are other factors. Firstly, he had qualified as a doctor and had established his family (parents, younger brothers and sister) in comfort. He had a room to work in. Secondly, his first experiences of professional life were profoundly altering him. Then, in November 1884, he coughed blood for the first time. Never in the nineteen years that were left to him could he ever have forgotten that his days were numbered. The sense of doom was heightened by his brother Nikolay's growing addiction to morphine, and their friend the artist Levitan's first signs of the paranoia that was to lead to suicide. As a doctor, Chekhov began to look closely at the society around him. As his letters of September 1885 show, the economic servitude of the peasants in the countryside around Moscow and the death rate of forty per thousand in Moscow itself coloured his outlook more subtly than the spectacular evils of railway crashes, frauds and murder trials with which his *Oskolki* writing had dealt.

In the summers of 1884, 1885 and 1886 Chekhov managed to escape the pressure of the city and to recapture a little of the country pleasures of his boyhood. The first summer was spent working as a locum in the little town of Voskresensk (now Istra), forty miles west of Moscow. The next summer, Chekhov's sister Maria made friends with the Kiselev family,[1] who rented a *dacha* on their nearby estate of Babkino. Maria Kiselev was the daugher of Begichev, the Director of State Theatres in Moscow, and of one of the women celebrated by Pushkin; she herself had literary pretensions and was the first of many people to encourage Chekhov to develop as a serious, responsible writer. Babkino gave him landscapes (now largely flooded by the Istra reservoir) which recalled the idyllic summers of his boyhood and his lifelong passion, fishing. Much of this is directly reflected in the *Petersburg Newspaper* stories. *Nalim* (*The Burbot*) of July 1885 recounts within a joke framework a real incident; so does *Myortvoye telo* (*The Dead Body*) of September, which tells of a corpse and two peasants who are obliged to watch over it until the authorities arrive. Medical practice gave Chekhov little joy : suicides, rickets, festering wounds all pointed to an underlying disorder of society itself. He hated decisive actions; he put off operations; medicine increased his awareness and despair of the evils inherent in life itself. For him, the interesting side of medicine was to be found in sociological and psychiatric research; the imaginative rather than the practical[2] aspect of medicine was to make it a philosophical substratum in his work.

If Chekhov's work in Voskresensk and Babkino gave rise to an almost mystic depression that fills stories such as *Son svyatochnyy* (*A Christmas Dream*) and *Zerkalo* (*The Mirror*), the river Istra, the woods and fields express an ecstatically romantic feeling for nature, the reverie of a solitary walker. Other human beings only cloud the landscape. Levitan's psychosis was symbolised for Chekhov when the great painter shot for sport a doe, a hare and a snipe. Only the taciturn recluse finds his place in nature, and this we can see in the figure of the ice-carver in *Khudozhestvo* (*Artistry*) of January 1886, or *Yeger'* (*The Huntsman*) of July 1885. A new experience of nature creates a new sort of hero for Chekhov, and this was the novelty which caught and held the attention of literary critics in Petersburg.

The Huntsman in fact was partially responsible for Chekhov's introduction to Suvorin at the end of the year. A mere two thousand
words long, the story is anything but slight. The hero, Yegor, is one
of the singleminded, unintentionally cruel types that Chekhov often
portrays, romantically, as hunters or sometimes as millers. Utterly
absorbed in shooting game, he encounters the wife he has been
married to for twelve years. He explains his indifference to her in
terms which make his mania for hunting very much like the demonic
creative urge of the artist : 'If they take away my rifle, I'll use my
rod; take that away, I'll catch things with my hands . . . Once a
man gets the free spirit in him, nothing in the whole world will get
it out. It's just like someone going in for acting or some other art;
he'll never make an official or a landowner.' The ruthless purpose
of the huntsman as he walks off into his private paradise, leaving
a weeping woman, is to imbue almost all the strong heroes of
Chekhov's work in the mid-1880s. Yegor's language may be the
barbaric, half-educated jargon of a peasant who has outgrown his
rank, but it has the brutal directness which, for a time, Chekhov
is to admire in literary prose and in the work of the explorer-scien-
tists, Darwin and Przhevalsky.[3]

The objectivity of the story, which in other hands would have
condemned the huntsman and commiserated with his wife, is not
its most remarkable feature. Chekhov has managed to condense in
his terse, third-person narrative a whole ode to summer and a de-
tailed, concrete reconstruction of sights, sounds and smells. The
opening phrases are so laconic that he revitalises the trite device
of personifying nature and imbuing it with the mood of the heroine :
'A sultry, close midday. Not a cloud in the sky . . . The grass, burnt
by the sun, looks sad, hopeless : rain or no rain, it won't grow green
again . . . The forest stands silent, motionless, as if looking somewhere with its tree tops or waiting for something.' It is an evocation
of a Russian summer as sensuous as the opening of Gogol's *Sorochintsy Fair*, but in a twentieth of the space. It is one of Chekhov's
first attempts at outdoing Gogol', attempts which were to culminate
in that epic of summer, *Steppe*. The ending is equally masterly.
The huntsman walks off and Chekhov follows his vanishing form
through the eyes of his heroine, a technique he is to use constantly
in his late prose, where all the sights and sounds of the narrative are
filtered through the eyes and ears of one of the characters. First, the
body loses its shape as it recedes : 'She can see his shoulderblades

moving, his youthful neck, the lazy, casual gait . . .' Then the colours vanish : 'But now the red of his shirt fuses with the dark of his breeches, his footsteps are invisible, you can't tell his dog from his boots. You can see only his cap'—and a few phrases later, his 'white cap' ends the story and the reader is left as forlorn as the neglected wife. Levitan, who was not given to praise, wrote to Chekhov to say that he admired his stories for their portraits of landscapes. Chekhov had the same feeling for perspective, shape and colour as are to be seen in the drawings and paintings of Nikolay.

Six months later, in a mid-winter landscape, the demonic recluse recurs in the story *Khudozhestvo (Artistry)*, incarnated as the ice-carver, Seryozhka, who is entrusted with the construction of the cross, the lectern and the figure of the Holy Ghost as a dove out of the ice on the middle of a frozen river, to celebrate the baptism of Christ in the Jordan. Most of the story is taken up with his bullying the churchwarden into doing all the donkeywork of cutting ice and hauling wood. Like the huntsman, Seryozhka would be contemptible were it not for his mania, his art. When the work is finally erected and painted, the story ends in an explosion of colour that justifies all the meanness, drunkenness and idleness of its creator; never at any point did Chekhov have such a high, romantic regard for the artist : 'In himself Seryozhka is nothing, an idler, a drunk, a squanderer, but when he has his red lead or his dividers, then he is something higher, a servant of God.' We can see in Seryozhka Chekhov's dilemma when faced with the genius of his brother Nikolay or of Levitan, a genius that seemed inseparable from moral squalor and destructiveness. The creative achievement is undeniable : it is a religious exultation, and for Chekhov, as for his mentor Leskov, art was never more genuine than when in the service of the church : 'With a shaking hand Seryozhka pulls off the matting . . . and the people see something extraordinary. The lectern, the wooden circle, the pegs and the cross on the ice are transfused with a thousand colours. The cross and the dove emit rays of light that hurt you to look at.'

Artistry and *The Huntsman* express a solitary romanticism. But we can find a more gentle and human sense of joy in stories that reflect life in the country at Babkino. By far the most famous is *Nalim (The Burbot)*; it is a combination of two very common subjects – the fish that gets away, and the trivial problem that attracts one man after another until a crowd is gathered. Yet *The Burbot* is memorable, perhaps because it is a vivid recollection of an actual event, perhaps because Chekhov for the first time succeeds in rendering the peasants' dialogue without any condescension or striving for effect. Out of the story comes a sense of an ordered and harmonious, if comically absurd, society. Two peasants damming up a bathing-pool in the river find a burbot hiding in the tree roots on the bank. (The burbot is a much sought-after edible fish.) They struggle in vain to grab it by the gills. Along comes the shepherd, who abandons his sheep, horses and cows in order to help. He is followed by the coachman and finally by the landowner himself. The burbot has involved everyone when, just as the landowner is feeling its fat liver, it springs back into the water and vanishes. Simple though it is, *The Burbot* strongly expresses the harmony of man and nature. The 'thick sickly-sweet honey smell' of the tall grass in the baking sun is echoed in the 'honeyed smile' of the onlookers when the fish is caught. A few touches of imagery and a perfect ear for speech turn a comic sketch into a romantic idyll.

Life in Babkino with the burbots, bream and perch, the caper-caillies and woodcocks, the hares and pine-martens, had a less idyllic obverse. Though only a summer visitor, Chekhov felt the harshness and miseries of the life of the permanent inhabitants, the peasants. Their servitude appears in a number of the *Petersburg Newspaper* stories of 1885—sometimes they are victims of super-stition or of the economic structure, but more often than not their distress arises when their world collides with the superficially humane but deeply impersonal ideas of justice and order which the authori-ties try to impose. The collision of humanism with humanity, of doctor with patient, of the law court with the prisoner, of the land-owner with the peasant, is a theme which preoccupies Chekhov in the mid-1880s and the late 1890s. In some stories, it merely extends his general idea of the difficulty of bridging two human or social minds; in others, there is a certain bias, sometimes to the calm, civilised procedures of western law and western medicine, some-times to the authentic, instinctual justice that, like most Russian novelists, he found in the Russian peasantry. In nearly every case, he expresses a conflict of sympathy which, though it may leave us dissatisfied, spares us rhetoric or polemics. *Myortvoye telo (The Dead Body)*, on the surface just an autumnal sketch of a real incident, brings out the alien quality of peasant life that, in Chekhov's work at the turn of the century, gives a nightmare sensation of a rift between 'them' and 'us'. Two peasants, one the village idiot, are guarding a corpse until the authorities come to hold an inquest. A pilgrim going through the forest disturbs them; horrified at a corpse which may be that of a suicide, he asks one of the guardians to show him the way through the woods. The dumb resignation of the wake, the superstition of the pilgrim, and above all the corpse that dominates the three living figures, project a sensation of horror, and omens, familiar to audiences of Chekhov's plays, add to the atmosphere : the hunting owl, the autumnal migration of the cranes.

Unter Prishibeyev (*NCO Prishibeyev*), about a self-appointed policeman who mercilessly bullies the peasants and is then, to his own bewilderment, taken to court is perhaps the best known of the stories of 1885. His paranoiac tyrannising seems a hyperbolisation of the rule of the State, and his inability to understand that the court is sentencing him and not the peasants is a poignant example of the meaninglessness of western legality in the world of the Russian peasant. The censors may well have reacted to the story in this way, for they refused to pass it for *Oskolki*. 'This story,' wrote the committee, 'is one of those that describe monstrous social forms, arising out of the police's intensive observation. Owing to the sharp exaggeration of the harm of such observation, the article [sic] cannot be authorised.' Chekhov changed the title *The Supernumerary Guardian* to *Klyauznik* (*The Caviller*), rewrote the story and sent it successfully to the *Petersburg Newspaper* three weeks later. (Its final title, that made its hero, NCO Prishibeyev, a household name, came in 1900, in the Collected Works.)

With the coming of winter, Chekhov could give his readers the familiar plot of the poor peasant freezing to death. *Gore* (*Grief*) is lifted out of the rut of such a well-worn theme by its dispassionate mixture of compassion and irony; Chekhov seems so familiar with the peasant's hardships and his muted reactions that he can present them as naturally as he can present the idyllic side of country life. An old woodturner finds that his wife, whom he has maltreated all his married life, is dying; he tries to take her to hospital through a blizzard; she dies, his horse gives up, and the old man wakes up in hospital, with fatal frost-bite. What gives the story its quality is the spark of humanity and the 'otherness' of the peasant that are revealed in the cruel, cunning old man. When he finds that his wife has died, he suddenly wants to live his life all over again; told

by the doctor that he has had his time, he begs to live a little longer
in order to bury his wife and return the borrowed horse. The moral
priorities of the Russian peasant and his calmness in the face of
death had been brought out strongly enough by Tolstoy, Turgenev
and Nekrasov, but never so disarmingly casually as here by Chekhov. It is the normality of the suffering that makes the picture so
convincing. *Grief* attracted the comment of Pal'min, an occasional
poet who worked for *Oskolki*, and he wrote to Chekhov : 'This is
the best you have written so far. One gets a strange impression from
this sketch, so full of true life; one feels amused and sad.'

The *Petersburg Newspaper* also allowed Chekhov more personal
themes. In a number of stories the idea of the tyrannical or dis-
placed father-figure appears to exorcise a demonic force in Chekhov's own life. The problem is never so great in his work as it was
in Dostoyevsky's, for instance, and by autumn of 1886 it is resolved
in the story *Tyazholyye lyudi (Difficult People)*, when we see father
and son realising that they share the same genetic make-up and that
their conflict is quite natural. But two stories of 1885 tempt one to
read into them something of Chekhov's displacement of his father's
parental authority. One is *Otets semeystva (The Father of the
Family)*. The dyspeptic father vents his pain, guilt and frustration
on his little boy and later, when he recovers, is puzzled by the boy's
trembling shyness. His brutal vindictiveness at the table reveals a
pathetic weakness on which nobody in the family dares to comment. In December 1885, Chekhov published *Svyataya prostota
(Sacred Simplicity)*. An old country priest is visited by his son, who
is now a famous lawyer. The old man cannot believe the allusions
to wealth and high living in his son's talk, and pride in his son's
achievement is mingled with a helpless inability to talk to him. The
originality of the story is that we commiserate with and laugh not
only at the naïve old priest, but also at the great lawyer who has
forgotten how to enjoy himself or his family. *Sacred Simplicity* is a
title that can be taken seriously as well as ironically; the story is
important, for it is the first in which Chekhov broached the loneliness of the successful man—the theme of a number of his major
works, such as *A Dreary Story* (1889) and *The Bishop* (1902).

Reading the stories printed in the *Petersburg Newspaper* in 1885
and 1886, one notices that those depicting ecstasy or harmony are
only interludes in a closed circle of subjection, frustration and death.
It is at the end of the year, in the season for ghost stories, that

Chekhov allows his depression to expand into almost mystic visions
of evil. One is *Son svyatochnyy* (*A Christmas Dream*);[4] the other
is *Zerkalo* (*The Mirror*). The first is perhaps only half-realised.
It was written for Christmas 1884, for *Oskolki*. Leykin held it over
till the following winter, suggesting that Chekhov rewrite it, but
instead Chekhov withdrew it and printed it in the *Petersburg Newspaper* on Christmas Day 1885. He never reprinted it. It is perhaps
over-ambitious, told in the first person, a technique Chekhov rarely
used until the late 1880s. Superficially it is Dickensian. The narrator
works as a nightwatchman in a pawnshop; he dreams that people
break into the shop and that, when he surprises them, he is so overcome by their poverty that he lets them take away clothes and
valuables. The next morning, however, his dream turns out to have
been reality and he is sentenced to forced labour. The morality of
the story, a little crude, comes in the narrator's plea : 'I was tried a
month later. Why? I assured the judges that it was a dream, that
it's wrong to try a man for a nightmare.' Poverty—the word echoes
through the story—is the nightmare responsible for the pawnshop
and the burglary. Society, not the individual, is the real culprit;
here for the first time is one of the constants in Chekhov's philosophy.
For him, evil is to be found more in the structure of society or the
family than in the individual himself. To this extent, Chekhov's
ethics are romantic, Marxist, rather than classical or Christian.

But the best, artistically speaking, of *A Christmas Dream* is not its
sense of social injustice, but its feeling for things. The narrator is
overcome by emanations from the objects in pawn. The guitar has
been pawned for money to buy drops to treat tuberculosis; the
revolver has been used for an alcoholic's suicide; a bracelet has
been stolen, and so on : the scene is reminiscent of the miser's survey
of his trunks in Pushkin's *Covetous Knight*. The narrator feels in the
pledges 'irreparable grief, disease, crime, debauchery for money',
and the objects themselves come to life, as they do in Chekhov's late
plays. The guitar's strings snap, like the breaking string in *The
Cherry Orchard* or the violin string in the story *The Bride*. The
wind howls in the chimney, as in *The Bride*. The half-real, half-
phantom break-in by the poor is like the nightmare in *On Official
Business*, when the peasants march on in the brain of the lawyer.
In this evocation of the power of things and of dreams, the story is
far ahead of its time, as it is also in its convincingly dim narrator.
The difference between this story and the stories of the 1890s is

only in technique. Horror at life may not be continuous in Chekhov's work, but it has deep roots.

Five days later, the new-year story *The Mirror* was printed. The young heroine, Nelly, is looking in the mirror, as folklore demands, to see what the future holds. Instead of the face of the beloved, a whole nightmare looms up out of the 'grey background' (*seryy fon*) in the mirror. Most of the story is taken up with Nelly (in the mirror world) pleading with a doctor, himself ill with typhus, to come and treat her sick husband. (This theme, of the doctor as much in need of treatment as his patient, is not developed, but it is to be found in the stories of the following year.) Nelly then sees her husband die; she anticipates a life full of debts, bailiffs, sick children and death, when suddenly the mirror falls from her hands and she wakes up. The 'grey background' has gone and she can see her unhappy face again. Naturally, the dream dominates the story, and the mirror world, with its senseless permutations of misery, has entered Chekhov's imagination never to leave it. It is the first of the visions of horror that can intrude on the mind of the prosperous and contented only in the form of nightmare, and it is this which makes the melodrama of *The Mirror* forgivable.

These stories initiate the trends of Chekhov's mature work. The bulk of those of 1885, in the *Petersburg Newspaper* and elsewhere, exploit seams that are already becoming exhausted. One type, particularly popular, was the sentimental story about children. The subjects are well observed and the tales more carefully written than Chekhov's farcical pieces, but they are geared to arouse stock responses in the reader,[5] and Chekhov's humorous pieces for Khudekov's paper are just as calculated. They meet the demand for titillation. The Feydeau-farce eroticism of his lighter work only shifts his themes of the incompatibility of the sexes and the perversity of life on to a lighter level. In fact, it is only tone that separates farce from drama. A story like *Ninochka*, in which the narrator is the lover of his best friend's wife, gets thanks from the husband for his guidance in their marriage, and ends by moving into the marital bedroom and putting the husband in the former pantry, may be cynical but it is not false. The shallow, casual Ninochka, the pathetic husband, looking only for peace and quiet as a background to his work, and the amiably ruthless lover and friend are all characters who reappear in more serious contexts—as in *Ariadna* (1895).

Much of Chekhov's comedy for the *Petersburg Newspaper* is black.

The 'Melpomene' stories of drunken, spendthrift actors continue; hen-pecked husbands and reluctant bridegrooms are still their mainstay, but into these stories comes the characters' own consciousness that they are third-rate and faced not with glory but with death. In stories such as *Poslednyaya mogikansha* (*The Last Mohican Squaw*), the characterisation is sharpened until the husband becomes a curious specimen of moral degeneration. A story such as *Kontrabas i fleyta* (*The Double Bass and the Flute*) takes a Laurel-and-Hardy pair of ill-matching orchestral players and makes of their slapstick incompatibility a wry comment on the fragility of friendship.

Sometimes the humour turns against the reader. *Tsinik* (*The Cynic*), a story which the censor refused to pass for *Oskolki*, describes a keeper conducting a tour of the zoo, jeering and mocking at each animal in turn, until his audience is aroused to fury and stops him. But the whole joke is at the expense of the public, indignant because the cynic is only expressing his own secret arrogance at the animals' expense. There is an element of self-justification by the author and of condemnation of the reader if the zoo is seen to represent life and conducted tour literature. Certainly, some of Chekhov's other, lighter pieces protest at the role into which the writer is forced. Stories such as *Kon' i trepetnaya lan'* (*The Horse and Quivering Hind*) or *Dva gazetchika* (*Two Newspapermen*)—the latter published in *Oskolki*—show a Muscovite New Grub Street in which decency, aspirations and talent are sacrificed to the routines of journalism. The jester is protesting at his role.

In much of the work of 1885, particularly the 'second-best' which now went to *Oskolki* and the Moscow weeklies, Chekhov's signature let him get away with much that was cheap or mediocre. But there are flights of absurdity which make three or four of the 1885 farces worth rereading. *Bumazhnik* (*The Wallet*) has three actors finding a wallet and murdering each other in their attempt to have sole possession : when Chekhov reprinted it in 1899, he added a moral which showed how little his experience of the theatre had altered his hostility to actors : 'When actors with tears in their eyes talk about their dear colleagues, about friendship and "solidarity", when they embrace and kiss you, don't get too carried away.' But despite flashes of invention, the stories of 1885 show us that humour has now become merely a profitable, automatic sideline in Chekhov's work. It was stories like *The Huntsman* that had caught the attention of the literary world.

5
New Times

In December 1885 Chekhov was invited to Petersburg by Leykin.
Here he was introduced to two men who were to play an important
part in his life. One was Dmitri Vasilevich Grigorovich, who had
made his name as a realist writer in the late 1840s and who was
one of the grand old men of letters. It was Grigorovich who did
more than anyone to convince Chekhov that he had a duty to himself, to art and society, to develop as a serious prose writer. Aleksey
Sergeyevich Suvorin was perhaps even more important. He very
soon took the place of father, elder brother and confessor in Chekhov's life, and their friendship was one of the most productive relationships in the whole of Russian literature. Suvorin, who was
twenty-six years older than Chekhov, is usually portrayed as a reactionary newspaper tycoon who exploited his protégé's good
nature, more subtly than had Leykin. This is only part of the truth.
Suvorin owned the most substantial newspaper in Russia, *Novoye
Vremya* (*New Times*). Precisely because it was reactionary,
nationalistic and anti-semitic, it was less restricted in its report-
ing of foreign affairs and political ideas than the more liberal, and
therefore more suspect, newspapers, but it disgraced itself on three
counts : it fought Darwinism as a pernicious science, it printed an
attack on the poetaster Nadson as he lay dying, and it fought against
the acquittal of Dreyfus. Nevertheless, it was a great newspaper and
perhaps only the Russian political system and limited readership
prevented Suvorin from making it as potent a force as *The Times*
of London. Suvorin was, moreover, as much the W. H. Smith
and Allen Lane of his time as he was the Northcliffe or the
William Hearst. He had interests in railway bookstalls and in cheap
editions of Russian classics which helped to spread literacy and
culture.

Not only was Suvorin good for Chekhov; he was also congenial

to him. Once a provincial schoolteacher in Voronezh, he had the
same humble, southern origins. He had a restless, melancholic
temperament and he was, like Chekhov, loyal to but alienated from
his family. He admired Western civilisation; he had an open if
sceptical mind. For Chekhov to attach himself to Suvorin might
well have been ruinous. As it was, his relations with the more liberal
journals, particularly the monthly magazines, became strained and
there were often clashes of loyalties with fellow-writers. But not until
1897, when the Dreyfus affair proved that Suvorin would do
nothing to alter his paper's anti-semitic tone, was the friendship
impaired.

Suvorin invited Chekhov to contribute to *Novoye Vremya*. Between February 1886 and March 1887, until he made his pilgrimage
south, Chekhov contributed twenty-one stories, more carefully composed and more ambitious than anything he had so far written.
They mark his irrevocable entry into Russian literature : of the
eighty other pieces published in this period, few can be compared
with the *Novoye Vremya* stories.

Grigorovich's immediate influence was perhaps stronger. It was
he who had read *The Huntsman* and decided to rescue great talent
from extinction in the *Petersburg Newspaper*. During 1886 he wrote
a number of letters to Chekhov, praising his prose extravagantly,
and always urging him to find a strong moral position to defend.
His first letter, of 28 March 1886, transformed Chekhov's whole
view of himself and his future with its reference to 'a talent that is
way above that of the modern generation of writers', its pleas that
Chekhov should give up 'writing to order' and save his impressions
for 'a thought-out, polished work, written over several sittings, in
happy hours of inward predisposition'. Chekhov's response is almost
embarrassing. 'I almost wept . . . If I have a gift . . . I confess to
the purity of your heart I have not been respecting it', he wrote.
Within a month, his self-confidence swelled to arrogance : he wrote
long letters to Aleksandr and Nikolay, reproaching the first for his
idleness and lack of principles, and preaching to the latter a
morality which consisted of respecting individuals, compassion,
property, and truthfulness; of not complaining or seeking fame; of
looking for the mother rather than the whore in a woman; and of
keeping a healthy mind in a healthy body. To his country cousin
and his uncle, Chekhov was to boast of his income, of being the
most fashionable writer in Petersburg. An astonishing, touching

emotional immaturity is revealed. Even more astonishing is Chekhov's recovery from this first impact of success; by spring 1887, he had become a literary thinker and moral philosopher so objective and so open-minded that his contemporaries never caught up with him.

Chekhov's letters of the period throw light on this delayed metamorphosis. 'My reception in Petersburg made my head spin for two months,' he wrote. The pride of being an 'artist, one man in two million' alternated with remorse—'If I'd known this was how they read me, I should not have written to order'—and priggish superiority: 'Who would have thought that such genius could come out of an earth-closet?' On his return from Babkino, in August 1886, Chekhov rented an expensive flat on the Garden Boulevard in Moscow. For the first time he let himself become sufficiently involved with a woman to propose marriage. (The girl was Dunya Efros,[1] whose spirited temperament and whose Jewishness appear in a number of Chekhov's heroines in 1886.)

The intoxication of success gave way to the hangover. Chekhov decided to dedicate himself to literature and medicine and to give up the ordinary pleasures of life. Phrases in his letters, particularly to his hostess at Babkino, Maria Kiseleva, have the sad naïvety of a Trofimov: 'I'm above marriage . . . I've now renounced worldly vanity and earthly pleasures and have given myself entirely to literature and medicine.' More important still, he realised that the literary world into which he had been initiated was all but dying: it consisted of a handful of survivors—Leskov and Grigorovich, for instance—and a handful of initiates—himself, Garshin (who was to influence him), Korolenko and the grossly overrated, moribund young Nadson. The only great figure of Russian literature, Tolstoy, had publicly renounced art in favour of preaching. Chekhov saw Russian prose, including his own, as a second-rate craft which could do little more than follow the lines laid down by Maupassant and Zola: entertaining and instructing, but no longer inspiring the reader.

After a second visit with his sister at the end of 1886, Chekhov found Petersburg less enthralling; his letter to Burenin (the leading feature-writer of *Novoye Vremya*) shows his disappointment with literature: 'The young lady has calculated that at present Russia has 174 poets. From a medical point of view, this profusion is extremely ominous: if there are many treatments for a disease, then it is a very sure sign that the disease is incurable.' The aphorism, taken from a medical textbook and applied to literature, must have stuck very deep in Chekhov's mind for he was to repeat it, almost word for word, in one of Gayev's speeches in *The Cherry Orchard* seventeen years later. By early 1887, his correspondence with Maria Kiseleva shows that he has come to see literature and society in terms of palliatives and painkillers for an incurable illness.

Maria Kiseleva watched with trepidation her protégé's rise to greatness. Some of the stories written for *Novoye Vremya*, particularly the stories with highly sexed heroines, made her indignant. Chekhov's replies to her criticism are his most enlightening self-revelations. Accused of raking the 'dunghill' for material and therefore of corrupting his readers, he defended himself by pointing out that reticence was only a passing convention in literature and that life demanded to be represented honestly. His main point was that 'finally no literature can outdo actual life in its cynicism : you can't make someone drunk on a glassful when he has already drunk a barrelful.' All his life Chekhov believed that literature had no ultimate effects, pernicious or beneficial, on life : it could only make it more lucid or more bearable. This is the nearest that he came to being an aesthete : he was never to delude himself into a prophetic or legislative role. His letter to Maria Kiseleva on 14 January 1887 is perhaps his frankest declaration of faith. If literature must reflect life as it is, he says, then he is as bound to show the dirt in life as is his friend Levitan to paint the bark and dead leaves on the trees, or a chemist to handle chemicals. For Chekhov there was no point in censorship—'There is no police that could consider itself competent in literary affairs'—or even in self-censorship—'I rarely converse with my conscience when I'm writing.' The response of critics and readers must provide the only censure of a writer.

This very modern and rational view of writing made Chekhov peculiarly susceptible to the vagaries of his critics. His empiricism seemed to his contemporaries to show a lack of principle and as early as 1886 they were tempted to take him down a peg or two.[2] The more subtle his re-creation of reality, the more deplorable to the Russian critic was his failure to lead, to judge and to blame. That he had made his début in *Novoye Vremya*, instead of in the 'thick journals' that were the self-appointed conscience of Russia, seemed suspect to many. Thus Chekhov could arouse a furore of enthusiasm and then be treated 'like a bone they've thrown to the dogs'; he was one of the few major writers to feel that critics had a right to dislike and misunderstand his work.

The work of 1886 and early 1887 differs mainly in degree from the best of 1885 : it is more carefully composed. But in one respect there is a radical departure from pieces written before his meeting with Suvorin. Chekhov no longer fears ideas. They are never the ultimate *'quod erat demonstrandum'* of the stories, but the expression of his hero's character, and the most important are those of Tolstoy, in particular his 'non-resistance to evil' and faith in the individual conscience as the means to a total reconstruction of society. Tolstoy may have deserted literature, but his ideas shattered the literary world as powerfully as they did politico-economic and religious thought, and Chekhov was later to admit to the hypnotic spell which Tolstoy had exerted over him from about 1885 to 1891 : his style, especially in 1887, shows that Tolstoy's hammering methods of exposition and his minutely observed descriptions were more hypnotic than his ideas of self-redemption by a literal application of New Testament ethics. Nevertheless, in stories such as *Good People* (first entitled *My Sister*), Tolstoyan ideas are the first example of a system of thought breaking into the lives of Chekhov's characters.

Novoye Vremya encouraged Chekhov to free himself from Leykin. In early 1886 he was already referring to Leykin as 'that lame devil', and in 1887 as 'Quasimodo'. The quality of his 'Chekhonte' stories, both for Leykin and for Khudekov of the *Petersburg Newspaper*, fell away. On a personal level, Chekhov's relations with Leykin improved : they shared an interest in dachshunds and cigars; but by 1888 Chekhov was to have the courage to write only what he was artistically involved in. In an effort to raise *Oskolki*'s level, he proposed a literary competition to Leykin : a competition for the best love letter was set, but only two replies were received—one obscene, one illiterate.

In the whirl of 1886, which was an *annus mirabilis* of productivity and quality, it is easy to lose sight of the darkening horizons in Chekhov's life. His first love, Dunya Efros—judging by what little we know—had a fiery temperament which tormented as much as it attracted him, a feature common to all but the last of his loves. If we use the unreliable criterion of his treatment of love and the heroines in his fiction of that time, Dunya Efros must have given him more pain than joy. Sickness was the other factor. The typhoid epidemic at the end of 1885 killed six of Chekhov's year at the university; in summer 1886 he was plagued by haemorrhoids and toothache (he used the pain of toothache to describe the agony of typhus); in March 1887 his brother Aleksandr summoned him to Petersburg: all around him, in the households of Leykin, Suvorin and Aleksandr, people were dying. Grigorovich had a heart attack caused by the joy of meeting Chekhov. Petersburg became for him a 'town of death', and his own body a *memento mori*.

The bondage of sexual love and a nightmarish atmosphere of mental and physical disorder provide the main themes of Chekhov's first twenty stories for *Novoye Vremya*. The sexual theme in the stories of 1886 is not only due to his own awakening or to the undoubted interest of the readers of *Novoye Vremya*: it is also one of the predominant themes of Tolstoy's late work and, in fact, in the contemporary novel, where sexuality rivals the pursuit of wealth as a motivating force for the characters. The influence of Tolstoy shows itself in a story such as *Neschast'ye* (*A Misfortune*), in which the heroine, a married woman, becomes uncomfortable as she realises that she is encouraging a family friend to become a lover. Her reaction to her husband, 'I love him, but why does he chew in such a revolting way?' recalls Tolstoy's Anna Karenina, as does the image of a goods train passing along like the monotonous days of her life. Her innate insincerity, her 'leech-like' sexuality, the author's condescending comments on the 'triviality and egotism of a youthful nature' all betray a too recent reading of Tolstoy. The theme of sexuality is at its most dramatic in the earlier 1886 stories. *Ved'ma* (*The Witch*) and *Agaf'ya*, both written in March, show, respectively, a deacon's wife and a railway guard's wife helplessly in thrall to their instincts. The 'witch' unconsciously lures the mail-coach to her door during a blizzard and nearly seduces the postillion. The old deacon cursing his young wife and the sorcery by which she attracts the mail-coach are of little importance compared with Chekhov's powerful evocation of sexual languor and his romantic technique of projecting the tormented passion of the 'witch' into the blizzard raging outside. *Agaf'ya* is a more prosaic heroine, returning like a beaten cat to her husband after an evening with her lover; but she too, in the perspective of a calm, all-knowing narrator, is presented as a dramatic portrait of the female rampant.

The most interesting of these slightly meretricious stories is *Tina* (*The Quagmire*). On the surface it is comical and even a little pornographic. It led to Maria Kiseleva's remarks about 'the dunghill'; Lavrov, the editor of the prestigious *Russkaya Mysl'* (*Russian Thought*), commented that it was fit only for *Novoye Vremya*. The 'mire' is the world of a Jewish woman who lives alone on her estate, ignoring convention. A young officer comes to see her to collect on an IOU the money he needs to marry on. She takes his IOU back, but does not give him the money and forces him to fight her for it; the fight turns into lovemaking and the officer stays the night. In the second half of the story, the same thing happens to the officer's cousin who also tries to recover the money. In the end, the young officer revisits her, only to find his cousin and all the men of the district also there, in the 'mire'. One could agree with Maria Kiseleva that the story is only a dunghill without any pearl, mere pastiche of Maupassant, were it not for the intensity and the originality of the portrait of Susanna, whose sexuality emerges in her masculine bravado, in imagery that is simultaneously repellent and alluring : there is a suffocating smell of jasmine; goldfinches fly about in the conservatory-living-room; clothes are strewn over an unmade bed; the heroine's slight hump, curly hair, pale gums excite the hero because he does not like them. The 'mire' is sexuality itself.

If Susanna's tempestuous Jewishness tempts us to link her with Dunya Efros, we can find a number of autobiographical traits in the best of these stories, *Verochka*. The heroine falls in love with a young statistician, Ognev, who is tied to his work and has never before fallen in love. Now, after an idyll with Verochka's family, he finds on the eve of his departure that he cannot reciprocate the love which she suddenly blurts out. His reticence, his dedication to his work and his fear of involvement show features both of the author and of Chekhov's later introspective heroes. He feels that the present is strangely unreal : it is the idea of a meeting with Verochka in ten years' time that interests him, just as the hero of *A Dreary Story* and those of the plays are more curious about life in ten or a hundred years' time than the present. In contrast to this spiritual impotence, masked by gentility, Verochka's forthright expression of love makes the female seem more honest and courageous than the male. Here, as later in Chekhov, the male can only wonder at his weakness : 'He had now known for himself the position of a decent and warm-hearted man who causes his neighbour, despite himself, cruel, undeserved suffering.' But even in the poetic, melancholy Verochka there is something degrading when she takes her stand : 'She seemed to him somehow lower, simpler, darker . . .

Vera's raptures and suffering seemed to him cloying and to lack seriousness.' Something cerebral in the hero resists the emotional, sexual and poetic forces that Vera lets loose : love is just as much a 'mire' here as in the story of the Jewess, Susanna.

If love 'lacks seriousness', the serious side in Chekhov's work of 1886 comes out in stories that portray life as a purgatory in which no one has a right to individual happiness. Here, too, the influence of Tolstoy on the theme as well as the technique is visible. *Skuka zhizni* (*The Boredom of Life*) suffers from this influence : an old woman remakes her life as death approaches. On the other hand, the Tolstoyan formula of the well-intentioned young man suddenly appreciating the enormity of his own life and its disparity with others' lives works well in *Koshmar* (*The Nightmare*). The hero comes to the country determined to do good, and tries to enlist the local priest in his efforts. But the priest seems interested only in drinking his tea and eating his biscuits. The hero is disgusted and not until the dénouement does he discover the terrible poverty of the village : the priest is himself starving, saddled with debts; the doctor is so poor that his wife has to wash her linen secretly in the river. As in Tolstoy's work, the rich man is as incompetent to set right the wrongs of society as is the camel to pass through the eye of the needle.[3] The ending is a pure sermon : 'His whole soul was filled with a feeling of oppressive shame at himself and at the invisible truth . . . Thus began and culminated a sincere impulse for useful activity in one of those well-intentioned but excessively well-fed and unreasoning people.' The vision of poverty and degradation was powerful enough to give the story a reception that amazed Chekhov. Country doctors saw themselves in the story, just as provincial women were to identify themselves with the unhappy three sisters of the play. The correspondence columns of *Novoye Vremya* were filled with letters confirming that Chekhov had revealed a new field for social action, and the impact of *A Nightmare* led the critics to associate him with contemporaries such as Korolenko and Uspensky, whose whole work was devoted to giving an accurate and moving picture of the sufferings of the under-privileged.

But Chekhov's intentions were not nearly so didactic as Tolstoy's or Uspensky's. His hero's impulses are shattered as soon as they are awakened. For Chekhov evil was never eradicable; it erupts in dreamlike sequences. *Mechty* (*Dreams*) of November 1886 is as full of autumnal mists as *Koshmar* of late March was full of a false

spring. It has only three characters—two soldiers and the prisoner
they are escorting, an escaped convict who does not give his name.
The convict dreams of a life of work and religious observance in
exile in Eastern Siberia, determined not to give his name so that
he cannot be returned to forced labour for the crime he has committed.
One of the soldiers escorting him talks to him and thus brings out
his life story : the dreamer is the son of a peasant woman by her
master, half-educated, divorced from the worlds of both peasant
and gentry; his mother murdered her master and he was convicted
as an accomplice. But his life history is not the point of the story :
the weak and insignificant dreamer is utterly spellbound by the
rivers and the forests of Siberia. Chekhov has endowed him with
his own love of fishing and of trees, as well as with the loneliness
of the *déclassé*. The irony of the dreamer's walk to the east is pointed
out by his escorts; he has not a hope of enduring the journey to
the promised land of exile. Between him and paradise lie 'the drawn-
out court procedure, the transit and forced labour prisons, the convicts' barges, the wearying waits on the journey, the frozen winters,
the deaths of comrades'. As he realises this, the dreamer's world
crumples : 'he writhes like a trodden caterpillar.'

There is far more in this short story of four thousand words than
a commiserating portrait of an honest criminal. The dreamer is an
allegorical figure : his dreams are those of humanity and of the
artist, and the terrible journey to Siberia is life itself : the graphic
imagery of the dreamer and the soldiers tramping in the mists gives
the story a Kafkaesque intensity. The mist isolates them in a moving,
permanent world of their own :

The travellers have been walking for a long time now but they cannot
move off a small fragment of earth. Before them lie about ten yards of
dirty, blackish-brown road, behind them the same and further, wherever
you look, is an impenetrable wall of white mist. They walk and walk,
but the earth is the same, the wall is no nearer and the fragment stays
a fragment.

This is reality in contrast with the dreams of Siberia :

In the autumn silence, when the harsh, cold mist overlays the soul,
when it stands before your eyes like a prison wall and demonstrates
man's limitations of will, it is sometimes sweet to think of broad, fast
rivers with free, steep banks, of impenetrable forests, unbounded
steppes.

The romanticism of Chekhov's yearnings for the open country of the south that he was to revisit in spring 1887, or of Siberia which he crossed in 1890, can be traced back to *Dreams*. Some of his critics could see in the story an imaginative intuition of the cosmos as well as a compassionate portrayal of suffering. Old men like Grigorovich could only consider the technique in the landscapes and characterisations; the new generation, for instance the future Symbolist critic, novelist and philosopher, Merezhkovsky, could get closer to the truth, writing in 1888 that Chekhov 'combines a broad mystical feeling for nature with sober, healthy realism'. But few of Chekhov's readers had any use for mystical feelings : literature for them had psychiatric and political functions—it had to heal and to reform its material. They found two categories of the 1886 stories which met their needs : stories of personal conflict, in which right clashes with wrong and reaches some sort of synthesis, and 'problem stories' in which contemporary philosophical topics are given mouths and legs and made to talk and act as characters. *Tyazholyye lyudi* (*Difficult People*) of October 1886 and *Vragi* (*Enemies*) of January 1887 show a vivid clash of personalities : so does *Khoroshiye lyudi* (*Good People*) of November 1886, but it is better understood as a 'problem story', like the famous *Na puti* (*On the Road*), which *Novoye Vremya* printed on Christmas Day.

Both *Difficult People* and *Enemies* have protagonists who can be identified with the author. In *Difficult People*, the hero is the student who has to fight his bullying father for the means to keep alive at the university. The mother is a helpless victim of the crossfire between father and son, whom we begin to see as two people embodying the same stubborn male individualism. The version printed in *Novoye Vremya* is both brutal and conciliatory. The story ends with the mother struck by a blow intended for the son, 'flapping her arms like a duck with its throat cut'. Shocked by their violence, father and son quieten down. The son suddenly feels sympathy for his father and sees their conflict as a natural Darwinian process : spring has to be paid for by autumn, humanity and meekness have to be reached by sacrifice and harsh lessons. Fifteen years later, when Chekhov revised the story for his Collected Works, he would not let the clash resolve itself so harmoniously. The episode of the blow and the last paragraphs were cut, and, in accordance with the unresolved and unfathomable nature of Chekhov's later outlook, right and wrong remain inextricable; the revised version ends : 'He didn't blame his father, he did not take his mother's side, he didn't torment himself with remorse : he understood that everyone in the house was feeling the same pain and God knew who was wrong, who was suffering most or least.'

Enemies has a doctor for a hero. (The doctor in the 1886 stories is an infrequent hero, compared with the lawyers and notaries who are the centre of a score of tales. He is a rough diamond whose idealism is imposed on and whose rough edges are mistaken for callousness.) It uses material which Chekhov outlined in *The Mirror* of late 1885 : the doctor is himself badly in need of treatment when an importunate visitor drags him out. There is a comic outline, but a tragic substance. Doctor Kirilov's only son has just died of diphtheria; a visitor insists on taking him ten miles to treat his wife. He uses all possible arguments and finally succeeds, but when they arrive, there is no patient. The wife has faked a heart attack so that she can leave with her lover. Kirilov is overcome with rage at the outcome and, like the student in *Difficult People*, is changed for life by his anger at the 'satedness and elegance' of the man who dragged him out. As so often in 1886 and 1887, Chekhov cannot resist a moral : 'Time will pass and so will Kirilov's grief, but this conviction, unjust, unworthy of the human heart, will not, and will stay in the doctor's mind till the grave.' Love of humanity, as the doctor is made to say earlier, is a two-ended stick. Chekhov is demonstrating that it is human nature, not ideas of justice and humanity, that is intractable and in need of treatment. His point of view becomes all the clearer when he writes stories that appear to deal with the world of ideas. *Good People*, originally entitled *My Sister*, introduces us through the narrator to a brother and sister. The brother is a literary critic, with commonplace ideas; his sister, who has suffered the death of her husband and son, falls under the spell of Tolstoy, particularly his notion of non-resistance to evil. Brother and sister begin to argue, but their arguments do nothing but destroy each other. She leaves; in the 1902 version, he dies and is forgotten. The version in *Novoye Vremya* makes Chekhov's (or the narrator's) stand-point more obvious : in a passage deleted from the final version of 1902, the narrator states that the brother's mistake is not that he thinks 'non-resistance to evil' absurd, but that he has not yet assessed his own competence to look at the question. The narrator then makes a declaration which should be remembered whenever we meet a system of ideas expounded by a Chekhovian character :

It is wrong to practise as a doctor if you don't know medicine or to try a thief without any preliminary acquaintance with the case, but it is odd that it is not considered dishonest in community life when people who are not equipped, not initiated, who are inadequately developed morally and intellectually, take it upon themselves to lord it about in a field of thought in which they can only be guests.

Chekhov deleted this passage either because he became reluctant to impose a narrator's interpretation on his readers or because he knew it was pointless to try to convince the Russian reader, so often a philosophical dilettante, that he was not competent to assess philosophical ideas. For the reader of 1886 or the 1900s the point of the story lay in the victory or defeat of Tolstoyan ideas. In the 1900s Chekhov had to insert phrases to remind his readers that the 1880s were the times when vegetarianism, celibacy and non-resistance to evil were becoming fashionable. The brother's views represent the consensus that if resistance to evil were abandoned, the world would be destroyed and only 'bashi-bazouks and brothels' would remain. The reader of 1886 would believe that Tolstoyan ideas won the battle, simply because the sister has 'suffered out' (*vystradala*) her ideas, becoming a woman doctor, losing her husband and son, attempting suicide and going off to serve her ideals. The reader of the 1900s would perhaps believe this, too, on the grounds that the brother is clearly a literary hack and, once dead, is forgotten. But the Tolstoyan bias shows only that Chekhov felt the lure of Tolstoy's new evangelism, not that he has surrendered to it. The essence of the story is that ideas have made their exponents false, sour and sterile.

Chekhov's readers were pleased to see 'serious questions' enter his prose. His other 'problem story', *Na puti* (*On the Road*), his brother Aleksandr wrote to him, 'produced a furore in Petersburg'. Chekhov himself boasted of his 'courage' : 'I'm writing about "something clever" and I'm not afraid.' *On the Road* was also by far the longest of the stories he had written for *Novoye Vremya*—over six thousand words—and by far the most conventional in having a hero very much in the tradition of the 'superfluous man' (a recognisable reincaration of Turgenev's Rudin), and a chance encounter and sudden burgeoning of hopeless love in the best Tur-

c

genevian traditions. It moved Tchaikovsky to write a fan-letter (which went astray in the post) and, twelve years later, Rachmaninov was to compose on it a *Fantasy for Orchestra*. Its appeal should remind us that in *On the Road* Chekhov's creative energies were spent in varying a well-known theme, not in breaking new ground. As in *In Autumn* (1883), he introduces us to a ruined gentleman, *progorevshiy barin*, taking refuge from the weather in an inn. With overtones of the nativity a blizzard rages outside, while Likharev and his little daughter try to get through the night. A young woman is held up, too, by the weather and she brings out the life story of Likharev: we see that he, like the characters of *Good People*, is wrecked by ideas, by faith. First, he confesses, he believed in science; then the infinity of scientific knowledge disillusioned him and he passed to political thought, nihilism, Slavophile populism and, lastly, non-resistance to evil. Each faith has brought with it a sacrifice of money, health and marriage, and with each change, betrayal. All that is left now is his painful realisation that the females who followed him are even more stupid than himself, superior only in their fidelity and endurance. Likharev thus makes between the sexes the distinction that Chekhov draws again and again: the superiority of the male lies in an ability to disabuse himself and declare himself morally bankrupt. The woman, like Likharev's previous women, cannot resist his idealistic charm even in this short time. The only wisdom, perhaps, comes from the little girl who breaks in with her complaints: 'Lord, he won't let me sleep with his talk.' Likharev is doomed this time: he is, like so many Chekhovian heroes to come, too old at forty-two. The heroine leaves him in the morning and he has to go to his final job as a mine-manager, a fate which recalls one of the episodes in Turgenev's *Rudin*. Likharev is the last of the 'superfluous men'; the blizzard covers him with snow until he is fossilised—'a white rock, but his eyes still kept looking for something in the clouds of snow.' Chekhov's aim appears to have been to dispose completely of the superfluous man. But like the hero of *Ivanov*, Likharev was unintelligible to Chekhov's contemporaries. They could not accept that the ideas as well as the man were a dead end. They either persisted in seeing Likharev as a man with the political enthusiasm of the 1860s who has been stranded in the sceptical, cynical 1880s, a victim of chronology, or they tried to see him as a traitor who uses ideas only as a means of seduction. The second view is a little more justifiable, but misses the sheer physical and spiritual restlessness of Likharev's nature, of which philosophy is only one feature. Merezhkovsky, for instance, wrote : 'Add to Likharev the feature of simple, naïve caddishness and take away the futile pretence, the desire to appear a hero and you get an utterly contemporary type of very many Russian "social activists".' In vain did Chekhov reply by saying that 'separating people into successes and failures means looking at human nature from a narrow, prejudiced point of view' (letter to Suvorin, 3 November 1888). This is a characteristic misunderstanding of Chekhov and in their search for 'types', for signposts, the critics were to misunderstand much more.[4] Rachmaninov's *Fantasy for Orchestra* showed more comprehension of the relationship between Likharev and the blizzard that maroons him on his last journey to a living hell than anything that Russian criticism had yet produced on the subject.

It is the very variety of the stories written for *Novoye Vremya* that makes summary difficult. They are 'literature', they look to the ultimate demands of the material, and of literary tradition, rather than to those of fashion. The essential difference between these stories and Chekhov's earlier work is that in them there is no consciousness of genre : their tone is dictated by the landscapes, the characters and their thoughts, not by the concept of an erotic, a farcical, a melodramatic or a *chinovnik* story. Many of them have a narrator who is himself a character, no longer the busybody, the impresario, the know-all of the early work, but a sensitive, tactful observer, sympathetic to his characters but reluctant to interfere with them. The narrator in *Agaf'ya* or in *Good People* is as close to the author as he can be without becoming confessional in tone, and it is the presence of a narrator that raises the almost plotless 'country sketch' to a high art form. Perhaps the most magical of the stories of 1886 is *Svyatoyu noch'yu* (*On Easter Night*). The narrator takes the rope ferry across the river to the monastery for the service on Easter night. The ecstasy of spring is fused with the celebration of the Resurrection and the narrator's tension in simply being awake at night and thinking about the monk who works the ferry. This is the frame story. Within this, the monk Iyeronim provides a contrasting tale of grief. Instead of celebrating Easter he has to work the ferry and to mourn his closest friend, the monk Nikolay who has just died. Iyeronim's memories of Nikolay, which he tells to the narrator, are an elegy for a poet. The dead monk was the composer of *akafisty*, psalm-like songs of praise, and Iyeronim quotes from them, in all the florid poetry of their Church Slavonic. Absurd (and untranslatable) though the baroque intricacy of the *akafisty* may be, their very strangeness tells us that poetry depends for its meaning on its apartness from ordinary life and usage.

On Easter Night shows how remarkably religious was Chekhov's idea of art. Again and again, in *The Student* (1894), in *The Bishop* (1902), for example, the church's language and myths incorporate all poetic utterance. *On Easter Night*, like the other ecclesiastical stories, uses various strata of language—the narrator's slightly pompous, disingenuous style; the monk's half-colloquial, half-monastic phrases; the pure poetic Church Slavonic of the *akafisty*—these make a progression from ordinary life to the life of the artist and hermit. There is a symbolism in the crossing of the river to the monastery, the river so often in Chekhov's work being both a prompter of melancholy and a division between two worlds. The imagery of spring vegetation in the night and of the barrels of tar set alight to illuminate the monastery helps to create the strange magical atmosphere of regeneration and elegy. Contemporary critical response was blinded by the plot. 'Shades of Turgenev', 'pantheism' were two of the phrases used in an attempt to explain the religious utterance of a doubter like Chekhov. But *On Easter Night* is to show the way to the greatest work of the next two years, *Steppe*; it is one of the most Leskovian[5] of Chekhov's works, and Leskov, whose name recurs in Chekhov's stories, is perhaps the Russian writer to whom he is closest.

Some of the stories of the *Petersburg Newspaper* show Chekhov still using topical material. The rabies epidemic of 1886 led to *Volk* (*The Wolf*), whose imagery of moonlight Chekhov used to instruct Aleksandr how to write, and to characterise the techniques of Trigorin. Another epidemic led to a highly dramatic study, *Tif* (*Typhus*); medical expertise is added to pathos; a young man recovers from typhus only to find that he has infected and killed his nearest and dearest.

Contemporary fashions in reading also affect Chekhov. It is in 1886 that we see the impact made by Maupassant's stories. The central character in *Khoristka* (*The Chorus Girl*), who is bullied by a wronged wife into handing over all her jewellery, owes much to Maupassant's *Boule de suif;* so does the poor prostitute who goes to a dentist she once knew, dares not reveal her name, and loses a tooth for no good reason. Chekhov respected Maupassant rather more than he had respected Gaboriau, and his influence, once assimilated, was to lead to a novel treatment of themes of sex and prostitution.

Some of the pieces written for Khudekov raise themes which Chekhov had yet to exploit fully. The railway and its horrors appear in an episode in *Strakhi* (*Fears*), in which a goods wagon without an engine arouses an irrational cosmic fear. The wrecked and ruined estate, the setting for Chekhov's plays, can be found in stories such as *Chuzhaya beda* (*Someone Else's Troubles*), in which a newly married couple buying an estate have their happiness soured at the sight of the despair of the ruined owners. The amiable but frustrated professor longing for his boyhood, who is to develop into the hero of *A Dreary Story*, is already outlined in *Ivan Matveich*.

By early 1887, Chekhov was feeling exhausted physically and mentally : he realised that his experience was being used up faster than it could be renewed. The last two stories written for *Novoye Vremya* in March 1887, *Doma* (*At Home*) and *Vstrecha* (*The Meeting*), show a noticeable falling-off of tension and involvement; the second, a Tolstoyan confrontation of two peasants, displeased Chekhov so much that he refused to reprint it in his Collected Works. By now he had settled his life : his family was installed in comfortable quarters; Aleksandr had been rescued from the customs and given a job on Suvorin's staff; he himself was an established figure in literary life. He approached Suvorin for approval and for financial help to revisit the towns and monasteries that he had known as a boy. The journey south to Taganrog gave him material and self-awareness : it was to make him a major writer.

6

The Steppe

Chekhov travelled for six weeks : first to Taganrog to relatives and friends, then north to the hills of the Donets 'Switzerland'. At the end of April he spent a few days at the monastery of Svyatyye Gory near Slavyansk, returning to Taganrog before the long journey to join the family at Babkino. His impressions were mixed : squalid provincial narrowness contrasted with the splendid emptiness of the open steppe, a contrast that was to polarise everything he wrote about man and nature hereafter, endowing his work with a recurrent motif and giving a core of sense to his rhapsodies on nature.

The most important work written as a consequence of the journey is undoubtedly the 'history of a journey', *Steppe*, which was published in the March 1888 issue of *Severnyy Vestnik* (*Northern Herald*); it is Chekhov's masterpiece. But in the course of the journey itself and in the summer of 1887 a number of preparatory pieces—stories is a misleading name—were written which already demonstrate how the journey south had widened Chekhov's perspectives. He wrote a very good account of it in his letters to his sister Maria. The phrases and thoughts he records were deeply etched on his mind; they reappear in his late stories and plays. The country around Taganrog and the Donets hills is the setting for *The Cherry Orchard*; the unseen mine-shafts that honeycomb the countryside, the sheep and the panpipes, the filthy kitchens and servants' quarters of the Ranevskaya household were all first noted in 1887. Chekhov's explanations have the indignation of Trofimov's and the mocking-bird dreaminess of Lopakhin's. He describes life in Taganrog (7 April 1887, to Maria)—'60,000 inhabitants are occupied only with eating, drinking and multiplying . . . How dirty, empty, idle, illiterate and boring is Taganrog'—as he is later to describe it in *The Bride* and other works.

The human scene was especially horrible in the Donets valley which at this time was being rapidly scarred by mine-workings, railways, steelworks, industrial tenements, deforestation and the use of grazing-lands for wheat. This made Chekhov the first Russian writer to link Malthusian and Darwinian theories with ideas of nature conservation. It made him all the more aware of natural beauty as something as frail as it was infinite: 'I left the carriage in the night to see a man about a dog, and outside there were sheer miracles: the moon, the boundless steppe with its burial mounds and the wilderness; the quiet of the grave, while the carriages and rails stood out sharply in the twilight—it seemed the world had died.' The overtones of death are important in the pictures of the steppe; very often, Chekhov's landscapes and seascapes, especially at night, breathe a lunar sterility[1] which stresses that nature is sometimes hostile and alien to man. The steppes have the *kurgany* (burial mounds) to remind the observer that his civilisation may be obliterated as completely as were the Scythians buried in them. The steppe country had been repopulated only recently, after centuries of desolation: the desolation is part of the attraction and mystery in the story or prose-poem *Steppe*.

During the whole journey, and for most of the year, Chekhov was plagued by illness: intestinal catarrh, what he still called bronchitis, an ear infection, piles and varicose veins as well as alleged 'excesses in Baccho et Venere' made the squalid sanitation and the moments of freedom from pain deeply felt. His sensitivity became acute, until he magnified the rough provincial life into a horrific cycle: the 'rational economy' of one farm is sarcastically characterised as

continuous killing, that doesn't stop for a day or a minute. They kill sparrows, swallows, wild bees, ants, magpies, crows, to stop them eating bees; they kill the bees to stop them spoiling the fruit blossom; they cut down the trees to stop them exhausting the soil. Thus you get a rotation which may be original but is based on the latest scientific data.

This is Chekhov's first jibe at science, which is to lead to the rhetoric against destructive modernity in the mouth of Astrov: at this point it germinates in Chekhov a feeling of being a lone explorer among aborigines. The names of explorers—Miklukho-Maklay and Przhevalsky—begin to figure in his letters. Conscious of his own superiority, freed in fact from memories of his youth, he becomes more sure of himself. In 1887 the stories he wrote with most enjoyment are those whose roots lie in the journey south and whose main character is nature: *Schast'ye* (*Fortune*), *Svirel'* (*The Pan-pipes*), *Perekati-pole* (literally *Field Eryngo*; figuratively *Thistle-down, Rolling Stone*) all prefigure *Steppe*.

These three stories and the five other works that Suvorin printed in *Novoye Vremya* between April 1887 and March 1888 show that Chekhov's best work was almost the monopoly of Suvorin. The stories for the *Petersburg Newspaper* clearly deterioriate ('I wrote foully, for money,' Chekhov explained to Leykin); later he excluded a number of them from his Collected Works. *Oskolki* received fewer and fewer, and at the end of 1887, Chekhov felt secure enough to write to Leykin a discreet letter of resignation. His work of 1886, his steppe stories, the invitations to write *Ivanov* and *Steppe* (for the highly respected *Severnyy Vestnik*), unofficial hints at the award of the Pushkin prize all gave him confidence to break away from the drudgery of the weekly story and to release creative energy for themes and genres of his own choosing. His income was by now substantial (though his southern loyalty to the family kept him insolvent); Suvorin paid him twelve kopecks a line and would accept up to six thousand words at a time; *Ivanov* earned him a thousand rubles, as did *Steppe*. For the first time he had an income from his books: *Pyostryye rasskazy* (*Motley Stories*) were edited by Leykin in 1886 and *V sumerkakh* (*In the Twilight*), a selection of the *Novoye Vremya* stories, was published by Suvorin.

To appreciate *Steppe* it is necessary to look at the evolution of Chekhov's thought during the eight months in which the work lay dormant. By 1887, he was writing many letters and his addressees were keeping them: they provide some useful evidence. A line here and there shows that he had broken with Dunya Efros: an attraction towards a vivacious and spirited young woman was abruptly suppressed by a fear of losing his privacy and his freedom of movement, and this desire for self-sufficiency is even more marked in his relations with Aleksandr, whom he turned into his agent at the offices of *Novoye Vremya*. Meanwhile, his literary friendships followed their previous pattern: he became close to two more 'grand old men'—Pleshcheyev, who had been sentenced to death with Dostoyevsky, and the last Russian romantic poet, Polonsky; he exchanged flattering letters with his contemporary Korolenko, with whom he was to share the 1888 Pushkin prize, but he remained outside the mainstream of literary life.

There was naturally a melancholy side to this private world. Family life at Babkino, gathering raspberries and fungi, rearing leverets, dispensing medicine to peasants and literary advice to amateurs, was not enough. A letter to Aleksandr, since destroyed, apparently spoke of the depression that was to lead to *A Dreary Story* and never quite to leave Chekhov's work: 'I'm alone, have nobody to talk to . . . I hear and read lies, petty but endless lies . . . I'm incapable of working . . . my youth has finished.' Although he frequently recovers his balance, the idea of lost youth and the dislike of what he reads and hears swell into a lyrical lament for lost time and honesty. Without these disillusionments, he would not have used the character of the little boy who connects the episodes of *Steppe* with anything like the intensely envious passion that he shows. Much of the lyricism of *Steppe* is escapist: if the story had been continued, Chekhov meant to make the little boy, Yegorushka, come to Moscow or Petersburg and end badly.

This *Katzenjammer*, as Chekhov put it, was not relieved by anything he read. Only one work makes a genuine impression on him: Thoreau's *Walden*, then being serialised, which shares with *Steppe* a thirst for nature that can dwarf man. All through the winter of 1887–8 Chekhov made plans to escape: to go to the Cossack Kuban' in March, to the Volga with the aged Pleshcheyev in spring, and to the Ukraine in summer. That his wanderlust does not look beyond the Russian empire is significant. The steppe had convinced Chekhov that the relationship of man and nature in Russia had no parallel with that in the populated and organised West. Europe began to seem to Chekhov an irrelevant, if agreeable, neighbour, and he did not visit it until the Suvorins took him. To Grigorovich, who had retired to Nice for his health, Chekhov wrote, explaining the difficulty of treating Russian psychology in prose:

The artist's entire energy must be directed at two forces: man and nature. On the one hand, physical weakness, tense nerves, early sexual maturity, passionate thirst for life and truth, dreams of activity as wide as the steppes, restless analysing, a dearth of knowledge together with wide-ranging thought; on the other hand—a boundless plain, a harsh climate, a dreary, harsh people with its heavy, cold history, Tatar yoke, officialdom, poverty, ignorance, damp capital cities, etc. Russian life bashes the Russian till you have to scrape him off the floor, like a twenty-ton rock. In Western Europe people perish because life is too crowded and close, here they perish because it is too spacious.

This was meant as an explanation of Russian suicides, but it amounts to a specific characterisation of Russian life. Here is a new dimension. In *Steppe*, as in Chekhov's later work, man is the prisoner of his antecedents and surroundings, as well as of his passions and past actions. The journey south had brought not only new material, but also a sense that the spiritual was weighed down by the material world.

After an absence of eight years, Chekhov's response to Taganrog was immediate. On his arrival he wrote a sketch *Na strastnoy nedele (In Easter Week)*, seeing Easter confession and communion through the mind of a nine-year-old boy narrator : the joy of absolution and the appeal of the half-intelligible language of the church comes over strongly through the child's mind. The ecclesiastical strain persisted as long as Chekhov was in Taganrog, and another of the *Petersburg Newspaper* stories, *Pis'mo (The Letter)* has a Leskovian trio of priests. Neither of these stories is a work of art, but the material of the impressionable boy and the authoritarian, good-natured clergy is to be used to the full in *Steppe*.

Before he left Taganrog, Chekhov dashed off another piece of two thousand words for Khudekov's *Petersburg Newspaper*. *Oby-vateli (The Philistines* or *The Average Man)* catches the sleepy degeneracy of the south, as the German schoolteacher and a Pole play cards and berate the idle Russians. The same graceless inertia characterises the postillion in the story *Pochta (The Post)* written in October, only here the opposition of man and the glorious earth which he sullies is brought out far more clearly. The postillion, a surly character, is thrown out of the mail-coach by the ruts in the road and the lively horses. In the newspaper text (which Chekhov shortened three years later for publication in *Khmuryye lyudi— Gloomy People)*, nature clearly resents human intruders : 'The river looked sternly and sadly; it seemed to be plotting someone's death in the shadows, together with the stars which were reflected in it, and now in its grumbling beneath the wheels could be heard restlessness and wrath at the breakers of its peace.' *Steppe*, too, has 'breakers of the peace' among its characters, together with the same conspiratorial resentment on the part of nature. But three stories of June, July and August anticipate its sultry tension far more closely. All were published in *Novoye Vremya*. The first, *Schast'ye (Fortune* or *Happiness)*, was in Chekhov's eyes and in his critics' the best piece he had so far written. It already shows the daring plotless-

ness, the relaxed pace, terse but unhurried, the full-blooded lyricism
that mark his maturity. 'A product of inspiration, quasi-symphony',
Chekhov called it. He dedicated it a year later to the poet Polonsky
as a picture of the steppe: 'the plain, night, pale daybreak in the
east, a flock of sheep and three human figures discussing fortune.'
To his brother Aleksandr, Chekhov belittled the technical achievement: 'The reader likes it because of the optical illusion. The whole
trick is in the ornaments inserted, like the sheep, and in the polish-
ing of individual lines. You can talk about used coffee grounds and
amaze the reader by means of tricks.'

By relegating the characters to a minor role, Chekhov can move
the plot to the descriptive level: opening with the sheep and the
Milky Way both dozing in harmony, ending with the stars fading,
a scarlet sun rising, and the sheep suddenly rushing off in 'some
uncomprehensible horror', a horror which ties up with the shepherds'
musing on fortune. The horror passes, like the conversation of the
two men with the estate manager, and we are left with the human
beings living their separate lives and the sheep thinking unknowable
thoughts. It is night on the steppe, with the grasshoppers and quails,
that produces conversation in men and thought in sheep. The
sheep's thoughts have a melancholic dignity; the old men's talk revolves round the old sorcerer who has died and the buried treasure
he has been hiding. Happiness, or fortune, is for them nothing but
spell-bound, buried treasure, and they think of it when they are
too old and sickly to have a hope of finding it. Like their sheep,
they respond to the sky and the plains, and their obsession with
treasure is like the panic of their flocks. The action is in the breaking of day. As night ends, life ends. The steppe becomes visible:
the 'invincible sultry heat' and the burial mounds make it seem
deadly. There is an unseen world in the mines beneath the ground,
in the railways and the ranches of the settlers—a motley of Germans, Russian sectarians, Ukrainians and Greeks—which suggests
a fungus-like infiltration of the wilderness. From this and from the
talk of sorcery comes the same aura of imminent doom as we feel
in *The Cherry Orchard*, of which there are also two specific anticipations in the tale. Just as Firs is to say that the stove howled and
owls shrieked before the 'catastrophe' of the emancipation of
the serfs, so here the shepherds talk about a rock howling before the
emancipation. Then there is a strange noise in the stillness. As the
sound dies, the young shepherd says: 'It's a tub that's broken away

in the mine-shafts': this is Lopakhin's explanation of the 'broken
string' noise.

This tub also appears in *Perekati-Pole* (*Thistledown*); it is one
of the many disasters that happen to the baptised Jew whom the
narrator meets in the monastery of Svyatyye Gory (Sacred Hills).
Thistledown has a dual world. It is a poetic evocation of the wholeness of ecclesiastical life, its harmony with creation and with the passage of the seasons; it is also as much a study of 'the outsider' as was
On the Road of six months previously. But while Likharev's nomadic
progress from one faith to another, until he ends like a desolate
snow-covered rock, has tragic grandeur, Aleksandr—once Isaac—
Ivanych is a pathetic example of the wandering Jew. He lacks the
charm of Likharev and the traditional 'superfluous man'; he writes
himself off in endless apologies and self-justification; he has lost his
sexual appeal. Chekhov has in fact subtly altered his heroes and
villains in his steppe stories, simply by depriving them of women.
Without female characters there can be no tragic interpretations of
failure, and the most important stories of 1887 and early 1888 are
all-male. Not only *The Letter, Fortune, Thistledown, Panpipes*,
but also many of the *Petersburg Newspaper* stories, such as *The
Post*, have no women characters. This is one of the most Gogolian
characteristics of Chekhov's most Gogolian period. The misfit is
reduced from romantic desolation to social write-off in the image
of a wind-dispersed weed, the eryngium *perekati-pole*. But there is
a darker side to the story of the converted Jew. The *perekati-pole* in
Russian folklore is a weed that turns blood-red when a murderer
touches it; Aleksandr Ivanych, a victim and a witness of murderous
forces, has the same aura of fatality. He is disowned by his family,
let down by his friends, and crippled when a tub crushes him in
the mine-shaft, the living hell beneath the paradise of the monastery.
The story uses Aleksandr Ivanych to bring out the peaceful sanc-
tuary of the monastery, and the narrator shows the same detached
love of the monks and the processions as does Chekhov in his letters.
Like him, the narrator slips away from the services, and communes
in solitude with the sun-bathed river Donets beneath the monastery,
which stands not so much for the Christian faith as for a golden
age in which man and nature were in harmony. Leaving it, the
narrator is once more faced with the endless steppe and with the
Quixotic image of the windmill, which is to be so important in
the first part of *Steppe*.

The third steppe story, *Panpipes*, like the first, uses human figures
only as secondary material. On a gloomy summer morning, a man
out shooting with his dog hears panpipes and meets a shepherd
with his flock. The panpipes have the unbearable anguish which
they were meant to induce when Chekhov introduced them as background music at the end of the first act of *The Cherry Orchard*.
They expand into the words of the old shepherd, who laments the
passing of the game, the drying up of the rivers, the cutting down
of the forests and the degeneration of the people in terms that
Chekhov, a decade later, is to put into Astrov's mouth in Act 3 of
Uncle Vanya. Like the old man in *Fortune* and old Firs in *The
Cherry Orchard*, the shepherd believes that the new order which
came with the emancipation of the serfs in 1861 began the decline.
Panpipes is a lyrical catalogue: of the birds—geese, cranes, ducks,
grouse, snipe, eagles, screech owls; the mammals—elk, wolves, foxes,
bears, mink; the fish—ides, pike, burbot, perch—which have vanished
from the impoverished countryside. The list is repeated in Chekhov's letters, Astrov's maps and the memories of Chekhov's old men
as they look for their boyhood.

Here the drying up of the rivers is not only linked scientifically
with the massive deforestation of the south: the shepherd also seems
an apocalyptic sign in the total eclipse of the sun (which occurred
on 7 August 1887 and was used by Chekhov in a number of comic
stories). The panpipes at the end weep for 'the disorder that had
been noticed in nature', and then suddenly fall silent, leaving in
the huntsman and the reader a painful, Chekhovian pity for the
world.

Even in the immensity of *Steppe*, which covers a journey of a
thousand miles from Taganrog to Kiev, we meet the fragility of
nature, as well as its immortality and vastness. Little of the journey
takes place in the day; most of Yegorushka's epic trek to school is in
the cool of the night, when the steppe is at its most alive and
mysterious. *Steppe* is one of the last pieces of romantic prose, and
in many ways it is constructed on the principles of the romantic
prose of, for instance, Gogol'.

Gogol's influence is, in fact, the most prominent of all the influences on *Steppe*. Writing to Grigorovich, Chekhov said that
Gogol', 'the tsar of the steppes', would be envious. The evocation
of summer, the sweeping imagery of sky, birds and earth recall
Gogol's *Sorochintsy Fair*. The loose construction of the story, in

eight episodes linked only by the main character; the light carriage (*brichka*) in which he sets off; the piling up of encounter upon encounter with characters who later disappear from the story; the arrangement of assorted peasants and other characters to make a miniature cosmology; the almost entirely male world in which the female is represented only by the extremes of a beautiful countess and two women who mother Yegorushka—everything reminds us of Gogol's *Dead Souls*, with its picaresque threading of episodes around Chichikov's light carriage. There are other motifs equally traditional. The veil of anonymity, as the carriage leaves the town of N. in the province of Z., is one early nineteenth-century tradition, as are the reflections on Russian humanity in general and the reminders to the reader from the discreet narrator that Yegorushka is to grow up and find a new understanding of his experience. But the observance of old conventions gives *Steppe* a period charm; it is Chekhov's formal entrance through the front door of literature, and Gogol', Turgenev and early Tolstoy indicate the way.

The eight episodes could in fact all exist in isolation. Apart from the journey and the boy, the plot that links them is tenuous. The boy, his uncle, the driver, and Father Khristofor are not only on their way to Kiev to see the boy into grammar school; they are also dealing in wool and preparing to meet the grazier and dealer Varlamov. The search for Varlamov is an intermittent quest in four episodes. When he appears in episode six, he turns out, to Yegorushka's amazement, to be a very ordinary man and, together with Yegorushka, the reader loses interest in this linch-pin of the plot, which is merely the motivation for a series of events and scenes: it is, if you like, an anti-plot.

The first episode has the *brichka* leaving Taganrog. The outskirts of the town—first the prison, then the cemetery and last the brickworks—are to give Chekhov the plan of so many of his nameless provincial towns that sully the countryside. Then the immensity of the steppe opens up, with a Gogolian emphasis on the macrocosmic harvested fields and the microcosmic detail of insect life. The tricks of focus, the romantic apostrophes—'How close and how melancholy!', the anthropomorphism of the kite high in the sky meditating upon the boredom of life, the driver's encounter with a peasant woman asleep on her haycart are as much Gogol's as Chekhov's. What is particularly Chekhovian is the subtle deceptiveness of nature, symbolised by the windmill that is so far away that it neither approaches nor recedes. Peculiar to Chekhov, too, is the characterisation of the priest, Father Khristofor, who attempts to console the nine-year-old boy with gentle platitudes about the value of education. The intellectual limitations of Chekhov's priests seem part and parcel of their calm, soothing sincerity.

Yegorushka comes to life in the second episode. Here the child's eye view works more convincingly than in any other of Chekhov's stories which have children as central characters. Yegorushka is neither particularly clever nor particularly appealing and so his idle play with grasshoppers and butterflies, his watching of the birds and seeds of *perekati-pole*, his silent encounter with a peasant child have a fascinating, mindless stillness, in which objects take on a reality they cannot have for an adult observer. The child's eye view makes it possible for Chekhov to personify nature without archness : a cloud exchanges glances with the steppe—' "Right", it said, "I'm ready", and frowned', and we feel the excitement of a storm that gathers but does not break.

In the evening the travellers reach a Jewish inn. This, the basis of the third episode, goes back to Chekhov's own chidhood, when he fell ill with peritonitis and was nursed by a Jewish innkeeper. It centres around the innkeeper's brother, the tubercular intellectual Solomon. He is the first of two revolutionary figures in *Steppe*; he protests against his brother's servility, against the hierarchy of power and money. But his mordant wit is of no avail. Yegorushka's uncle and Father Khristofor are so far from Solomon's views that they cannot even understand them; they can only deplore his tone. Dying and despised, the intellectual freethinker has no place in the world of the steppe : Solomon, alas, is to be the prototype philosopher in Chekhov's work—a man whose moral bankruptcy and moribund appearance tell us that philosophy can be nothing more than a symptom of physical, social or spiritual malaise. The treatment of Solomon and, later, of the *ozornik* (troublemaker) peasant Dymov, is not a reactionary gesture. Chekhov did not believe in the possibility of revolution, nor, therefore, in the future of the revolutionary.

Suddenly, the line of the plot is broken. Travelling at night, the carriage meets a convoy of woolcarts and Yegorushka is handed over to the six peasants driving the convoy, while the other characters vanish from the story to meet Varlamov, and reappear only in the last episode. Of the six peasants, two become especially important to Yegorushka. The old sectarian Panteley protects him and tells him his life story, while the young Dymov terrifies him with his rough mockery and latent violence. The nocturnal steppe also changes mood : the chirping insects are replaced by the burial mounds, the Scythian stone female figures, the evocation of Russian folklore figures such as Robber-Nightingale, crosses that mark the graves of robbers' victims. With Tolstoyan sharpness, the difference between the peasant and the genteel world is drawn. Panteley muses about death with the calm solemnity of a man for whom it is the most important event in life. 'Death is all right, it's good, only I wouldn't die without repentance. There's no worse evil than sudden death.' His stories reveal a whole mythology that mingles Christianity with a pagan cult of death; Chekhov excuses their romantic fiction by ironic comments from the narrator. But the blood-curdling effect on the reader of the stories of murder and rescuing angels is as strong as it is on Yegorushka.

Throughout the next two episodes, the impact of Dymov grows stronger. His tremendous energy, as he catches fish, picks quarrels, kills a snake, jeers at the 'little lord' Yegorushka, reaches a climax when a storm strikes the convoy and Yegorushka's hatred of him leads to helpless hysteria. Suddenly Dymov relents, offers to let Yegorushka hit him, and then lapses into despair. His fury and re-rebelliousness are as impotent as Solomon's intellectual protest.[2] The storm is perhaps the most magnificent set-piece in Chekhov's work; starting with the phrase 'as if someone had struck a match across the sky', terrifying Yegorushka with hallucinatory shapes, knocking him unconscious with fever, it is the final triumph of nature over the travellers. After that, Yegorushka's reunion with Father Khristofor in Kiev and his new home seem an unimportant epilogue.

It is not only the imagery of the steppe, felt with all the child's senses—sight, hearing, smell and touch—that makes *Steppe* remarkable. It also has a prose rhythm unprecedented in Chekhov, and, except in *The Bishop*, unique.[3] The sentences have a Gogolian stretch and a sensuous recreation of movement, whether of the decrepit carriage leaving town, the hypnotic stillness of the hot afternoon, the lumbering woolcarts or the violent storm. They imitate the richness of the steppe's animal life and the simple directness of Yegorushka's sense-impressions. The peasants quarrelling or reminiscing, the Jews, the Ukrainians have their linguistic peculiarities recorded faithfully enough to mark their apartness from Yegorushka and his class, but not so pedantically as to be curious in themselves. This diversity of language, from the clerical speech of Father Khristofor to Varlamov's curt commands and Pantely's archaic utterances, makes the interdependence and comparative harmony of the characters all the more effective. In the immense world of the steppe, all human beings fit into a hierarchy. The protesters, Solomon and Dymov, are not allowed to disturb the pyramid, whose summit is Varlamov and whose base is the peasants along the road. The human world, in the end, is as unified as the natural world.

Chekhov knew he was stretching himself as never before. 'I'm writing,' he told Pleshcheyev in January 1888, 'with feeling, with sense, taking my time'. He was deeply interested in critical response. He had a letter from Ostrovsky (the step-brother of the great playwright) which delighted him with its careful analysis; as Chekhov put it, it was written 'with feeling, with sense and taking his time'. Writers, critics and publishers who knew Chekhov greeted *Steppe* in ecstatic terms. Like the author, they were bewitched by its strangeness, its encyclopedic vision of the steppe, the power of each page to stand as a prose-poem in its own right, the distance between its acceptance of the world and the protest of current literature, its combination of the Romantic tradition and an almost Symbolist allegory of an awesome venture into the unknown. But after the first impact Russian criticism found that it could not fully understand *Steppe*. N. K. Mikhaylovsky, who was perhaps the most influential repository of received ideas in Russia, thought that the story was a dissipation of creative powers, lacking purpose, theme and soul. Oddly enough, the negative reactions marked Chekhov's arrival, even for the philistines, in the Russian literary canon. Readers now felt they had a right to demand from him a strong narrative line, psychological analysis, and ideological signposting. The real strengths of *Steppe*, such as the reduction of the mysterious Varlamov from the goal of the travellers to a little man on horseback who can't pronounce his 'r's, or the elevation of the landscape into the role of hero and heroine, seemed faults to the critics and it was fortunate that by spring 1888 Chekhov was sure enough of his abilities to take no notice of public opinion. He refused to rewrite *Steppe* on the lines suggested and began to toy with the idea of a private guerrilla war against '12,000 false schools of criticism'. But he did not continue *Steppe*, as he had intended to do; nor, until Siberia captivated his attention in 1890, did he write anything more along the same poetic lines.

The stories of 1888 and 1889 make a concession to critics in that they turn to psychological analysis and to problems of contemporary life. In their themes they take up topics that are first raised in the *Petersburg Newspaper* stories of 1887. By far the most important of these is a study of an adolescent tormented by his sexuality and his rebelliousness—*Volodya*. But the final version of this story, written in 1888 for book publication, so extends and alters the limited scope of the *Petersburg Newspaper* story that it is best discussed in the next chapter. The psychological stories of 1887 come close to melodrama; much fine material from Chekhov's hospital experience in Voskresensk is spoilt by crudely built-up suspense or sentiment. But two of the serious stories, apart from those connected with *Steppe*, are interesting for their treatment of hallucinatory states. One is *V saraye (In the Shed)*, in which a child plays with the servants at cards while the corpse of a suicide awaits the police. The other is *Spat' khochetsya (I Want to Sleep)* (January 1888), in which a servant is driven insane by her perpetual lack of sleep and murders the baby she is supposed to nurse. Both see a world of horror through the eyes of a child; both confuse fact and fiction, the past in the countryside with the present in the town. *In the Shed* conveys a peculiar terror in the terms of the card game, 'I beat and pile on', which seem covertly to refer to the suicide's death. *I Want to Sleep* shows hallucinations turning clothes on the line into scenes in the forest, until the girl loses all sense of reality. Much of its imagery, in particular the green light that is to be associated with death in all Chekhov's future work, loses its power in the decadent sensationalism of the murder : 'She looks up at the blinking green light and, listening to the yelling, finds the enemy that stops her living. This enemy is the baby.' After this, Chekhov placed nothing of any substance with the *Petersburg Newspaper*. He relied less and less on one particular outlet, moving from *Novoye Vremya* to the monthly *Severnyy Vestnik* and, four years later, achieving total independence from editorial policy by switching from one paper to another.[4]

Chekhov was never to write anything longer than *Steppe*, but he had discovered his range. If *Steppe* is a miniature epic, many of the later works are miniature psychological novels. Freedom to choose his own length, whether of three or thirty thousand words, led Chekhov to discover a way of developing the psychological novel or novella into something more than the pastiche that we still find in 1887.

7
Into the Impasse

Chekhov's prose of 1888 and 1889 is very different from his previous work, in quantity[1] as well as in theme. It develops an analytical, psychological trend that may be detected in some of his work of 1887 such as *Vragi* (*Enemies*), or in the portrayal of the Jewish outsider, in *Perekati-pole* (*Thistledown*) or the third chapter of *Step'* (*Steppe*). Philosophical analysis ousts lyricism: in 1888 and 1889 the moon, the birds, the trees and the sea are suppressed background noises that only become audible when the hero's thoughts break down.

How may we account for this change, that was to lead Chekhov into something very like despair? The impressions of *Steppe* do not die away completely: many stories, such as *Ogni* (*Lights*) and *Krasavitsy* (*The Beauties*), are set in the south. But the narrator, whether telling the story in the first person or whether seeing the word through the eyes of his heroine (*Imeniny—The Birthday Party*) or his adolescent hero (*Pripadok—An Attack*), interests us in the confusion of his own mind rather than in the complexity of the outside world. To some degree, Chekhov now writes prose of psychological analysis because he is aware of the demand for it, because he feels competent and experienced enough to say something new, and because he has fallen under the spell of Tolstoy's technique of monitoring characters and analysing every twitch of their bodies and every lie on their lips.

A lost letter to Aleksandr (of September 1887) shows Chekhov's obsession with 'petty, continuous lying'. To expose lies involves analysing the thoughts and motives behind the spoken word, and makes it impossible not to employ Tolstoyan techniques. Lies in philosophy, in criticism, in private life, and lies to oneself obsess and distress Chekhov throughout 1888 and 1889, perhaps the most desperate years of his life.

For Tolstoy the moment of death was always the supreme victory of physical truth over psychological deceit: that is why the death of Andrey in *War and Peace* and the death of Levin's brother in *Anna Karenina* are so crucial to the salvation of Tolstoy's heroes from untruth. Without experience of death, no real thought about the meaning of life is possible. If we accept that this is so, then Chekhov had every reason to turn to philosophical enquiries in 1888. Death enters his personal life and clouds it. His letters to Suvorin and to his brother Aleksandr show at times a real agony. The first shock was the death of Garshin,[2] the most talented of Chekhov's contemporaries. Young, naïve and high-minded, he reacted to the horror of life, whether in the army or in a St Petersburg tenement, by taking refuge in madness. His stories, particularly *The Red Flower*, influenced Chekhov's portrayal of insanity in *Ward No. 6* and *The Black Monk*. The two writers had met in December 1887 and Chekhov later learnt that Garshin's last days had been 'renovated' by reading *Steppe*. But on 24 March, Garshin threw himself down the well of his staircase, which Chekhov had noted as 'horrid, dark and filthy'. *Volodya* (in its final version) and *An Attack* are tributes to Garshin.

In the spring of 1888 it became clear that Aleksandr's common-law wife was dying. Chekhov had to arrange for the children to be looked after, and in May the household moved—not to Babkino, but to the north-east Ukraine, to the estate of the Lintvarev family. The Lintvarevs provide much material for Chekhov's later work: they included three unmarried daughters, the two eldest doctors, the youngest a schoolteacher. Chekhov was soon regarding them as possible raw material: 'The Lintvarevs are marvellous material: they're all clever, honest, knowledgeable, loving, but all this is perishing for nothing . . . like sunbeams in the desert.' The eldest Lintvarev daughter was blind with a brain tumor, calmly waiting for death. That summer Aleksandr's wife died, and in spring 1889, Nikolay caught typhoid and his tuberculosis became fatal. Chekhov had to take his dying brother with him to the Lintvarevs and to face his own inability to halt the terminal process. Enduring and causing enormous suffering, Nikolay died in June, and Chekhov left the Lintvarev estate at Sumy for a brief and pointless tour south to Odessa and the Crimea; that winter his own tuberculosis became virulent enough to interfere with his freedom to travel and to write.

The experience of death was undoubtedly the cause of Chekhov's new interest in stoicism; he turned to Marcus Aurelius, as well as to *Ecclesiastes*, Schopenhauer and Goethe. Disillusionment with the literary world and its cowardly critics, a sudden surge of sexual disgust at Aleksandr's setting up house with Natalia Golden only months after the death of his wife, the complicated pressures that arose when Chekhov involved himself with the theatre (*Ivanov* and *The Wood-demon*) could only intensify the change. He knew that *Steppe* had ended, as well as begun, a stage in his career. He said he was worried at being 'a man who had given great expectations'. In a long letter to Suvorin (30 May 1888), after describing the idyllic Ukrainian countryside, he turns on Suvorin for having complained that his story *Lights* did not solve the problem of 'pessimism as a demoralising philosophy' that it posed. Chekhov attacks the assumption among Russian critics that the writer must lead. For him, his narrator's conclusion, 'You can't make anything out in this world', is a step forward :

An artist must be . . . only an impartial witness . . . the jury, i.e. the readers will do the evaluating . . . It's time writers, especially artists, admitted as did Socrates, and as Voltaire used to, that you can't make anything out in this world. The mob thinks it knows everything and understands everything; the sillier it is, the wider its horizon seems to be. But if an artist trusted by the mob decides to declare that he understands nothing of what he sees, that will make at least one piece of knowledge in the realm of thought and a great step forward.

Everything that Chekhov says reinforces this classical scepticism. He found that Yelena Lintvarev, with whom he practised medicine in Sumy, read Schopenhauer. Greek tags appear in his letters, just as Greek tags such as 'know thyself' are to figure in his fiction. In April 1889 he recommends to friends the stoicism of Marcus Aurelius; we can trace a line of thought that is to dominate *A Dreary Story* in remarks to Suvorin such as 'Ecclesiastes gave Goethe the idea of writing *Faust*.' The very phrases of Ecclesiastes, 'Vanity of vanities, all is vanity', echo in his letters and stories, and the Faustian disillusionment with knowledge, success and, eventually, life itself colours his outlook.

Taking refuge from literature in the countryside of Sumy, in a life that was half a fisherman's paradise and half a doctor's hell, Chekhov wrote little. But his thoughts take bold strides. First he shakes off any apologetic feelings : Russian literature may be settled in 'tundra, wrapped in mist, portraying a dismal, typhoid life' in the 'dampness of the gutters', while he himself leads 'a tramp's life, avoids compulsory service, describes nature and satisfied man', but he no longer feels wrong or inadequate as a writer. A letter to Pleshcheyev in October 1888 virtually breaks with the literary world and for the first time expresses that faith in personal freedom which was to sustain all Chekhov's later work : 'I can see . . . pharisees, stupidity and tyranny in science, in literature, among the younger generation . . . My holy of holies is the human body, health, intellect, talent, inspiration, love and the most absolute freedom from force and lies.'

A few days after being awarded half of the 1888 Pushkin prize, Chekhov was arguing in the same vein to Suvorin, declaring that the correct posing of a question did not mean a solution, and bringing Tolstoy's *Anna Karenina* and Pushkin's *Yevgeniy Onegin* into the argument as examples of literature that was great because it refused to solve problems. This was a battle that Chekhov fought and never won against Russian criticism; in very slightly altered form it is still being fought and lost today. It soured Chekhov's relations even with his 'grand old men' : in Grigorovich he began to see nothing but 'virtuoso insincerity'.

Lies in literature were only the outward form of lies in private life. Chekhov saw lying as an addiction like 'alcoholism, psychosis, morphine addiction, onanism, nymphomania'. He saw it as a symptom of his elder brothers' moral and physical degeneration, and it introduces into his work the themes of isolation, frustration and tragedy, all caused by addiction to lies. The elderly professor of *A Dreary Story* or the husband in *The Birthday Party* have become incapable of sharing and relieving unhappiness. The same absolute freedom is needed in life as in art. In January 1889 Chekhov wrote a violent letter to Aleksandr, denouncing his whole way of life with Natalia Golden. 'Despotism and lies crippled our childhood, ruined our mother's youth,' he began, and then went on to berate Aleksandr for treating Natalia as if she were a prostitute. Overt sexuality is intolerable. That Aleksandr should be 'ironic about relations in bed' meant to him 'corrupting woman and removing her from God'. Wives and mothers had to be treated with ceremony; for Chekhov, 'between a woman who sleeps on clean sheets and one that wallows on dirty sheets and laughs uproariously when her lover screws her there is a difference as wide as between the living-room and the pub.' This polarisation of women, a little Gogolian in its idealisation, is characteristic of Chekhov; it helps him to enter Garshin's mind when he uses a Garshin-like hero in his story of a man revolted by brothels, *An Attack.*

It must be said at the outset that none of Chekhov's prose of this period corresponds to his intentions. Throughout 1888 and 1889 he planned to write a novel;[3] it was to be based on the Sumy area, to cover in its first version a whole family and in its second version episodes in the lives of a group of friends : it was to show the good life—another Gogolian touch in Chekhov's intentions. Part of this novel probably survives in the play *The Wood-demon*; but Chekhov's time with the Lintvarevs was spent nursing the dying, consoling the bereaved, and fishing in the river Psel. The novel was scrapped, and with it the 'good life' in literature.

What Chekhov wrote displeased him; of the stories of 1888 and 1889, only the last, *A Dreary Story*, is as faultless a work of art as *Steppe*. There is too little balance in *Volodya* or *An Attack*, too much mannered writing in *Lights* or *The Birthday Party*, and indignation too badly suppressed in those stories such as *An Unpleasantness* or *The Princess* in which an overworked, uncompromising doctor battles with an idle, dishonest society. Plays and the unwritten novel sapped his energy; by March 1889, only the moral framework of the novel survived : 'This framework is absolute freedom of man, freedom from violence, from prejudices, from ignorance, from the devil, passions etc.' The ephemerality of fame begins to obsess him as much as it does the hero in *A Dreary Story* : his work, he says, 'won't live ten years in human memory'. Only science and its future remain certain.

In *A Dreary Story*, we can see the arid wasteland when all the lies have cleared; the earlier stories of 1888 and 1889 have tried to disperse the various lies that cloud human vision. The first, in Chekhov's view, is the social and sexual lie, the lubricant of human contact. This is the lie that Chekhov deals with in *Potseluy* (*The Kiss*, 1887) in which a gauche young officer is suddenly kissed by an unknown girl waiting in the dark for her lover. The young officer's whole life is tortured by speculations about the kiss, and his self-consciousness in society becomes neurotic. In *Volodya*, as Chekhov finally wrote it, the torture ends with suicide. In 1888, a wave of adolescent suicides in Russia prompted Grigorovich to ask Chekhov to write on the topic, and thus to prove himself a writer concerned with the problems of the day. Chekhov therefore turned his story *Volodya* into a work of protest, in which the schoolboy hero discovers his own clumsy sexuality and his mother's shameless dishonesty. He expanded a scene in which Volodya loses his virginity to a plump, blonde friend of his mother; he is so hurt and disgusted by his 'fall' that he loses all self-possession. He suddenly interrupts his mother's conversation, screams an indictment of her social lies and pretensions, then goes next door and shoots himself. His suicide is similar to, if less inevitable than, Konstantin's in *The Seagull*: Chekhov was cramped by the difficulty of dealing with feelings more extreme than his own. To Grigorovich he had listed the ways in which other writers would deal with an adolescent suicide: 'X, without knowing it, would quite sincerely write slanders, lies and blasphemy, Y would let petty, pallid tendentiousness creep in, while Z would explain it by psychosis. To master that personality [i.e. the boy's], you have to know what suffering is yourself, but modern singers can only whine and snivel.'

Accordingly, Chekhov's other story of adolescent revulsion ends in an attack of hysteria, which can be taken, like the madness in *Ward No. 6*, merely as an outburst of sanity in a mad world. *An Attack* was written for a memorial book under the influence of Garshin's prose and his death. As it was to be illustrated, it was subject to strict censorship and Chekhov's problems were made worse. He wanted to show a youth of Garshin mentality—pure, crystal-clear, benevolent and uncompromising—and then bring him into contact with evil by taking him to the notorious Moscow brothels of Sobolev Alley. This makes the story one of many indictments of state-tolerated prostitution in Russia. The criticism of regulated prostitution—the 'yellow ticket' was one of the great reforms of the 1860s—was regarded not only as sensational but also as a political matter. Chekhov himself felt he was 'a specialist in whores' from his student days and, in contrasting two poles of his own being, could write a story that was at the same time an indictment, self-analysis, and a tribute to Garshin. *Pripadok* (*An Attack*) is pruned to parable simplicity, and Garshinian lucidity and sparseness here become one of the best features of Chekhov's narrative style. A medical student and an artist take the law-student Vasil'yev to the brothel quarter. Each brothel revolts him more than the last; he tries to talk to the whores and, to his horror, he discovers that he can no more look on them as human than can their other customers.

He goes through a Tolstoyan crisis as he mulls over his experiences. But he is too honest to accept Tolstoyian solutions. He does not marry one of the prostitutes or preach to their customers and the cabmen; he gives way to despair. The point of the 'attack' comes in the last chapter; the artist and medical student take him to a psychiatrist, who treats his horror and sends him away with a prescription for bromide and morphine. This is not only Chekhov's first attack on psychiatry; it is also the first of his stories to diagnose evil as inherent in the social system (something quite different from Tolstoy's conception of evil), and not susceptible to individual reaction against it. The Garshinian idealism of the hero is, perhaps, not Chekhov's, but neither is the psychiatrist's cynical acceptance of normality. To Suvorin Chekhov wrote that prostitution 'is the most terrible evil. Our Sobolev Alley is a slave-owner's market', but he offered no solution. His feeling is most apparent in the careful description of the first snow that falls in the alley, indifferent, as nature usually is in Chekhov's world, to human good or evil.

For some time, in 1888, Chekhov can be seen resisting the pessimistic helplessness in which *An Attack* and *A Dreary Story* result. The first story after *Steppe* which he wrote for the *Severnyy Vestnik*, *Ogni* (*Lights*), is mainly a first-person narrative by an engineer constructing a railway, and shows how earlier pessimism led to moral turpitude. It is not a convincing illustration—Chekhov denied that it was meant to be—but the anti-pessimist holds the floor and his opponents are hardly allowed a word. The engineer, Anan'yev, is talking to his pessimistic young assistant and to the doctor-narrator who is standing in for the author. Anan'yev admits that the railway, whose lights stretch into the distance like the campfires of the Philistines, will vanish in two thousand years as surely as did the Philistines themselves. But he refuses to admit that this is cause for despair. Only Shakespeares and old men have the right to pessimism. To convince his listeners, he relates an episode from his youth. Then a pessimist, without the 'Christian substructure and personal experience' necessary for noble pessimism, he allowed himself to seduce a married woman he had known as a schoolgirl, to tell her he loved her and then to flee the town and abandon her to her misery. His pessimism tells him that nothing matters, and thus it leads to destructive self-interest. Now, as a railway engineer, he can glory in the schools, hospitals and factories that are going to follow his railway line in the next hundred years. The most hypnotic feature of *Lights* is not the seduction story, despite its partial anticipation of the love story in *The Duel*. It is the lights of the railway under construction, the sense of time translated into space, and the Chekhovian question of whether the next hundred or thousand years will justify the sufferings and ignorance of the present. For Chekhov the future plays the same role as the Second Coming in a Christian writer's work.

The problem of pessimism is unsolved; Chekhov has not yet given in to Ecclesiastes or Marcus Aurelius. But even in a story as clumsily told as *Lights*, the way out is discernible. Nature is not wholly suppressed; it speaks in the seduction story, when the narrator's pessimism unites with the loneliness of the 'infinite, harsh steppes, forests and snows' : Russian man is attuned to Russian nature. The roar of the sea orchestrates the young Anan'yev's words of consolation and the woman's sobs. As in *Gusev, The Duel* and *The Lady with the Little Dog*, the sea reminds us that man lives and dies in obscurity; all Anan'yev's contempt for his ruthless past cannot overcome the melancholic effects of listening to the waves.

In *Nepriyatnost'* (*An Unpleasantness*), published by Suvorin in June 1888, nature subtly undermines the hero's arguments in the same way. Here he is a doctor, Ovchinnikov, embodying rural rough simplicity in a complex world. (Ovchinnikov had been the name of the doctor who calms the hero of *The Wolf* (1886), who thought he had rabies.) Ovchinnikov publicly hits his assistant in the face for drunkenness. He is overcome by remorse and, unable to control his emotions or to reach a decision, ends up by having the case hushed up by the authorities and being expected to resume an impossible *status quo*. Like the hero of *An Attack*, he alone is outraged by what everyone else considers normal. Like the snow on the brothels, or the sea in Anan'yev's provincial escapade, nature mocks him and his turmoil with its purity and life :

Through the green of the birches, slightly quivering in the wind, you could see the blue, bottomless sky . . . the starlings, having decided to be frightened, one after the other with a cheerful shriek, as if making fun of the doctor who couldn't fly, made for the tree-tops.

Thus the engineer and the doctor who fight their own and other people's moral cowardice are Don Quixotes who ignore reality and fight sheep : they have turned away from nature. In *Steppe* there were peasants so sharp-sighted that they could recognise a bird before anyone else could see it, or watch vixens playing with their cubs miles away; in the world of the townsman or the intellectual, nature passes by unheard, unseen and misunderstood. It is a mark of Chekhov's rapid development that while in 1886 the railway engineer (in *The First-class Passenger*) is an absolute hero and Doctor Ovchinnikov (in *The Wolf*) is wisdom incarnate, in 1888 they are only high-minded, misguided misinterpreters of experience.

Nature is fully integrated into psychological narrative in *Imeniny* (*The Birthday Party*), which Chekhov wrote in September 1888. It is a carefully, frigidly constructed story : a hot, sticky summer's day in the country ends with a storm, while the heroine's tense, protesting emotions and her corseted seven-month pregnancy finally erupt into a blazing row and a disastrous premature labour. The atmospheric detail, the husband's hay-making, the heroine's resentment and her playing of the role of hostess, the physical pain of labour, the stresses of marriage are all rendered with a virtuoso attention to technique. Chekhov was immensely proud of entering the mind and the body of his pregnant heroine, Ol'ga, and revelled in the praise of his multipara readers. Ol'ga is incensed by lies : her husband, who faces a court case, pretends to be light-hearted; she herself pretends to be hospitable. Chafing, she sees nothing but mediocrity in her guests and their views. Thus Chekhov can satirise through her eyes the self-proclaimed radical of the 1860s, the Ukrainophile, the liberal and the conservative. (By doing so, he incurred the annoyance of the critics for whom the 1860s and political idealism were so sacred that even fictional characters who abused or caricatured them were forbidden.) When husband and wife are left alone and their quarrel breaks with the storm, we are meant to sense a return to the reality of thunder, the doomed foetus and the helpless hero and heroine.

The Birthday Party suffers not only from frigidity. As Chekhov admitted, it is too ambitious for its scope. Its beginning is expansive, its middle 'crumpled' and its end 'a firework'—faults of over-condensation that Chekhov detected in a number of his stories. Worse is the influence of Tolstoy. The authoritative Tolstoyan manner is unique in convincing the reader that the characters' involuntary gestures, their flushing and their postures, reveal to the author the falsity of their words. Chekhov lacks Tolstoy's self-confidence, and the result is an embarrassingly high number of coincidences which seem derivations from *Anna Karenina* rather than original insights.

There is a scene in which the husband scythes hay, amazing the girls who watch him as Levin amazes himself in Tolstoy's novel. The heroine talks with the gardener's wife about childbirth, as does Tolstoy's Dolly. She hates the back of her husband's neck with a Tolstoyan suddenness. The satire on the guests is a Tolstoyan satire on the Europeanised lawyers who try to govern the provinces. Even the world Tolstoyan, *Tolstovets*, springs to the heroine's lips. Tolstoyan moralising runs through Ol'ga's mind—'Lies are just like the woods, the further you go, the harder it is to get out'—together with the Tolstoyan love of proverbial wisdom.

Years passed before Tolstoy's spell weakened; it paralysed other stories, for instance *Knyaginya* (*The Princess*) of 1889, in which a high-minded doctor speaks his mind to the princess who maintains a façade of Christian charity while she soullessly exploits humanity. Throughout 1889, preoccupied with his dying brother (an experience very much like Tolstoy's) and aware of the weaknesses of his prose, Chekhov could not write. Only when his brother was dead could he produce what is in effect a lament for life and love so powerful that Tolstoyan method cannot dominate it. That lament is *Skuchnaya istoriya* (*A Dreary Story*)—perhaps the most ironical of Chekhov's 'throwaway' titles. It is told by a dying man who finds all his fame, ability and innate goodness useless to help himself and others. Much argument has been spent in attempting to identify the original for the professor of medicine, Nikolay Stepanovich (no surname), who narrates the story. Chekhov's friends were tempted to see Suvorin or Babukhin, a professor at Moscow University, behind the portrait. Indisputably the ironic tragedy of a professor of medicine unable to halt his own death coincides with the last months of the great Russian professor of medicine, Botkin, who died a month after the story was written of a liver disease he would not diagnose. It would not matter, were it not for the illusion of reality given by the narrative and the introduction of the names of actual people.

The melancholy, the restless, sceptical yet conservative temper of Nikolay Stepanovich are certainly Suvorin's, but the Suvorin characteristics are in fact only those that he shared with Chekhov, and much of the portrait of the old professor of medicine has its origins in Chekhov's projection of himself as an artist who could see no way out. Many of the phrases of lament in Chekhov's letters are transposed into the professor's narrative. A letter to Suvorin of November 1888 complains: 'Nobody wants to love the ordinary person in us.' Likewise, the professor comes to feel that he and his great name are two aspects of a split personality. His name is revered; it tours the papers and will survive on his tombstone when he himself is ignored and forgotten; when he comes in the sixth and last chapter to ask himself what he is by asking what he wants, he says: 'I want our wives, children, friends, pupils to love in us not the name, not the firm, not the label, but the ordinary person.' Like Chekhov, he has risen from humble origins—he was a seminary student—and like him he is nostalgic for simple country food and family life. His indictments of contemporary literature read much like Chekhov's denunciations of mediocrity: like Chekhov, he has three criteria for great literature—wit, talent and nobility—and modern writing never satisfies more than two. Like Chekhov, he sees true art represented only by two or three old men, and turns, as Chekhov turned to Maupassant and Paul Bourget, to French literature, just because it is free, and not imprisoned by political preconceptions or prudery or critical narrow-mindedness.

The professor reflects on nature with the same irony and passion as does Chekhov. Both are agonised, knowing, as Russian poets such as Pushkin and Tyutchev repeatedly said, that 'all these pines and firs, birds and white clouds in the sky, in three or four months' time when I am dead, won't notice my absence.' The philosophies of the world are resumed by the professor with the same desperate concision as Chekhov's into a socialist commandment 'labour', a Tolstoyan 'give all you have to the poor', and a classical 'know thyself'. Like Chekhov, the professor prefers the last of these imperatives; he is taken aback when he realises that the oracle does not tell man what to do when he knows himself. The emotional climax of the story is reached when he cannot find words to console or advise the young woman who was his ward and is now his only friend. He lets her slip to perdition, as paralysed by his useless skills as was Chekhov himself, with nothing but ipecacuanha, atropine and creosote to delay his brother's death.

It is not necessary to isolate all the points of contact to realise that *A Dreary Story* is in fact a lyric work, a very personal, Ecclesiastes-like song. Chekhov maintained that its whole point lay in the dastardly son-in-law's opinion of the professor—'the old man's gone off his head (*spyatil starik*)'—but that would not account for the qualities of sympathy and substance that Chekhov has built into his hero to make him far nobler than his surroundings.

From a formal point of view, *A Dreary Story* is the most satisfying of Chekhov's works. The narrative is almost entirely in the present tense, as if to bring out the sensation of time being drawn out, which the professor notices as his last months of life drag by. Unparalleled elsewhere in Chekhov, this present tense gives the narrative a strange combination of relevation and tedium.

The first chapter is an ironical self-introduction. As he begins his eloquent discourse, the professor announces that he cannot express himself. The first theme he broaches is that of the last chapter : that his name and his self are two separate entities. The split strongly recalls Gogol's *Nose*, in which the hero's nose lives a separate life in imposing uniform, and the absurdity is just as spine-chilling. Left alone with his pathetic self, the professor takes on a child-like appeal. Further features borrowed from the author are his incurable physical twitch, his insomnia, his anguish at being in debt, his compulsion to work. To a certain degree he is a dramatisation of Chekhov, like Trigorin in *The Seagull*. For him the university is a refuge and lecturing his art. His power to control himself, his subject and his audience, now slipping from his grasp, finds its parallel in Chekhov's enjoyment of his material, his language and his readers. The parallels between his own writing and the professor's science had already occurred to him. In May 1889 he wrote to Suvorin to give his reactions to Bourget's *Le Disciple* which had appeared in *Severnyy Vestnik*. Repelled by Bourget's identification of science with unprincipled materialism, Chekhov felt that there need be no 'struggle for existence' between art and science, that 'in Goethe the natural scientist got on excellently with the poet.' But for the professor as for Chekhov, faith in science fades before the 'panic fear' of death. Throughout his narrative the professor discovers as he writes that without faith or love, the joy and interest of his science can be destroyed by the least physical or emotional upset. The porter at the university is happier than the professor, because he is that Quixotic figure, 'the man who lives', while the professor falls into the Hamlet category of a man unable to love or act until too late.[4] Thus the joy of teaching is overshadowed by the ominous entry into the lecture room of the corpse for dissection before the professor.

The second chapter is in two halves. The first is a satirical skit on the professor's visitors, mediocrities pleading for their degrees. Their inanities irritate the professor, just as the students who brought Chekhov their manuscripts irritated him by their 'pretentious, naïve,

high-minded and mediocre' work. The comedy dies out in a scream
of anger. Next comes a typical dinner-table conversation between
the professor's daughter and her future husband, the crab-like
Gnekker, on Brahms and Bach, fugues and counterpoints, told in
the present tense as if it were repeated each night, which gives a
Huis clos-like horror to the scene.

The professor's flight from his family takes him, again every
evening, to his ward Katya, the woman he loves, though he does
not realise this until the last sentence of the story. An ex-actress
embittered by failure, she provides the professor with a cynicism
diametrically opposed to, and just as unsatisfying as, the conventional respect of his family. Disillusioned and dying, he cannot accept
her unperturbed assumption of the worst, and cannot abandon his
faith in science. Katya's cynicism is reflected in that of their common friend, Mikhaii Fyodorovich, and together they seem like two
croaking toads. Again, the third chapter ends in flight.

The fourth chapter presents a typical day in the professor's vaca-
tion. Much of the family hell of the second and third chapter is repeated, in every detail, down to 'Brahms and Bach, fugues and
counterpoints' : this time it is allowed to burst out into an open row.
The professor quotes Krylov's fable to the loathsome Gnekker :

> Eagles may sometimes fly lower than hens,
> But hens will never soar up to the clouds

But, as one might expect in *Huis clos*, Gnekker ignores the challenge.
The professor is entirely alone, worshipping 'the feeling of personal
freedom' that his family rejects and the 'sensitivity and ear for art'
that Katya so plainly lacks. He remains a Nietzsche among *petit-
bourgeois*, an eagle among hens.

The picture complete, Chekhov disposes of his hero in two scenes.
The first is familiar to us from the plays, especially Act 2 of *The
Wood-demon* and *Uncle Vanya*. The sultry, stormy 'sparrow night'
wakens the professor with premonitions of death, aggravated by the
imagery of moonlight and his thoughts of owls screeching and dogs
howling. As in the plays, an inexplicable noise, *kivi, kivi*, heightens
the tension; the panic spreads, his daughter awakes in hysteria he is
no longer able to calm, the dogs howl, and Katya suddenly turns
up in the garden, distraught and penitent.

A little later, we find the professor in a hotel-room in Khar'kov
(an image of hell in *Uncle Vanya*), taking refuge in action. Too late,

he finds that Gnekker is an impostor, for Gnekker has already married his daughter. The professor has toyed with his three possible philosophies and does not know what to do with them. All he is left with is a simple one-man party game : 'Tell me what you want and I'll tell you what you are.' He lists his desires; the first is Chekhov's : to be loved for himself, not for his name; the second is also Chekhov's, to judge by the frequency with which it is expressed : to see what science will have achieved in a hundred years' time; the last desire is pathetic : to live about ten years more. He does not define himself. This is done for him when Katya bursts into his room and demands the help that he cannot give. His last, unspoken words to her have a gallows humour which is perhaps the best in his philosophy : 'So you won't be at my funeral?' He, at least, is happier than she.

A Dreary Story is a remarkably modern work; it is one of the first 'confession stories', which lay bare existential absurdity, rather than attack, defend or repent. Chekhov is pioneering a genre that is to be exploited by Gide, Duhamel and Camus—a genre to which he is to return in *My Life* of 1896. To avoid, as he and his successors do, glorifying or indicting the narrator can be done only by relegating the plot to a low level. In the professor's confession his intrigue passes almost unnoticed; another writer would have made much of the change from a paternal to an erotic note in his attitude to Katya, or of the revelation, when Katya drops a bundle of letters and the professor reads half a word, 'passio . . .', that Mikhail Fyodorovich is her lover. Existential agony takes first place in *A Dreary Story* : it is a lyric, a complaint rather than a story or a dramatisation of life.

A Dreary Story was, for all its greatness, impossible to develop. It raises themes of stoicism and pessimism in its references to Marcus Aurelius, its echoes of Schopenhauer, that can be developed only in a dialogue. Its vision of life is too complete to be enlarged : all Chekhov's pain and delight were put into the professor's love for Katya and for medicine. Like other stories of 1888 and 1889 it is interspersed with quotations and thoughts from Shakespeare's *Othello*. The distrust, the despair of a man vulnerable to evil machinations around him is a point of departure in 1888 to which *A Dreary Story* returns.

In *A Dreary Story* critics saw only an imitation of Tolstoy's *Death of Ivan Ilyich*, in which a very ordinary old man, screaming as he

D

dies, thinks over his own life and finally reconciles himself with truth
and death; they failed to see the chasm between Tolstoy's morality
and Chekhov's elegy of life; between Tolstoy's miracle play and Chekhov's irony. Everything Chekhov had said about 'pharisees, stupidity
and tyranny' rebounded on him; even praise, such as Mikhaylovsky's, condescended by deploring his failure to believe in the demo-
cratic and revolutionary idealism of the 1840s and 1860s. He was
accused of copying Tolstoy, of having no ideas, of preaching
pessimism. Acclaim for the achievement went together with obloquy
for not giving it a moral framework. Perhaps the equivocal reception of Chekhov's plays had something to do with the querulous
tone of the press; both led him to turn away from Moscow and
Petersburg to Siberia, from art to statistics.

Chekhov always reacted to staleness or disaster with wanderlust.
Just as in spring 1887 he had returned to Taganrog, so in summer
1888 he had left the Lintvarevs for a journey with Suvorin's son,
the 'Dauphin', to the Crimea and the Caucasus. In summer 1889,
immediately Nikolay had been buried, Chekhov fled to Odessa
and the Crimea, returning to Sumy when he found himself unable
to enjoy travel. After writing *A Dreary Story*, the idea of crossing
Russia and Siberia to its most distant possession, the island of
Sakhalin north of Japan, germinated in his mind. It was to be not
merely a diversion, but an exploit that would prove him an explorer as bold as Przhevalsky and a sociologist and statistician as
academically sound as any professor of medicine. It was a gesture
against literature, prompted by his own frustration and his critics'
incomprehension, and it was to enrich his work and wreck his pre-
carious health.

In January 1890 he went to St Petersburg to read everything
he could on Eastern Siberia, to get a press card, if not a
blessing, from Suvorin, and vainly to try for some official
introduction that would allow him to investigate the penal settlements of Sakhalin. In one letter written during his month's stay
in St Petersburg he declared that his main aim was to 'cross out a
year or eighteen months from my life', but in fact he was the victim
of *Mania sachalinosa* as he put it. Aleksandr and Maria were set to
visiting libraries and abstracting material on Sakhalin. He himself
turned into a geographer, geologist and meteorologist. 'My Sakhalin
work will show me to be such a learned son of a bitch that you'll be
dumbfounded,' he persuaded Suvorin. The bibliography to his

account of Sakhalin defies belief, when we see that there were barely three months in which to read through tens of thousands of pages, some highly technical, on the island and on the theory and practice of penal settlements. He was following in the footsteps of the American journalist George Kennan, whose accounts of Siberia and exile were circulated as underground literature in Russia in 1889 and 1890, and thus winning his credentials as a radical.

The benefits brought by Chekhov's journey to the prisoners on Sakhalin were small and measurable; the benefits it brought to his outlook and his creativity were immense and immeasurable. But Chekhov's earliest writing for the theatre precedes the momentous journey, and to his first plays we now turn.

8

The Dramatic Hero

Chekhov's departure for Sakhalin in spring 1890 closes a period of development as a playwright as well as a story-writer. His theatrical experience was far more turbulent and spasmodic than his career as a story-writer, and the aims and techniques of the dramatic pieces seem so markedly different from those of his narrative prose that the plays and stories are not easy to correlate chronologically.

It is important to bear in mind that all Chekhov's full-length plays are variations on one play; from his unnamed, youthful indiscretion, now called *Platonov*, to *The Cherry Orchard* over twenty years later, the general conception and many of the details remain the same. The estate on which most of *Platonov* is set is sold by auction and the gentle, feckless owners are disinherited, just as in *The Cherry Orchard*. The smell of patchouli offends Anna Petrovna in *Platonov* as it offends Gayev in *The Cherry Orchard*. The seasonal scale, the predatory imagery, the intrusion of clocktime on the characters' lives, the frivolity in the face of horror are the same in all the full-length plays, which are all comedies written out of tragic material. Yet a chronological division can be made. The plays of the 1880s differ in that they have a male hero (or anti-hero) at the centre of the action : Platonov, Ivanov, the Wood-demon and Uncle Vanya give the title and the central theme of their respective pieces. The fundamental question is whether the hero is a scoundrel, a victim of environment or, nearest to the truth, an acute case of existential disease. The later plays, *The Seagull*, *Three Sisters* and *The Cherry Orchard*, are emasculated, in that they no longer revolve around a sexually magnetic hero (Trigorin in *The Seagull* is perhaps an exception), and their action is complicated by three or four female characters. The plays of the 1880s are 'mono-heroic', while those of the 1890s and 1900s have no heroes, and a polyphonic structure that is independent of the characters.

We do not know when *Platonov* was written; Chekhov's brother Mikhail and most critics place it in the summer of 1881 but there is evidence in the text that it was written in 1883, by which time it seems likely that Chekhov could have acquired facility in dialogue and dramatic incident. *Ivanov* and *The Wood-demon* can be dated November 1887 and summer 1889 respectively, but *Ivanov* was rewritten twice and *The Wood-demon* once, so that we are dealing in fact with an *Ivanov* of January 1889 and *The Wood-demon* of December 1889. *Uncle Vanya* is the most difficult of all Chekhov's work to date. Most readers will know that it is a revision of *The Wood-demon*, which Chekhov suppressed and refused to publish or have performed. Four quite important characters are removed; the play is shortened by a third; the focus moves from the doctor (the wood-demon himself) to the uncle, Zhorzh or Vanya; a few subtle alterations of tone and technique make the play virtually unrecognisable. Yet two-thirds of *Uncle Vanya* exists word for word in *The Wood-demon*. *Uncle Vanya* was first mentioned as a title in 1896, first printed in 1897. By 1898 the play was being performed in the provinces; its technical subtlety and its fourth act, showing a protracted disintegration of the household, place it firmly with the plays of the 1900s. Chekhov himself told Diaghilev in 1901 that he wrote *Uncle Vanya* in 1890.[1] This seems likely : *The Wood-demon* was a flop and at that time failure would have spurred Chekhov to cut back and rewrite his play. On his return from Sakhalin at the end of 1890, until he began to work on *The Seagull* in 1895, there seems no reason why Chekhov should return to the script of *The Wood-demon*, a play which he 'hated'. Nevertheless, there are in his notebooks for 1892 to 1897 phrases which are used in Astrov's speeches in *Uncle Vanya*. Probably *Uncle Vanya* was salvaged out of *The Wood-demon* in 1890, more by cutting than by writing, and was filled out with new material, such as the old nurse, Astrov's speeches, and Vanya's extra monologues, when Chekhov returned to drama in 1895. Our chief consideration of the play will be contained in the present chapter.

Platonov, unstageable, crowded and far too long, is nevertheless a remarkable testimony to Chekhov's originality and consistency as a dramatist. Its setting, a rural estate far from any easy route of escape, and its hot sticky atmosphere are to be used many times. Casual stage properties and casual remarks have the same irrelevancy and thus the same eerie symbolism as we find in the later plays.

Platonov opens with the sight of a piano and the sound of a violin, the ambling musical commentary which empties dialogue of its meaning—whether the piano and cello of *Ivanov*, the piano and song in *The Wood-demon*, the guitar in *Uncle Vanya* and *The Cherry Orchard*, the violin in *Three Sisters*. A Jew, Vengerovich, in *Platonov* remarks on the heat in Palestine, with the same uncalled-for excursion into absurdity as we find in *Uncle Vanya*, in Astrov's remarks about the heat in Africa. Chekhov has begun his dramatic *oeuvre* by giving to sound effects and stage properties an importance equal to that of the characters. The study which is the setting of Act 4 of *Platonov* has the same accumulation of bric-à-brac as Ivanov's study or Uncle Vanya's room and office, bric-à-brac which creates dramatic tension as we wait for a gun or cage-bird to act its part in the drama.

The similarities of *Platonov* with the later plays can be explained if it is assumed that Chekhov deliberately re-used its material, especially for *Ivanov*. Certainly the two heroes are very close, and their involuntary dissipation makes them look alike, but the differences are so great that *Platonov* must be looked at as a separate work.

Platonov is the most conventional of Chekhov's dramatic heroes; once an idealist, he has married a simple country girl and taken a post as a village schoolteacher. Boredom, idleness, emotional rather than sexual promiscuity place him in the tradition of the 'superfluous man'. In the course of the play, he arranges to elope with his best friend's wife, Sophia, for 'a new life', but he almost succumbs to the best friend's stepmother, the young widow Anna Petrovna Voynitseva, and he flirts with and assaults the rich and eligible Grekova. He is a catastrophic disrupter: his wife, Sasha, tries to kill herself by throwing herself on the railway line (on stage) and then by eating matches (off-stage); the horse-thief Osip, in the nature of familiar spirit to the other characters, tries to murder Platonov; his friend, Sergey Voynitsev, nearly dies of despair; Sophia is so angered by Platonov's betrayal that she kills him. He sparks off such kaleidoscopic action that it would be difficult for the most experienced dramatist to portray him convincingly. Chekhov solves the problem by the use of comedy. Platonov's gestures of despair, boldness or love flare up only to be ludicrously snuffed out as soon as he wins sympathy, leaving a self-satisfied, helpless dependence. Four women are desperately in love with him; one nearly kills herself, one kills him—yet *Platonov* is a comedy. This is not due to eccentricity or to monumental incompetence on Chekhov's part. *The Cherry Orchard* is subtitled a comedy, as was the first version of *Ivanov*; so is *The Wood-demon*. 'Comedy' meant to Chekhov 'not tragedy'; it implied that the death or suppression of the central character lets normal life resume; it implies a satirical distance from the characters. When Chekhov felt for his characters (the final version of *Ivanov*, *Three Sisters*) he used the neutral term 'drama'. Chekhov did not write tragedies;[2] the murder of Platonov, like the death of Ivanov and the suicide of Zhorzh in *The Wood-demon*, liquidates a problem and restores normality, without giving us any pity or fear. How can one pity a man so grotesquely funny as Platonov or Zhorzh? How can one fear a fate so absurd that it cannot make sense? Sophia's murder of Platonov, like Ivanov's death, whether by a stroke or by a revolver shot, happens on the spur of the moment. If there is a real tragedy, none of the characters notices it. It lies in the disintegration of the rural estate. The general's widow, Anna Petrovna, is so preoccupied with Platonov and his affairs that she ignores the financial crisis closing in on her; her guests are planning to marry her off for money, to get her estate by auction, to buy her coal-mines. Yet the play moves on through a succession of parties, and the real business is conducted only in asides.

The best of *Platonov* lies in its setting, effects and stage properties —anticipations of later plays. It is worth looking at its defects, in order to understand the problems of creating a new mixed dramatic genre. First of all, it is three times as long as *Uncle Vanya*: it would take over four hours to stage, even at the pace of comedy. It has twenty-one speaking parts; many characters double as father and son, having no part in the main plot. Secondly, like *The Wood-demon*, *Platonov* reads like an abandoned and hastily dramatised novel. It makes incredible demands on stage effects; it devotes too much time to analysing the enigma of Platonov. As one of the characters says, Platonov is 'the hero of an unwritten novel'. Thirdly, the play suffers from too fresh a memory of the repertory of the Taganrog theatres. Shakespeare, in particular *Hamlet*, is a dominating presence in all Chekhov's plays; Platonov cannot bear the weight. Voynitsev proposes to Platonov that they all act *Hamlet*, with Sophia as Ophelia. As Lopakhin to Varya in *The Cherry Orchard*, he ironically declaims: 'Ophelia, nymph, in thy orisons/Be all my sins remember'd.' Like Ivanov, Platonov sees himself as Hamlet, differing only in that he fears life, while Hamlet fears dreams. The catastrophic ending in which Platonov tries to shoot himself and is shot by Sophia, while the onlookers are prostrate with grief and the body of Osip lies offstage, as throughout Act 4, requires a Shakespearean talent to handle it : 'So many princes at a shot So bloodily struck.'

Chekhov learnt later how to cope with Shakespeare : the Hamlet theme is used with ingenious boldness in *The Seagull*. But *Platonov* suffers from memories of classical comedy, particularly the Russian comedies of Fonvizin, with their *raisonneurs* and bludgeon-like satire. Like Fonvizin's *Brigadier*, *Platonov* has a wastrel son, crazed by love of France, and father-figures aghast at the destructiveness and ignorance of their sons. Griboyedov's famous *Woe from Wit*, which influenced the construction of *Ivanov*, suggests to Chekhov both the characterisation of Platonov along the lines of Griboyedov's Chatsky and the portrayal of a debased and superficial society : Platonov himself is called 'a Chatsky of our times', without being given any of the sparkling wit of Chatsky or Uncle Vanya.

It takes Chekhov far longer to explore the irony of Platonov than to sum up, say, Uncle Vanya. Platonov is a 'second Byron, a Christopher Columbus' whom fate has cast as a village schoolteacher, just as Uncle Vanya thinks he might have been another 'Dostoyevsky, Schopenhauer', if Professor Serebryakov had not reduced him to the role of a farm manager. The Uncle Vanya problem is laughed away when his idiotic old mother tells him that he used to be 'a radiant personality (*svetlaya lichnost*')'—the ideal of Russian radicalism. Platonov's past and potential are cast in the clichés of the Russian radical movement of the 1860s; Chekhov already looks at the terminology with irony, but the irony is serious. Platonov used to think of himself—and Sophia believes in him—as a 'toiler, martyr (*truzhenik, stradalets*)'. Both characters are pinned down by outmoded doctrines of the emancipation of women and service to an ideal, and Platonov's tragedy is that, though he knows these ideals are 'nice phrases, but just phrases', he cannot stop using them to seduce Sophia and delude himself. Very early, far earlier than in his prose, Chekhov has stumbled on a way of using a character's philosophy to show his moral disintegration, but the method is too slow, as yet, to be dramatically acceptable.

Much of Platonov's characterisation does hold good. Fear of old age—he is twenty-seven—hurts him as it hurts Ivanov and Uncle Vanya. Uncontrollable talk—'*zaraportovalsya*, I've let my tongue run away with me'—leads him, as it leads Vanya, into collision with the other characters. As do Chekhov's later stories, *Platonov* shows us 'attacks of lying' taking possession of the hero, leading him to clutch at straws. The straws are the same as those in Chekhov's stories: running away to a new life, *novaya zhizn'*—the cry of Platonov, of Ivanov, of Uncle Vanya, of all three sisters of Trofimov —as if a new environment and another woman could drown his inner complaints.

Platonov could never have been acted when it was written. Indeed, none of Chekhov's plays except his vaudevilles would have been staged, had it not been for his reputation as a story-writer. He himself is partly to blame. *Platonov*, like all his plays, is hostile to the theatre; reading it, we cannot forget Chekhov's frequent comments on the degradation and limitations of actors; the fossilised adherence to genre—tragedy, melodrama, comedy or farce; the artificiality of the repertoire and the stupidity of the audience. *Platonov* makes its attack by mixing the tragedy of Platonov with the melodrama of the horse-thief Osip, the comedy of the intriguing guests plotting profitable marriages, and the sheer farce of the hero's incompetent handling of four infatuated women. Much must generously be assumed to be parody, like the melodrama of Chekhov's novel, *Drama at a Shooting-party*. The body of Osip, murdered by the peasants, is left lying by a well, so that characters can point through the window and use it as a moral. 'There lies a man who has paid for his sins.' The dialogue is ludicrous: 'The peasants have killed Osip!—Already?—Yes . . . Near the well.— So what? He asked for it.' Robbery, bankruptcy, attempted suicides and murder have no effect: no policemen appear, no one in authority except the bailiff who summons Platonov for assault. The doctor, Triletsky, who is the brother of Platonov's wronged wife, is as incompetent and heartless as the doctors Dorn and Chebutykin in the late plays, but his casual attitude is farcical: When Platonov is shot the doctor asks for water, and instead of trying to give it to Platonov he drinks it himself and throws the carafe away.

The anticipations of the later plays, especially *Ivanov*, make it unlikely that Chekhov wrote *Platonov* before 1883. Too many phrases—'What's the time?', 'You've got tears in your eyes', 'How foul, low and filthy life in this world is', 'A man without women is

a locomotive without steam', 'What am I to do? Teach me. I won't
be able to live through it', are to be found word-for-word in the
later plays and in stories of 1888. The irony, right down to Platonov's
words before he tries to shoot himself—'That's one clever swine
less'—is too mature for 1881. There is one piece of internal evidence
for dating the play: waiting for Platonov, his religious, good-
natured wife Sasha picks up a book, reads a little and puts it down.
The book is by Sacher-Masoch, the author of *Venus in Furs*, who
became known to Chekhov when he was planning his doctoral
dissertation on the history of sexual dominance in September
1883.

Between writing *Platonov* and being asked to write *Ivanov*,
Chekhov's drama was limited to reworking his early stories. The
sketch *In Autumn* of 1883 became a melodrama, *On the Highway*, by the addition of a scene in which the drunken landowner
meets the woman who left him and ruined him. After writing *Ivanov*,
Chekhov was to have considerable success with vaudevilles made
out of one or more of his *Oskolki* stories. They gave him pleasure
to write and they were profitable—*The Bear* brought in so much
money that he felt he should have called it *The Milch-Cow*. They
refine the technique of farce by their skilled timing, but they do not
alter the history of the theatre.

Ivanov was hastily written in less than two weeks of October
1887, for a private Moscow theatre owned by the astute Korsh.
Chekhov rewrote it twice, but it never fully recovered its reputation
after Korsh's production. Korsh subscribed to the cult of the great
actor and actress. It was impossible for Chekhov to get over to the
actors or to his audience the fact that Ivanov is neither a great
victim nor a great villain, and that Dr L'vov who denounces him
is not a saint: the actors knew no other way of playing them. To
a certain extent, *Ivanov* suffered in its later versions from Chekhov's
concessions. He added a substantial monologue, so that the lead
actor could have his aria without music; in the final version Ivanov
shoots himself, whereas in the less dramatic first version, he has a
stroke, and in the second version he is abandoned on the eve of his
second wedding. In *Ivanov* Chekhov first met the contemporary
theatre head-on; this time he changed his play instead of changing
the theatre.

Nevertheless *Ivanov* is by far the most important Russian drama,
tragedy or comedy, since Ostrovsky's best work of the 1850s. It has

the terseness, the richness of texture, the total integration of every detail that is the hallmark of Chekhovian drama. As soon as he had finished it, in October 1887, Chekhov wrote, 'I wanted to be original: I didn't bring forward a single villain or angel (though I couldn't restrain myself from having clowns), I didn't blame or justify anyone.' The instant he realised that Korsh and his actors were determined to play *Ivanov* in their routine way he regretted having written it. 'If I'd known, I'd have kept out of it.' But he drew eight per cent of the play's takings, and he could not afford to withdraw it. A poster of the time shows how alien to the spirit of his work was Russian theatrical tradition: in enormous letters stands the title, *Ivanov*; the male lead, Svetlov, has his name in thick black capitals; Chekhov's own name appears in type smaller than that of the director, the minor actors or the date.

The very title, *Ivanov*—the most common of Russian surnames—suggests that the play is not about one man, but about a type, a hero of our time.[3] Thus the critics understood it; but they judged Ivanov either by his own monologues of defeatism and self-hatred or by the malicious interpretations of the other characters. Ivanov is married to Anna, who left her Jewish family, faith and name to marry him and who is now dying of tuberculosis. He is bored, tired and guilty. To escape from his dying wife, his cynical uncle and his manager, the clown and petty demon Borkin, Ivanov starts visiting the Lebedev household. He has let himself get heavily into debt to Zinaida Lebedev, and allows their daughter Sasha to fall in love with him. In its final version, the play—now a 'drama', not a 'comedy'—shows Ivanov fleeing to the Lebedevs in Act 1, and declaring his love to Sasha at the end of Act 2, when his wife bursts in and collapses at the sight. In Act 3, Ivanov, morose and guilty, is loathed by his wife and the high-minded Doctor L'vov, while in Act 4 (Anna having died) a year later Ivanov tries to back out of his wedding to Sasha and, publicly denounced by L'vov as a murderer and confidence trickster, shoots himself. There is all the dramatic interest and conflict that the theatre of the 1880s could desire. Once again the shadow of Hamlet hangs heavily over the play: Anna, like Ophelia, sings sadly and mysteriously, and the doctor who has been treating her denounces Ivanov as much out of revenge as for the sake of honesty. But for Chekhov the fundamental point lay not so much in suspense and the clashes of Ivanov, L'vov and the two heroines as in a diagnosis of Ivanov. Even Suvorin could not see Ivanov as Chekhov meant him to be seen, and at the end of 1888, when the final revision of the play was nearly finished, Chekhov wrote to him, giving his own interpretation—almost the only one of any of his plays: 'If you can't understand why Sarra [Anna's original Jewish name] and Sasha love Ivanov . . . then there is no question of putting the play on . . . Ivanov is a gentleman, with a university education, not remarkable in any way: an easily aroused nature, ardent . . . honest and straightforward, like that of most educated gentlemen.' Chekhov then quotes speeches by Ivanov and Anna which show Ivanov as an active, socially useful man— unique in a decrepit money-grabbing, drunken, card-playing provincial society. Then, 'At thirty to thirty-five he begins to feel langour and boredom . . . he doesn't understand what's happening to him and what has occurred . . . Narrow people put all the blame on the milieu or enrol as superfluous men or Hamlets and content themselves with that. Ivanov, however, a straightforward man, publicly declares he doesn't understand himself.'

Chekhov felt it important to note that Ivanov is Russian; for Suvorin he drew a graph of the Russian temperament, in which there are short spasms of arousal followed by periods of apathy, each peak of arousal being lower and each period of apathy longer. Ivanov's love for Sasha is merely a second peak of arousal, and not a cynical decision to marry his creditor's daughter now that his wife, whom everyone thought he married for a dowry, is dying. He is thus a type in the once-fashionable science of racial psychology, while L'vov, the doctor, is a sign of his time, rather than of Russia. He is the intellectual whose rigid principles are not softened by experience. He only sees 'saints and cads'. He

is honest, straight, doesn't pull his punches, hits below the belt. If need be, he would throw a bomb under a carriage, bash an inspector in the nose, act the cad . . . People like him are needed and are attractive . . . True, caricature is sharper and therefore more intelligible, but better to leave half-drawn than to daub.

The last phrase is particularly important to an understanding of Chekhov's characterisations: unfortunately it required a Stanislavsky, not a Korsh, to complete the drawings.

Chekhov intended Sasha to be as ignorant of life as is L'vov; she is 'a female whom males conquer not by the brightness of their feathers, not by being supple or brave but by their complaints, whining, failures.' In vain Chekhov argued; like Doctor L'vov, Chekhov's audience and actors could not separate good or neutral intentions from the evil in the characters' world.

Evil is perhaps the best realised side of *Ivanov*. All the wickedness that gossip attributes to the morally paraplegic Ivanov is incarnate in his manager, Borkin. Borkin, like Yepikhodov, is a comic incarnation of Satan. Just as Yepikhodov (suggesting 'episodic', or 'walking about') walks to and fro through *The Cherry Orchard*, absurd and repulsive with his malapropisms, his revolver, his breakages and his talk of spiders and cockroaches, so Borkin runs through *Ivanov*, an ever-flowing stream of evil nonsense. He plans to extort money by threatening to dam the river; to infect cattle with pestilence and collect the insurance; to marry old Count Shabel'sky to the rich heiress Babkina and collect a percentage; to help the French fight the Germans with an army of rabid dogs. His first appearance in the dumb-play that opens Act 1 shows him taking a rifle and threatening to shoot Ivanov point-blank. Act 2 has a grotesquely farcical exit when Borkin and the Count lead the heiress offstage, both kissing her on the cheek. Like Shamrayev in *The Seagull* and Yepikhodov, Borkin has taken over : he refuses to give Anna any hay, just as Shamrayev takes his mistress's horses and Yepikhodov breaks the billiard cues.

As so often in Chekhov's plays, disasters slowly take place during the most banal events—tea, a picnic, a game of cards, a ball. In *Ivanov*, the parties turn into farces : the guests are starved by the mean Zinaida Lebedev, who keeps counting the sugar lumps and the candles; there is a maniac card-player who answers every question by talking about his hands and grand slams. But in them there is a Gogolian pettiness, the triumph of *poshlost'* over reality. It makes Ivanov's passion, however ephemeral, noble. 'In fishlessness a crab is a fish' is the Russian proverb that Chekhov chose to illustrate the point.

Ivanov has a lyricism stronger than any of the later plays. To a certain extent, this is due to the dying Anna : women do not die in any other Chekhov play. She plays the piano to Shabel'sky's cello through most of the first act, sings snatches of song, makes pathetic jokes in a Jewish accent. The cynical Count Shabel'sky, like Chekhov's Doctor Chebutykin in *Three Sisters,* lets his mask slip to reveal a vulnerable, loving heart. His tearful desire to go to Paris and weep on his wife's grave places him very firmly in the tradition of

Turgenev's sad old men. His cynicism is pathetic in its hopelessness. His proverbial remark to Anna, 'A baptised Jew, a pardoned thief, a doctored horse—all worth the same', is the knell of doom.

The lyrical effect is heightened by the offstage sounds: the screech of the owl and the banging of the nightwatchman are omens of time running out which Chekhov is to use many more times. The absurdity we associate with him is already apparent in the stage properties, particularly in Act 3 which takes place in Ivanov's study where the guns and maps are mixed up with the gherkins and herrings, olfactory 'props' that play such an important part in the aromatic effects of *The Cherry Orchard*.

But music and off-stage noises are not the things which make *Ivanov* important. If not perfect, the play has a structure and a wit that *Platonov* totally lacks. The way in which gossip attributes to Ivanov the plots of Borkin, so that he has Borkin as an *alter ego* he cannot sack; the construction of Act 4 in which hostility to Ivanov spreads from the minor characters until it is uttered and concentrated by Doctor L'vov in a few words powerful enough to kill—a plan very like the gathering hostility to Chatsky in Griboyedov's *Woe from Wit*—give the play a tautness that the slightly clumsy monologues and asides of both Ivanov and L'vov do not spoil. Borkin's absurdities, Shabel'sky's cynicisms, and Ivanov's deflections of criticism give scope for considerable wit. Borkin's comment on his master, 'You have a wine cellar but no corkscrew', is a concrete image of Ivanov's impotence, far more effective than the Byronic description of Platonov 'turned into Hamlet or Manfred or something'. Ivanov's warning to Sasha that she should not love a weak man like him, 'You're spoiling the human breed—there'll only be whiners and psychopaths left', introduces a topical Darwinian note into the predicament. Chekhov has rid himself of the morality and sententiousness of *Platonov*. When L'vov enters, Ivanov comments: 'There it is, the triumph of virtue and truth', in a mocking tone very far from that of an eighteenth-century comedy-writer. Virtue is as illusory as the 'new life'.

One actor, Davydov, took up *Ivanov* with enthusiasm, and Chekhov gratefully wrote for him a dramatic monologue, *Kalkhas (Swansong)*. But even Davydov could not cope convincingly with the monologues. Ivanov had 'to sing' in Act 3 and to be 'furious' in Act 4; Davydov would not act in this way, and Chekhov drew a line under the play. 'With *Ivanov* I shall put an end to writings about whining, anguished people.' The fair success of *Ivanov* in its Petersburg version in January 1889 and the thousand rubles' profit did not change his mind.

Leshiy (*The Wood-demon*) is a regression. An appallingly un-dramatic work, it repays examination if only because it illustrates the merits of *Dyadya Vanya* (*Uncle Vanya*), which was salvaged from it. It was crippled as a play for two reasons. Firstly, it was begun as a joint venture with Suvorin, who produced most of a draft of the first act to Chekhov's plan before abandoning the project. Secondly, it embodies material that Chekhov had in mind for the novel he planned to write in 1888 and 1889—the life of good people in an idyllic rural setting. The rural setting is very like the Lint-varev estate near Sumy where he spent the summers of those two years: the mill that Dyadin works, the setting of Act 4, recalls the mill on the river Psel; when she talks to the nightwatchman Yelena refers to her husband, the professor, as *pan* (which suggests the Ukraine); while the two eligible girls Yulia and Sonya, married off in a traditional comedy finale at the end of Act 4, have a little in common with Yelena and Natalia Lintvarev. Suvorin suspected that he himself was the material for Professor Serebryakov. During his visits to Chekhov at Sumy his conservatism and his hypochondria were as evident as the conservatism and hypochondria of Sere-bryakov.[4]

Whatever the source of the material, *The Wood-demon* was 'a terribly strange play' even for its author, 'unbearable in its con-struction'. It may be relevant that in 1889 Chekhov's brother had tried his hand at drama and that Anton had reproached him for using plainly autobiographical material: 'Give people people, not yourself.' *The Wood-demon* certainly is packed with people. It also follows another piece of advice to Aleksandr, that the first act may last an hour, but the later acts must not exceed thirty minutes, and the third act must be the lynchpin of the action. *The Wood-demon* has its moment of crisis at the end of Act 3, when Zhorzh Voynitsky shoots himself. Whereas the dramatic climax of *Platonov* and *Ivanov* comes within seconds of the final curtain, in *The Wood-demon* and all Chekhov's later plays, with the partial exception of *The Seagull*, the third act brings the climax, making the fourth act a melan-choly addendum. In *The Wood-demon* the problem of Act 4 is badly solved. Chekhov was not able to let the characters drift back to their initial state as they do in *Uncle Vanya*: he takes them all to the romantic setting of Dyadin's mill, where Yelena is reconciled to her old professor, Sonya wins the good Doctor Khrushchov, the 'wood-demon', and Yulia marries the reformed rake, Fyodor Ivanovich. The only trace of horror is the fact that all this happens only fifteen days after Uncle Zhorzh has shot himself.

Apart from Act 4, the plot of *The Wood-demon* differs only in detail from that of *Uncle Vanya*. Professor Serebryakov has retired with his new young wife Yelena to the estate belonging to his daughter and brother-in-law by his first marriage. The daughter is Sonya and the brother-in-law is Uncle Zhorzh Voynitsky (a clear reminiscence of Voynitsev, the surname of several characters in *Platonov*), later to be called Uncle Vanya. Act 1 is a birthday party at the house of a rich landowner Zheltukhin and his marriageable sister, and the Serebryakovs and Voynitskys are guests, together with the Orlovskys. (The elder Orlovsky is a friend of Serebryakov; the son is a womaniser, after Yelena Andreyevna's virtue, as is Uncle Zhorzh.) Both the Zheltukhins disappear from *Uncle Vanya*, as does the elder Orlovsky; the younger Orlovsky is merged with the 'wood-demon', Khrushchov, to make Doctor Astrov.

Act 2 of *The Wood-demon* is virtually identical with Act 2 of *Uncle Vanya*. There is as yet no old nurse to soothe Serebryakov; Zhorzh has far less to complain about than Vanya and is far more antagonistic to the doctor's mania for forests, but the differences are all in minor details of characterisation. In Act 3 of *The Wood-demon* the essential action is the same as that of *Uncle Vanya* : the professor proposes to sell the estate, which is not his to sell, and to live off the money, and Uncle Zhorzh is driven to violence. The important difference is that here Zhorzh shoots himself, while in *Uncle Vanya* Vanya shoots at the professor, misses, and is shattered by his own lack of success. *The Wood-demon* has a sub-plot : other characters believe that Zhorzh has already seduced Yelena and that Serebryakov is planning to sell his estate to Zheltukhin so that Zheltukhin will marry his daughter Sonya. *The Wood-demon* thus portrays the provincial malice and gossip that play such a part in destroying Ivanov. At the end of Act 3, just before the shooting, the doctor or 'wood-demon' rushes in and pleads with Serebryakov not to sell his forests, but he is dismissed as a psychopath. This scene was replaced in *Uncle Vanya* by a far more subtle episode in which Astrov shows his maps of the district's deforestation and degeneration to Yelena, who tolerates his speech-making only because she is waiting to pounce. The moralising of the 'wood-demon' is transformed into a dramatic episode that makes the message of conservation all the more effective because it suspends the love intrigue.

The change of title is the best indication of the difference between the two plays. The wood-demon is a little too saintly to be credible : he is a knight *sans peur et sans reproche*, saving lives and forests, reconciling and stimulating his friends. Khrushchov is Chekhov's first and last 'positive hero'. In *Uncle Vanya* he not only loses his title-role : he also acquires the cynicism, the love of vodka and the lust for Yelena Andreyevna which characterise Orlovsky. Astrov is tired of medicine : his latest memory is of a patient dying under the anaesthetic; he goes off with the worst possible grace to tend an injured factory worker or to treat Serebryakov's gout. He gets drunk and teases Uncle Vanya mercilessly; he loses his temper when he catches Vanya trying to steal his morphine. He fails to respond to Sonya's love. In all, he is a thoroughly convincing human being and his sensuous love of his trees and his horror of destruction are all the more infectious. The forests become an even more important symbol of unspoilt creation than in *The Wood-demon*, where they catch fire, or in *Ivanov*, where they are felled for timber.

The Wood-demon is cruel to Uncle Zhorzh : he has more to say in *Uncle Vanya*, where an additional monologue reveals the agony of an intellectual who has had to worry for twenty-five years about curds, peas and vegetable oil, and turns his passionate hatred of Professor Serebryakov into an almost noble mania. In *The Wood-demon* he is maligned, driven to suicide and forgotten : the survival of the fittest almost constitutes the play's morality. In *Uncle Vanya*, Vanya survives as a tearful, almost silent wreck, back with his vegetable oil and grain accounts—almost the salt of the earth in a perpetual cycle of exploitation by the Serebryakovs and their kind. *Uncle Vanya* has far more biting wit—for example, Serebryakov's stroll through a sweaty summer afternoon in overcoat and galoshes, or Uncle Vanya's flashy tie—but it is nevertheless a play of far greater compassion, no longer a comedy, but 'scenes from country life'.

Despite the alterations, it would be wrong to see Uncle Vanya as the victim of the ruthless and unworthy Professor Serebryakov. Much of Serebryakov's characterisation is identical with that of the professor of medicine in chapter 5 of *A Dreary Story* (written shortly after *The Wood-demon*). The stormy, self-pitying, querulous professor in Act 2 is a man wronged by life—admittedly more wronged in *The Wood-demon*, where we are told the details of his career—who has worked his way up, like the professor of *A Dreary Story*, from the bottom, only to find himself unloved and unloving. Uncle Vanya is the victim not so much of the professor as of the mould in which he cast himself. Like Platonov and Ivanov, he had been 'a radiant personality', and in his tantrum before the shooting he declares 'I could have been a Dostoyevsky, a Schopenhauer.' He is but another victim on Chekhov's graph of arousal and apathy; in a way, he is the last, for Chekhov's later heroes lose Vanya's sexual drive, just as Vanya has lost the sexual magnetism of Platonov and Ivanov. The hero, like his author, is ageing.

Both *The Wood-demon* and *Uncle Vanya* develop the use of noises and 'props'. *The Wood-demon* gives Yelena a talent for the piano, and Act 3 opens with a tribute to Tchaikovsky,[5] as Yelena plays Lensky's aria before the duel from the opera *Yevgeniy Onegin*, and thus introduces the motif of death by shooting into the play. (Tchaikovsky and Chekhov had met early in 1889 and formed a high opinion of each other.) Death fails to enter *Uncle Vanya*; it erupts into *The Wood-demon* in Act 1 : a bird flies over and the characters decide it is a hawk. In Act 4, while all the survivors gather to make peace, the wood-demon himself starts drawing maps, only to notice an extraordinary sunset on the horizon. In Chekhov's mind sunsets were, as his letters show, always associated with coughing up blood, and inspire horror : here, the apparent sunset turns out to be the forests on fire, and the wood-demon goes off to save his trees—the true heroes and victims of the drama.

Uncle Vanya, only two-thirds as long as *The Wood-demon*, is more sparing in its effects, using them to economise on words. In the earlier play, Yelena decides that perhaps she is a free sparrow, not a caged canary; in *Uncle Vanya* we are merely shown a starling in a cage in Act 4. The forest fire on the horizon is replaced by the more easily staged map which conjures up Astrov's absurd and therefore significant comment on the heat of Africa. In both plays, the clocks and the banging of the night-watchman measure time to the last minute, but the outside world is more oppressive in *Uncle Vanya*; we no longer have the rich Ukrainian countryside around Sumy, and Astrov has to cope with starvation, railway accidents, typhoid. The seasons in *Uncle Vanya* run from late spring to autumn, while *The Wood-demon* takes place in one month of summer. The endearingly pompous Dyadin, the romantic miller of *The Wood-demon*, is reduced to the sadly ignoble hanger-on, Telegin, who can only strum his guitar while Vanya cries. Most important of the changes is the appearance of the nurse Marina : in Chekhov's later plays the old servants, with their constant cares, and their rock-like faith in God and order, throw into greater relief the idleness, the vacillation and disorder of their masters. Faced with Marina, Astrov has to question himself in a way that the wood-demon could never do : will the future in two hundred years' time show the slightest trace of his work and sacrifices?[6]

From Chekhov's stories, where the question of the future decides the value of the present, the theme of the golden age soon to dawn and justify all the darkness of this age creeps in. It becomes an alternative faith. The servant believes in God's gratitude as in her master's gratitude. The heroines, whether Sonya in *Uncle Vanya*, or Anya in *The Cherry Orchard*, or the sisters in *Three Sisters*, must create a rival religion, an Arcadia of the future or of distant Moscow to keep themselves sane in the present and in the provinces. *The Wood-demon* is still an idyll : it needs no religion of the future as a sedative. Sonya's consoling lies to Uncle Vanya about rest, mercy and transfiguration show a fresh version of the 'new life' that was promised to Platonov and Ivanov. How can we believe in it?

Chekhov's four pre-Stanislavsky plays are a development of an original, aggressive conception of the theatre. Of *Platonov*'s innovations one might say that fools rush in where angels fear to tread; but by constant refinement, tragedy, comedy, symbolism and the close reproduction of the minutiae of everyday life fuse into a viable dramatic technique. It took a Stanislavsky to make this acceptable, and without Stanislavsky Chekhov might well have abandoned drama. *Uncle Vanya* was published in 1897 before it had been performed and Chekhov took no active interest in the provincial theatres that first presented it. *The Wood-demon* appeared only in a lithographed edition in 1890. Chekhov accepted criticism of the play for its 'literariness', and evidently concluded that this was a fault inherent in his work : to the actor-manager Lensky he wrote in November 1889, 'I shan't write any more plays. I haven't got the time, the talent nor, probably, enough love of the craft for it.' He sold the play to a private theatre, and except, probably, for cutting it down into a prototype of *Uncle Vanya,* kept his word for at least five years. His disillusionment was one of the factors that impelled him in 1890 to desert the arts for a journey to Sakhalin.

9

The Trophies of Sakhalin

*For the world, I count it not an inn, but an hospital,
and a place, not to live, but to die in.*
                    Sir Thomas Browne, *Religio Medici*

Chekhov did not lack reasons for his self-imposed ordeal of a
journey to Sakhalin. We have seen in an earlier chapter how inexorable and thorough were his preparations, once the initial decision had been taken. Why Sakhalin? Perhaps because it was the
most arduous and longest journey he could undertake, without having to speak a foreign language; certainly because it was Russia's
Devil's Island, and as the most terrible of penal settlements it
seemed to Chekhov an inferno into which an artist must descend,
if he was to get at the roots of the evil and misery which beset him
on earth.

   To reach Sakhalin meant nearly three months' travelling across
Siberia, mainly in an unsprung covered wagon, in the cold, wet
spring of 1890. The monotonous plains, the flooded rivers, the
terrible roads and living conditions were only a foretaste of Sakhalin
itself, notorious as climatically the most unpleasant island on earth.
Its isolation across treacherous seas from the mainland and its desti-
tute remnants of an aboriginal population made it a fitting place
for the most desperate and recidivist criminals. Most of the prisoners,
once their sentence was served, had to stay on the island as subsis-
tence farmers, still the captives of a half-military, half-bureaucratic
régime which relied on floggings, fetters and starvation rations to
maintain order. Their families, whose undeserved fate concerned
Chekhov most, were forced into a depraved underworld of child
prostitution and beggary. To explore and record this cesspit of
Russia meant tracing the corruption, injustice and violence of
Russian society to its sources. Arguing with Suvorin, who naturally

felt Chekhov's expedition to be a pointless exercise in muck-raking
and self-mortification, Chekhov insisted on the almost religious nature
of his pilgrimage (8 March 1890):

Sakhalin can be superfluous and boring only to a society that does not
exile thousands of people there and does not spend millions on it . . .
Sakhalin is a place of the most unendurable sufferings which man,
free or deprived of freedom, is capable of. People whose work is to do
with, or on Sakhalin have been and are now dealing with terrible, responsible problems. I'm sorry I'm not sentimental, or I should have
said that we ought to go to pay homage to places like Sakhalin, as the
Turks go to Mecca.

Chekhov's wanderlust is understandable. *A Dreary Story* hints at
a writer who has mined his seam of experience to the end; three
years earlier, in 1887, it was a long summer's journey which had
brought new material, freedom and experience, and had made
possible new departures in writing, such as *Steppe*. There were, too,
more immediate reasons for travel; by early 1890, the Russian critical
monthlies were so often reproaching Chekhov for alleged indifference
to suffering humanity and to political and social questions, that their
attacks amounted to baiting. The editors of the 'liberal' *Russkaya
Mysl'* were the most virulent. ('Liberal' in the Russia of the 1880s
and 1890s meant 'free-thinking, reformist-radical, anti-aesthetic', as
opposed to the conservative nationalism of the government, the
socialism—Marxist or Tolstoyan—of the illegal movements, or the
decadence of the new generation of artists: for non-liberals in Russia,
'liberal' was a dirty word.) A month before Chekhov left, Vukol
Lavrov[1] stung him so badly in *Russkaya Mysl'* that for the first and
last time in his life Chekhov riposted (10 April 1890):

I read this phrase, 'Only a day ago, even the priests of unprincipled
writing, such as Yasinsky and Chekhov, whose names etc., etc.' . . . In
fact, I wouldn't have replied to the slander, but I am soon leaving
Russia for a long time and perhaps I shall never return . . .
    . . . there is not a single line I've written which might make me
ashamed. If we allow the conjecture that by unprincipledness you
mean the sad fact that I, an educated, much published man have
done nothing for those I love, that my activities have left no mark on
the rural councils, the new law-courts, freedom of the press, freedom
in general, etc., then in this respect *Russkaya Mysl'* must in all justice
consider me its colleague, not indict me, since it has done no more
than I have in this direction up to now—and this is not our fault.

The journey to Sakhalin was to prove by action what Chekhov refused to do by writing—that he was committed to alleviating human suffering.

Other motives may be cited: the death of his brother Nikolay in 1889 and a lull in the tense relationship with his eldest brother, Aleksandr, as well as his comparative affluence, loosened for a while the ties that bound him all his life to his family. He was also regretting his neglect of science for the arts, and the entire journey was planned and carried out as an expedition for sociological medicine, not as a journalist's scoop. It was heroic science, in the nineteenth-century tradition of Darwin and Przhevalsky,[2] whom Chekhov adulated. Eighteen months before, in October 1888, Chekhov had written Przhevalsky's obituary; in it the great explorer and zoologist emerges god-like, in contrast to the despairing intellectual:

One Przhevalsky or one Stanley is worth a dozen educational institutions and a hundred good books. Their aspirations, noble ambition, based on love of homeland and science, their stubborness, their pursuit of the goal they have set themselves, undeterred by any deprivations, dangers and temptations of personal happiness, their wealth of knowledge and love of work, their acceptance of heat, hunger, homesickness, exhausting fevers, their fanatic faith in Christian civilisation and science make them in the eyes of the people heroes who personify a higher moral force . . .

In our sick times, when European societies have been overwhelmed by idleness, boredom with life and unbelief, when everywhere a dislike of life and fear of death reign in a strange mutual combination, when even the best people sit back, justifying their idleness and depravity by the absence of a definite goal in life, heroes are as necessary as the sun.

After an obituary like this, Chekhov could hardly do otherwise than follow in Przhevalsky's footsteps across Siberia.

There was also considerable romanticism in Chekhov's motives. One or two of the stories written before his departure show how strong were his yearnings for new horizons. In *Vory* (*The Thieves*) (first entitled *Cherti, The Devils*), the central character, Yergunov, drunken, boasting fool though he is, expresses a romantic longing for wide open spaces, for the bold, amoral freedom of the horse-thieves and the poetry of irresponsibility. The adventure and novelty promised by Siberia were as attractive to Chekhov as the new material and new attitudes which his researches in Sakhalin might bring him.

Chekhov returned by sea, via Hong Kong, Ceylon and the Black Sea, at the very end of 1890. The stories he wrote after his return, admittedly, have only the faintest imprint of that year's experiences. If we read *Gusev, The Peasant Women, The Duel* or *Ward No. 6*, we shall detect only the most tenuous links with the Chekhov who toured the hell of Sakhalin, like an up-to-date Dante, with ten thousand sociological questions. On the surface Sakhalin nowhere seems as relevant to subsequent work as the journey south to the Don in 1887 was to *Steppe*. But in the background the island is very much there; Gusev is returning from a life worn out in Sakhalin; the Darwinist hero of *The Duel*, von Koren, plans an expedition to the Pacific coast of Siberia; the women in *The Peasant Women* feel the lure of a crime that can lead only to penal servitude in Sakhalin. In fact, Sakhalin played a much stronger part than these slight allusions imply. Its effect on Russian literature was less dramatic than, but just as pervasive as Tolstoy's 'spiritual crisis' fifteen years before. It changed Chekhov; his tuberculosis became much more virulent, and he returned aware that he would not see middle age. There is an intense poetry of death everywhere in the stories of 1891 and 1892, and a feeling, even stronger than before, of nature's indifference to man. Sakhalin gave Chekhov the first of his experiences of real, irremediable evil. Everything which he was to record in his dissertation on the island contributed to a vision of an irredeemable fall, and this vision ousts the Tolstoyan morality that underlies so much of the earlier work. No longer can Chekhov follow Tolstoy towards a rural Eden that will save mankind from the Sodom and Gomorrah of urban civilisation : in Sakhalin he sensed that social evils and individual unhappiness were inextricably involved; his ethics lost their sharp edge of blame and discrimination. After the journey he can no longer denounce the neurasthenic, nor can he exculpate the Przhevalskys of this world.

The scientific preoccupations behind his journey naturally influenced the structure of his work. It was four years before a sociological framework became apparent in his stories, but almost immediately he complicates the pattern of his narrative. Instead of one hero whose line of thought arouses our sympathy and criticism, the stories now have at least two conflicting outlooks which fight each other to a stalemate. While one argument may be more attractive than another, it would be a mistake to assume that it represents

Chekhov's viewpoint : the impasse is just as hopeless, whether it has two entrances or only one. In the stories of 1891 and 1892 almost every philosophy that Chekhov had ever toyed with or fought against is embodied in one or more characters; after the lifeless landscapes of Sakhalin, optimism and faith in common sense are weakened. The letters, like the stories, are full of lunar imagery : the world to Chekhov is as dead and absurd as the moon, and for long periods he loses his sense of life on earth. In the struggles of *The Duel* and *Ward No. 6* we now have a match with a hopeless end-game. Human salvation lies elsewhere than in the correct set of values for which the stories before Sakhalin search. After Sakhalin, relief comes only in flashes of absurd beauty, which hint at the mystical insight which Chekhov always declared he lacked, and in a listless hope that science and technology will open up some unsuspected prospect.

More positively, and most importantly, Sakhalin cured Chekhov of any lingering feelings of inferiority. He stopped apologising for his lack of leadership; he clearly accepted himself as a Russian writer whose initiation into greatness had been as tough as Push-kin's exile, Dostoyevsky's sentence of death, or Tolstoy's spiritual crisis. That he has accepted himself as a classic writer can be seen in the strikingly traditional modes in which his post-Sakhalin stories are written. *The Duel* has a plot as symmetrical as any of Gon-charov's or Turgenev's, while *Ward No. 6* has a cast-iron mould of tragic necessity and a well-matched clash of opposing philosophies which are classic in every sense of the word.

However indirectly, Chekhov had thus brought back across the world from Sakhalin more than a sense of social responsibility and a pet mongoose as trophies; he had instated himself as a major writer with responsibilities to a tradition. He had come of age (he was now over thirty), and his first action was to shake off the hypnotic effect that Tolstoy's writings and personal aura had for six years exerted on him. The change can be seen in his reaction to Tolstoy's brilliantly stupid *The Kreutzer Sonata*, which was circulated in early 1890 and in which bourgeois marriage, music and sexuality all conspire to destroy the hero's potential for good. (In *The Kreutzer Sonata* the narrator tells how he was lured into marrying by the unconscious sexual marketing of his bride, how the experiences of the bedroom gradually poison his life, distract him from his true goals, and, when his wife commits adultery with a violinist, turn him into a murderer.) *The Kreutzer Sonata* was a sensation all over Europe, partly because it was clearly aimed by Tolstoy against his own wife, partly because its diatribe against woman as an agent of evil was a fashionable piece of Schopenhauerian philosophy, and partly because it is a powerful work in its brooding, vindictive atmosphere.

A month after he had read *The Kreutzer Sonata*, Chekhov's doubts about it were overcome by Tolstoy's forcefulness; he wrote to Plescheyev in February 1890 :

Apart from its artistic merits, which are astounding in places, thanks to the story just for arousing one's thoughts to the utmost. Reading it, you can hardly stop yourself shouting, 'That's true!' or 'That's absurd!' True, it does have very annoying faults . . . the bold way Tolstoy deals with what he doesn't know or what he refuses out of obstinacy to understand. Thus, his arguments on syphilis, orphanages, the revulsion women have towards copulation etc. are not merely arguable, but simply reveal an ignoramus . . . But these faults disperse like feathers blown by the wind; because of the story's qualities, you just don't notice them.

In December, however, back from Sakhalin, Chekhov could write to Suvorin :

How wrong you were when you advised me not to go to Sakhalin! . . . What a sour-face I should be now if I had stayed at home. Before the journey *The Kreutzer Sonata* was an event for me, while now I find it ridiculous and think it senseless. Perhaps I've matured with the journey, perhaps I've gone mad—the devil knows.

Although Chekhov revered Tolstoy all his life, he now saw his bullying ignorance for what it was and, in his post-Sakhalin stories, he gradually argues Tolstoyan morality out of his system. We can see the process at work in the negative features of characters such as Layevsky in *The Duel* and Doctor Ragin in *Ward No. 6*. These stories demonstrate the catalytic effect of Sakhalin.

But *Gusev*, the only story written in 1890, already shows the sea-change that Chekhov has undergone. The chief character[3] is a simple peasant soldier, sent home from the Far East, after five years there as a batman, because he is dying of tuberculosis. Passive beneath the injustices of his life and the approach of death, he is a natural primitive, and the story contrasts his apathy and nostalgia with the impotent rage of Pavel Ivanych, likewise dying, who has contrived to get himself a passage with the soldiers. Pavel Ivanych berates Gusev for his ignorance, brutality and quietism : almost Dostoyevskian in his self-conscious unpleasantness, he is 'protest incarnate'. Yet as death comes, it is Gusev who accepts it, while Pavel Ivanych fails to come to terms with it. Thus the story is a rather Tolstoyan contrast of the healthy peasant and unhealthy bourgeois views of death. Like Chekhov's other post-Sakhalin works, it opposes rebellious scepticism with passive surrender to fate, but unlike the later stories, it is above all a static poetic vision. The arguments between Pavel Ivanych and Gusev do not matter much : Gusev cannot understand a word Pavel Ivanych says and is hardly allowed to reply. What matters is Gusev's burial at sea, when the body falls through the waves, is ripped from its sailcloth by a shark and sinks into the ocean. Here, as so often in Chekhov's mature work, the sea is the beginning and the end of life; ocean and sky communicate, and create forms which go beyond any human powers of expression. Chekhov conveys a thoroughly romantic vision of nature having its own spirit, language and poetry, in which human beings are an ephemeral anomaly :

But meanwhile, up above, where the sun sets, the clouds are packing; one cloud is like a triumphal arc, another like a lion, another like scissors . . . A green ray of light emerges from the clouds and stretches right into the middle of the sky . . . the ocean at first frowns, but soon also takes on gentle, joyful, passionate colours which are hard even to put a name to in human terms.[4]

Nature has all the beauty, emotion and communication that have disappeared from human life. What is clearly the point of *Gusev* is to become part of the lapidary structure of *The Duel* and *Ward No. 6* : the poetic imagery will recur in the seascapes and the death vision of the later works.

The year 1890 had cost Chekhov some four thousand rubles and had produced only one story. In spring 1890, he made another journey, his first to Western Europe, with the Suvorins. To pay for all his travels and to make up for his inactivity, he worked feverishly for the rest of 1891. Up to September, *The Duel* took up most of his time; simultaneously, he was tackling another, even more novel work, his dissertation on life on Sakhalin. These radically new efforts at more conventional modes of writing did not come easily, but in the same summer and autumn he threw off a number of stories from his previous mould, some like *Moya zhena* (*My Wife*) on the lines of *A Dreary Story*, others continuing on familiar Tolstoyan lines.

In *The Duel*, Chekhov freed himself from the influence of Tolstoy but he was still to write two of his most Tolstoyan works. One is *Baby (The Peasant Women)*. The women, two peasant sisters-in-law, one ugly with an absent husband, the other pretty with an idiot husband, bored and oppressed in their father-in-law's house, make the 'frame' story, while its core lies in the narrative of a visitor, Matvey. Matvey tells his story, quite unaware of its effect or its morality: he seduced a soldier's wife, and drove her to poison her husband. Matvey is a Russian Tartuffe in his hypocrisy, lechery and moralising; he also comes across as a parody of Tolstoy's Pozdnyshev, the narrator of *The Kreutzer Sonata*. To this extent the story is anti-Tolstoyan. But the 'frame' story dominates: the peasant women, after they have heard Matvey, feel an urge to kill the men who make their lives such a misery. The evil of the narrator infects the listeners in a truly Tolstoyan fashion. *The Peasant Women* plunges us into the language and hierarchies of a peasant household, with a Tolstoyan feeling for the layers of passion, inhibitions and ritual in its outlook. Most Tolstoyan of all, however, is the sensation of immense evil threatening to break through into action.

The other important Tolstoyan story is *Poprygun'ya (The Grasshopper—The Butterfly* in the Oxford Chekhov). Like *The Peasant Women*, it pleased Tolstoy greatly and he put it on his list of Chekhov's best works, together with every other Tolstoyan piece by him. It is a story of virtuoso narrative technique, even by Chekhov's standards, but it is marred by Tolstoyan defects in its overall scheme. As in *The Princess*, black is jet-black and white is snow-white. The 'grasshopper' herself is a satirical portrayal of a woman, Ol'ga Ivanovna, who lives on reflected glory and jumps from one celebrity to another in search of it; the satire is subtly coloured by the ingenuous way in which the narrator echoes the clichés and exclamations that Ol'ga herself utters. But in contrast to the satire, a morality story is in progress. Ol'ga frivolously marries a saintly, modest doctor and by her trivial exploitation, her adultery with an artist and her lies drives him to despondency, so that, over-worked and careless, he infects himself with diphtheria. Chekhov wrote *The Grasshopper* very quickly; the doctor, the grasshopper herself and the artist were modelled—perhaps unconsciously—on real people. The scheme of the story is as ill-digested as the raw material; only in an obituary, not in a short story, can the hero be so idealised and the villains so blackened. The result is a denunciation of woman's irrelevance and destructiveness as crude as *The Kreutzer Sonata*; nevertheless, the pretentiousness of the artist and the post-coital disgust of the lovers are cleverly evoked by such touches as the image of a peasant woman's filthy finger in the soup she serves to the lovers. Ol'ga Ivanovna's comments on art are turned into clichés simply by putting the words 'she said', 'she replied' in the imperfect tense, so that her statements become routine to the point of absurdity.

If the hero of *The Grasshopper*, Doctor Dymov, is the last ideal figure to appear in Chekhov's work, the story itself is the last of Chekhov's Tolstoyan moralities. He regretted it (especially as the originals recognised themselves in the principal characters), hovered between four possible titles for it and called it 'a little sentimental novel for family reading' when he offered it to Tikhonov, the editor of *Sever* (*The North*). It met, to be fair, with an enthusiastic reception, especially because it showed 'the simplicity and patience of a noble, truly great man'; Ivan Bunin, a most discriminating critic, thought it a good story with a terrible title. But undoubtedly it reflects too well Chekhov's intermittent misogyny and his distrust of aesthetes.

Chekhov's mind seems even more convoluted when his attitude to sex breaks right away from Tolstoy's in *The Duel*, which was nearly finished when *The Grasshopper* was written. His own experience of women may have been particularly troublesome in the summer of 1891; into his letters to his new love, the vicacious Lika Mizinova, a schoolteacher colleague of his sister, creeps a tone of real emotional involvement. All the bantering, ribaldry, mock courtship and reproaches do not quite conceal sentiment, even passion. Probably Chekhov's strongest feeling was fear—fear that sexual attraction would trap him into losing his freedom to a woman who could irritate as well as stimulate. His irreplaceable sister, Masha, was the only person who could have given an account of Chekhov's love for Lika Mizinova and, discreet to the last, she chose not to do so. All we can be sure of is Chekhov's cat-and-mouse treatment of Lika; even six years later, when his non-committal had brought her near to disaster, he could still be cruel. 'I always valued *Reinheit* (purity) and kindness in women, and you have always been kind', he wrote. The ambivalence in his treatment of his women friends is re-

flected in his heroines. The sexual delinquency of the 'grasshopper'
is condemned, while the delinquency of Nadezhda, the heroine of
The Duel, is compassionately condoned.

Duel' (*The Duel*) is one of Chekhov's longest works (over thirty
thousand words); it cost him considerable effort, and it is one of his
most carefully constructed stories. Its plot is unusually taut and
symmetrical. Into a dull seaside Caucasian town two newcomers
have introduced conflict and tension. The first is Layevsky, a self-
diagnosed Petersburg Hamlet in the tradition of the 'superfluous
man'; he has run away with another man's wife, Nadezhda. His
first intentions were to take refuge from the corruption of the city
and work like a Tolstoyan convert on the land; instead, his naturally
weak nature has led him to take his place as an idle civil servant
in the easy-going life of the local Russians. The second newcomer
is von Koren, a zoologist and a Darwinist, who is immune to Layevsky's charm and violently hates him and Nadezhda as 'macaques',
who should be exterminated in the name of progress. The story
opens when Layevsky, bored with Nadezhda, learns that her husband has died and that he now has to marry her or run away back
to Petersburg. Inevitably, he sees his salvation in flight, and much
of the story concerns his efforts to raise the money for his fare. The
mediator between von Koren and Layevsky is the kindly, naïve military doctor, Samoylenko, who lends Layevsky money and takes in von
Koren as a paying guest. Von Koren grows more and more convinced that Layevsky should be exterminated, as he sees him press-
ing Samoylenko for loans, and finally he takes advantage of Layevsky's hysteria and provokes him to a duel, which takes place at
dawn. Nature casts an eerie spell over the event, and von Koren just
misses killing Laveysky when his friend the deacon interrupts with
a shout of horror. The deacon, like Doctor Samoylenko, is a mediator, a peacemaker who is more profound, yet more stupid, than
the antagonists with whom he argues. Samoylenko is a naïve, bluster-
ing clown compared with the articulate Layevsky; the deacon is a
typically unworldly, childlike ecclesiastic compared with the ruth-
lessly logical von Koren, but our final impression is that they are
the true normal human beings.

The consequences of the duel may seem a little trite : Layevsky
is so shattered by the nearness of death that he becomes a reformed
character. He and Nadezhda work to pay off their debts, and expiate
their fornication by marrying. Von Koren takes back his insults

and departs with an apology. Layevsky's repentance is brought about not only by the duel, but also through the sub-plot involving Nadezhda. Neglected by Layevsky, she sinks into malaise and debts; she goes to bed with the local police chief and then prostitutes herself to the son of the shopkeeper to whom she owes money. Layevsky catches her in bed with the police chief on the eve of the duel; he immediately sees himself as the cause and, instead of experiencing a Tolstoyan revulsion from her, falls properly in love.

The plot is thus not only more eventful than most of Chekhov's; it is also very tautly put together. The main effort must have been expended on creating a full but objective characterisation of the duellists. The aggressive von Koren had to be detached from his real-life original, Wagner, a Moscow zoologist, whom Chekhov knew quite well. Chekhov insisted on a German name, not only because all the prominent zoologists in Russia were German, but also because von Koren's energy and dedication had to be un-Russian. Likewise, in Chekhov's original plan, Layevsky was called Ladzievsky, an equally un-Russian name. Only under pressure from his editor did he cancel this Polish name, which would have brought out better the contrast between the Russian minor characters and the non-Russian 'bearers of an idea'. Layevsky, as it is, is a difficult piece of characterisation, so close is he to the stereotype of the 'superfluous man', but Chekhov makes him convincing by bringing out his literariness; Layevsky talks in quotations, cites Tolstoy, calls himself a Hamlet, and acts like one of Lermontov's or Turgenev's heroes.

The success of the characterisation comes from the use of a technique that is later to be the backbone of Chekhov's plays; the hero's philosophy is expounded both by Layevsky and von Koren with the energy of hatred, and thus exaggerated slightly but irrevocably into comedy. *The Duel* is in fact even more dramatic than Chekhov's plays; not only is the story staged in five major confrontations, not only does the conflict emerge almost entirely in dialogue, but there is also a stage brilliance in von Koren's advocacy of the laws of natural selection when he justifies the liquidation of Layevsky which reminds us of Uncle Vanya's tirade against Professor Serebryakov. The serious argument is interrupted by the elaborate preparation and eating of the food which Samoylenko is serving and the dramatic laughter and protests of the others present. Layevsky's jaded arguments against woman and civilisation, that echo so patently his reading of Tolstoy, likewise make a dramatic impact, tragi-comic and self-satirising, that echoes Uncle Vanya's monologues. The antagonists belong essentially to Chekhov's dramas; if Layevsky anticipates Uncle Vanya, von Koren's brutal wit recalls Doctor Astrov. (It may well have been at this time, in 1891, that Chekhov undertook the revision of *The Wood-demon* into *Uncle Vanya*.)

Much of the narrative has the poetic intensity we associate with Chekhov : the roaring of the sea, the awe-inspiring mountains, the lighting, all combine to give an uncanny strangeness to what would otherwise be a romantic plot of a familiar sort. Typical, too, are the intrusions of everyday trivia into an abstract discussion : the sand in Samoylenko's boots and the smell of Nadezhda's bedroom break up the continuity of action. But nevertheless *The Duel* is virtually drama transposed into story-telling. For the first time, Chekhov's action arises out of dialogue. Even the descriptive passages are condensed into no more than an occasional dozen words, and it would require very little to convert them into stage effects—backdrops, off-stage noises, lighting effects. The climax of the story, when von Koren rides to fight with Layevsky, is lit by the same image as symbolises death in *Gusev* : two rays of green light. Here the image is in pure stage terms. The very structure of intrigue, climax and dénouement belongs to Chekhov's dramas. The pistol shot that fails to kill does, admittedly, seem to destroy the falseness in Layevsky, and thus makes for an apparently trite dénouement, but the effect is somewhat more subtle than the triumph of German action over Russian idleness would suggest. The rehabilitated Layevsky and Nadezhda are not quite alive any more. When von Koren takes his leave of them, he seems to sense that he has destroyed something in Layevsky, who is now a worn-out automaton : 'He's pathetic, shy, crushed, he bows like a Chinese dummy, and it makes me sad.'

True to himself, Chekhov does not persuade us that the duel leads to a clear-cut triumph. The impact of the story comes from the minor characters, the deacon and Doctor Samoylenko, and from the sexual ordeal of Nadezhda. The story begins with the sea drowning Layevsky's complaints, and ends with it resisting the oars of von Koren's boat as he leaves for good. Only Samoylenko, the deacon and the minor characters hidden in the mountains around the town, the Tatar innkeeper and the ghost-like tribesmen, live at peace with nature. Layevsky declares that he hates nature, von Koren fights it with his system, his science and his Darwinism. But nature triumphs over them. In the episode of the evening picnic that for the first time brings all the characters together, it reduces the conversation of the picnickers to exclamations and mute bewilderment; it isolates them. Across the river from the party, Caucasian tribesmen gather and sit in a circle, listening to a story. They are barely discernible in the dusk, and their language is unintelligible, but in the harsh scenery of rocks and stunted trees they are at home, while the European, posing, arguing picnickers seem creatures from another planet. It is one of Chekhov's post-Sakhalin 'lunar' episodes, and it sheds a quasi-religious light on human alienation. The deacon stares at the scene, plunged into a daydream which ends in a vision of himself as a bishop proclaiming, 'Oh God, see and visit this vineyard which thy right hand hath planted.' Idle reverie though this is, cut short by Samoylenko's shout of 'Where's the fish?', it is at the same time the poetic highwater mark of the story. It is one of Chekhov's most intense pleas for the revelation of meaning, for an explanation of nature's relationship to man. Truth is not to be found in some compromise between Layevsky's excuses for inertia and von Koren's campaign to exterminate the weak. It can only come in silence, as one listens to the forces of nature outside man.

The sub-plot of Nadezhda's experiences has a gruesome comic streak; giving in to Kirilin, the police chief, she infuriates the shopkeeper's son Achmyanov, who takes Layevsky along to catch her in bed with Kirilin. But in these half-farcical, half-pathetic episodes Chekhov's critics rightly saw a retort to Tolstoy. Certainly, Nadezhda is at the mercy of her sexual instincts and gives Layevsky a case when he blames her for the squalor of their life. Taking his cue always from literature, he echoes Tolstoy's words, 'The emancipation of women is not in courses or hospital wards but in the bedroom', shocking Samoylenko with his 'women need the bedroom most of all.' The sub-plot is full of sordid detail : Nadezhda's vaguely gynaecological illness, her tawdry clothes, her untidiness, all make sexuality seem demeaning. But Layevsky's reaction when he discovers her infidelities radically distinguishes Chekhov's hero from Tolstoy's. He feels no more resentment or revulsion, only tenderness. This is perhaps the only place in Chekhov where Christian love moves in when sexual love is dead; it is shown as convincingly as possible. Layevsky is, after all, *in extremis*; it is the eve of the

E

duel and he has to see himself for what he is. 'In the whole of my life I haven't planted a single tree' is a terrible indictment for a character created by a man who planted tens of thousands of trees.

Of all Chekhov's characters, von Koren is the strongest. He would dominate *The Duel*, were it not that the very lucidity and finality of his views implant the seeds of doubt in us. The peacemakers cannot match him in argument; only Layevsky, feeling the force of his hatred and having to justify himself, can undermine him in an exposé so witty that it undoes a good deal of Chekhov's character-isation and, using the phrases of Chekhov's obituary of Przhevalsky, makes von Koren seem a parody explorer, a monster :

He's a hard, strong, despotic character . . . He wants the wilderness, a moonlit night; around him in tents and under the open sky sleep his sick, hungry Cossacks, worn out by terrible marches . . . only he is awake, sitting like Stanley on a folding chair and feeling like the king of the desert and the boss of these people. He goes on and on some-where, his men groan and die one after the other, while he goes on and on, perishes in the end and still remains a despot and the king of the desert, since the cross over his grave shows up for thirty or forty miles to the caravans and reigns over the desert [as Przhevalsky's grave by Issyk-Kul dominates the Kirghizian scenery].

Von Koren's scientific defence of natural selection leads to para-doxes : the abnormal must be wiped out for love of humanity. This application of zoology and Darwinism to ethics and politics was very characteristic of Chekhov's day, and his letters and *feuilletons* (especially his denunciation of Moscow Zoo, *Fokusniki (The Trick-sters)*, 1891) brought him on to the fringe of the controversy that was raging among Russian thinkers abroad and at home. The extreme left and, in some cases, the extreme right saw Darwinism as a justification of war and suffering in human society. Works such as Robert Byr's *Der Kampf um's Dasein* (1875) spread neo-Dar-winism in Russia, with such von-Korenisms as 'Fight for existence consciously or unconsciously, by force or cunning . . . follow the eternal urge dominating us from birth to death—but don't lie about loving one another.' In Sakhalin Chekhov had seen all he wanted of the struggle to exist. That explains why he worshipped Przheval-sky in his obituary of 1888 and why he is disabused of heroics and neo-Darwinism in 1891. Seeing von Koren's boat disappear in the darkness, Layevsky thinks of humanity taking a step backward for

every two steps forward; while truth remains unfathomable, we can
be sure that von Koren's ideology is a step backwards. For that
certitude, we can thank Sakhalin.

Writing *The Duel* in conjunction with so much else, especially
the book on Sakhalin which dragged on for three more years, exhausted Chekhov. The autumn and winter were all the more gloomy
for the onset of the great Russian famine, which Chekhov tried to
relieve; for the death of several people close to him; and for the
end of the brief respite in his illness. Worried by the search for a
country estate, plagued again by influenza, headaches, haemorrhoids, a tubercular cough and depression, Chekhov had no need of
outside horrors to create the despondency of *Palata no. 6 (Ward No.
6)*. The story is a culmination of his Sakhalin experiences; its
austerity recalls the Sakhalin landscapes, and its view of the world
as a prison generalises the penal state of Sakhalin. Like *The Duel*,
Ward No. 6 is long; it took eight months to write, and, like *The
Duel*, it is unusually conventional in its structure. Chekhov saw
from the start that it was not typical of his work up to this time:
'There's a lot of argumentation in the tale and no love element.
There's a plot, an intrigue and a dénouement. Liberal in trend', he
wrote to Suvorin in March 1892. Its difference is emphasised by
the fact that Chekhov took great pains to have it published by
Vukol Lavrov, who had so bitterly attacked him two years before,
in *Russkaya Mysl'*. 'Liberal in trend' should, however, be taken with
a grain of salt, despite Chekhov's remark and the choice of a 'liberal'
magazine. Chekhov was not assenting to Lavrov's criticisms of his
'unprincipledness' so much as showing more explicitly in *Ward
No. 6* why he could not preach liberal ideas.

Ward No. 6 opens with a narrator's description of the ramshackle
provincial hospital and résumé of the lives of the five mental patients
locked up in Ward No. 6; in its free commentary this follows the
style of Chekhov's early period, particularly his *feuilletons*, and
gives the work, at first, a documentary flavour. Then the narrator
effaces himself and narrative style is adopted, merging with the
inner monologue of the protagonist. We are told how Ivan Gromov,
the only youthful, articulate and educated patient, came to suffer
from persecution mania and to end up as prisoner of the brutal male
nurse, Nikita. Then comes a portrait of the hospital doctor, Andrey
Ragin, who presides over and condones the cruelty and neglect in
his hospital. Gromov reacts to the world outside and inside the

ward with indignation and idealism; Ragin justifies his inactivity by a curious quietism, perverting the stoic ideal into an argument that suffering and death are inevitable and that it is pointless to alleviate one or delay the other; happiness lies only in introspection and the world is unalterable. If Gromov is an existentialist, Ragin is an 'essentialist', believing that if a mental ward exists, then patients must fill it.

The story proper begins with an ominous accident. Ragin meets one of the patients, an insane Jew, who is returning to the ward after a day's begging. Only then does he visit the ward and become interested in Gromov as an intellectual sparring partner. This is the fatal catastrophe to which his hubris and his easy-going nature have laid him open. Interest becomes a liking; his visits start an intrigue by his jealous assistant, and the rumour runs through the provincial town that Ragin, too, is mad. Driven by his superiors' suspicions to hysterical anger, he is trapped into becoming a patient in his own ward, where he dies soon afterwards of a stroke. Like *The Duel*, *Ward No. 6* has an unintentional dramatic structure, but it is more unequivocally tragic than any of Chekhov's dramas. The classical pattern of hamartia, hubris, catastrophe, catharsis and nemesis underlies Ragin's fondness for intellectual speculation, his visits to Gromov, his sudden fall and his painfully unstoic death. There is hardly any comedy in the story. Only the secondary character the postmaster, Ragin's supposed best friend, Mikhail Aver'yanych, who drives him mad with his catch-phrases and poses, and who helps to trap him in his own hospital, has a vaudeville verve. If there is comedy, then it is Gogolian in its grotesquerie, and the Gogolian atmosphere is reinforced by the virtually all-male set of characters and the locale of the story—a nameless, quintessentially provincial town, so typical of the Gogol' of *Dead Souls* or *The Government Inspector*. *Ward No. 6* is an austere work. The hospital is a prison. It has no landscapes or views. Only a grey fence, nettles and burdock and the town prison in the near distance make the story a *composition en abîme*, and thus a work unique in its allegorical and symbolical effect. The town itself, left almost undescribed, outside place and time, is as closed as the hospital; it is a symbol of the world. There are no sunsets, no cloud formations, no trees. Even the imagery of death, so important in Chekhov's post-Sakhalin work, is condensed into the last few sentences of the story. The 'green light' of *Gusev* and *The Duel* is alluded to in the colour of Ragin's eyes as he dies. Only one strange fragment of poetry lights up the gloomy fatal dialectic of Gromov and Ragin, as the latter's consciousness fades:

His eyes went green. Andrey realised that this was the end and he recalled that Ivan Gromov, Mikhail Aver'yanych and millions of people believed in immortality. Supposing it existed? But he didn't want immortality and he thought of it only for a moment. A herd of deer, unusually beautiful and graceful, which he had read about the night before, ran past him.

The absurd image of the deer is the sole stroke of beauty; it implies a lost nature, harmony and peace which are not to be found either in the humanitarian and Christian ideals expressed by Gromov or in the defeatism of Ragin. It leads on to the final image of the story, when the moon lights up the doctor's corpse on the mortuary table. Again, a picture of lunar sterility, so important in the post-Sakhalin works of Chekhov, provides the key to the real idea of *Ward No. 6*.

Contemporary critics generally took the view that Chekhov was anti-Ragin and pro-Gromov, anti-defeatist and pro-humanist. While he obviously sympathises with the vital, anguished Gromov and exposes the bankruptcy of Ragin's pact with evil, this is too simple an interpretation. There is too much irony in the portrayal of Gromov; like Ragin, he is an innocent, a bookworm and a provincial. It is necessary to look more closely at the story's construction and to take into account the circumstances in which it was written. Sparse in its prose texture, *Ward No. 6* is one of the few pieces that Chekhov barely altered when he revised it for his Collected Works. Not only are two philosophies matched, tested and left for our verdict; the story is also plotted with a deadly irony. This is the first time that Chekhov gives us a microcosmic setting—a universe made out of a handful of characters against a sketchy background. Most of his contemporaries understood it as an allegory. The aged Leskov exclaimed: 'Ward No. 6 is Russia', a hospital where the sane are locked up for their madness and the cynical serve the state by acquiescing. In Chekhov's day, the symbol of the world-as-a-hospital was already common in poetry—Baudelaire was beginning to find a decadent following in Russia—but in prose Chekhov is anticipating the nightmares to come of Sologub and Leonid Andreyev.

Once the narrator has shown us round the ward, with the Chekhovian images of spiked fencing, nettles and rotten wood that pervade the description, we are given our cue for response. The narrator takes a stance to be found in the earliest Chekhov, saying openly how he approves of Ivan Gromov: 'I like him, he's polite, anxious to help and usually considerate in his dealings with everybody.' Gromov's past experience of life is set out in such a way that a persecution complex seems the most logical reaction to the sight that germinates it: convicts being taken through the streets. His mad ravings are summed up in a passage that suggests they are no madder than any noble outpouring of idealism: 'He talks of humanity's baseness, of violence crushing truth, of the beautiful life that will one day come to pass on earth.' So far, so good. But to like Gromov is not to follow him blindly. In that last phrase, 'the beautiful life that will one day . . .', is to be heard an ironic reverberation of cloud-cuckooland; the beautiful future is the religion of the foolish and naïve in all Chekhov's work, and it is the one true symptom of insanity shown by Gromov.

The characterisation of Doctor Ragin is striking for the number of parallels between him and his patient, the fearful symmetry of guard and prisoner. Like Gromov, he reads as compulsively as he breathes; his knowledge of the world is bounded by a brief, unhappy infancy. Like Gromov, he sees the world only through the prism of his ideas. Gromov 'used only crude colours in his judgments of people, only white and black . . . there was nothing in the middle.' This was a criticism Chekhov often made—of Dostoyevsky in particular and Russian thinkers in general. The doctor, too, fits everything he sees into an inverted Panglossism, as though everything were for the worst in the worst of all possible worlds. And yet, if Gromov is not wholly right, Doctor Ragin is not wholly wrong. Like Chekhov, at this time working for famine relief, and like so many Chekhovian doctors, he realises that his efforts can leave no mark on human misery; he is unlike Chekhov and Chekhovian doctors principally in his logic: if efforts are useless, they should not be made. Much of his philosophy parodies Chekhov's own thoughts; the idea that prisons exist and must therefore be filled, that life on earth is an unfortunate and temporary absurdity in a cosmos that will soon revert to its primeval inanimate state, the feeling that the inevitability of death makes all attempts at embellishing life futile—all this can be found in Chekhov's life and letters. Where Chekhov differs is that he persisted in treating the sick, sowing corn and planting trees.

In 1892 it was impossible for a reader of *Ward No. 6* not to see Doctor Ragin as a caricature of Tolstoy's 'non-resistance to evil by violence'. But it is doubtful whether Chekhov was hitting at Tolstoy's Christian ethics so much as at the Schopenhauerian conviction that the material world is evil, which underlies much of Tolstoy's thought. In Tolstoy's study at Yasnaya Polyana, ever since the writing of *Anna Karenina*, there has hung a portrait of Schopenhauer. Unlikely bedfellows though they are, Tolstoy and Schopenhauer had much in common: their suspicions of woman as a traitor to the 'idea', a horror at the enormity of death, disgust at Western civilisation, a feeling for a life of the spirit, of Nirvana rather than Utopia, all made Schopenhauer extremely attractive to Tolstoy. Ragin is Schopenhauer in provincial Russia, with none of the heart-searching of Tolstoy—a conceited and glib reciter of *Aphorismen zur Lebensweisheit*. Only in his bigotry and his refusal to fight social evils can Ragin be seen as an attack on Tolstoy.

Ragin quotes classical authors, above all Marcus Aurelius, the stoic. In Chekhov's library, dating from 1887, is a much-thumbed and annotated Russian translation of Marcus Aurelius. Ragin is not a disciple, but a perverter, of the stoic; Chekhov knew very well that Marcus Aurelius felt existence to be finite and senseless and, like Ragin, sought only the pleasures of the intellect, but unlike Ragin he did not advocate total indifference to evil.

Gromov, naturally, expresses himself far less coherently than does Ragin; his views are based on his nervous instincts, and in his need to act, to follow his senses, no matter how irrational, he steps out of the pages of fiction and speaks for Chekhov, who at this very time was settling into a newly bought estate and planning for the future. Like Gromov, Chekhov felt that the ultimate stoic (and Schopenhauerian) could only be the fellow-patient in Gromov's ward, the fat peasant, a filthy, mindless vegetable, not even reacting to the stimulus of a beating. Right or wrong, Gromov is undoubtedly more noble and promising as a model. The fact that he lives and Ragin dies hardly gives him victory, his subsequent life is endless hell, while Ragin, even in his nemesis, is vouchsafed a moment of beauty and eternal relief. His stoicism is put to the test and fails, but it is scarcely purged, so quickly does his apoplexy kill him. His death is a subtle authorial intervention, for Chekhov, with his usual medical expertise, has unobtrusively given his character a whole series of little symptoms which lead up to the stroke. The final images as he dies make us wonder what he has done to earn this transfiguration; the moonlight almost sanctifies him.

Doctor Ragin and Ivan Gromov are in fact two facets of one personality. Ragin is a symbol of the contemplative but inert artist, while Gromov symbolises suffering humanity. There was undoubtedly a dualism of this kind in Chekhov's make-up, but there is no need to see a confessional purpose in the two men. If Ward No. 6 is the whole world, they are the only inhabitants deserving eternity : together, they add up to humanity.

Ward No. 6, like *The Duel* a year earlier, examines and finds wanting two philosophies, one noble, one ignoble. The noble failure may be honourable, but it can hardly attract converts. While *The Duel* leaves us with the consolation of natural man in Samoylenko, the deacon and the Caucasian natives, *Ward No. 6*, without its philosophers, leaves us only with idiots and walking gargoyles. Nature has deserted the scene; the only view from the window of the ward is cold and lunar: 'A cold, scarlet moon rose. Not far from the hospital fence, two hundred yards, no more, stood a tall white house, surrounded by a stone wall. This was the prison.' The only other feature described is the bone-processing works, which in Chekhov's townscapes often symbolises pollution and death. *Ward No. 6*, despite the indomitable hatred of Gromov for his captors, is the most desperate of Chekhov's works, for a vitiated humanity has not even the beauty of the earth to console it.

In Russia, *Ward No. 6* is the most influential of Chekhov's works : Solzhenitsyn's *Cancer Ward* is only the last of a long series of political allegories that are modelled on it, but Chekhov himself was not fond of it. Before he travelled up to Moscow to read the proofs in his hotel room, he wrote to Vukol Lavrov in October 1892, 'I ought to touch it up, otherwise it stinks of the hospital and the mortuary. I'm not fond of stories like that.' More revealing is a letter to Suvorin earlier that month, which confirms that Gromov and Ragin both exist in Chekhov's own personality :

You have seen a monochrome, colourless and melancholy life through the prism of my bonhomie. According to you, I am one thing, and my Monrepos [the new estate, Melikhovo] and seven horses is another thing. Dear chap, I'm not one to deceive myself about the true position of things; I'm not only at a loose end and dissatisfied, but even in purely medical terms—i.e. to the point of cynicism—convinced that we can only expect bad things from this life—mistakes, losses, diseases, weak-

ness and all sorts of foulnesses, but at the same time if you only knew
how nice it is not to pay for a flat and what pleasure it gave me to
leave Moscow yesterday . . . Today I have been walking over the
snow in the fields, there was not a soul around and I felt that I was
walking on the moon.

The 'vanity of vanities' of *Ecclesiastes*, and the feeling of lunar
sterility, never far beneath the surface of Chekhov's work, are plain
in that letter, as they are in *Ward No. 6*, then being printed. A week
later, Chekhov had to reply to Suvorin's reactions to the story. In
1904 Suvorin took back and destroyed all his letters to Chekhov,
but between the lines of Chekhov's reply we can guess at a typically
Suvorin reaction : 'Very good, old boy, clever, but it hasn't got the
fire and idealism of Tolstoy or Goethe.' Chekhov, modest as usual,
tried to discuss the merits of *Ward No. 6*, but produced a number
of judgements which applied to himself, to his fellow-writers and
to his contemporaries in painting. The failings of art in his time
are, he says,

due to a disease which is worse than syphilis or sexual exhaustion for
an artist. We lack 'something', that's right, and it means if you lift up
our muse's skirt, you'll find a flat place. Remember that the writers
whom we call eternal or simply good and who intoxicate us have one
common and very important factor : they are going somewhere and
calling you to come with them and you can feel not with your mind
but with all your being that they have an aim, like the ghost of Hamlet's father, which has come to disturb the imagination with good
reason.

Of all the comments made à propos of *Ward No. 6* this is perhaps
the most important : he disassociates himself from evangelism. *Ward
No. 6* is an allegory that analyses; it is not a parable that reveals
new truths.

Afterwards, Chekhov took little interest in the story. He did nothing to assist a project to translate it into English, and the praise
and questions of his correspondents roused only embarrassed dis-
claimers. A Taganrog classmate wrote in the spirit of most of Chekhov's critics to say how pleased he was that Chekhov in *Ward No. 6*
had moved from pantheism to anthropocentrism. Presumably he felt
that from nature, as in *The Duel*, Chekhov had switched his search
for divinity to suffering mankind, as personified by Gromov. To this
classmate, Dr Ostrovsky, Chekhov gave only the vaguest encourage-

ment, but made his usual point that the skill, not the intentions, counted in literature. He wrote, 'Everyone writes as best he can. I'd like to go to heaven, but I haven't the strength . . . The point is not pantheism but the extent of one's talent.'

There is a short sketch of a story, *V ssylke* (*In Exile*), which Chekhov wrote in April 1892, while *Ward No. 6* was getting under way. It shows how closely connected *Ward No. 6* is with memories of the journey to Sakhalin. Chekhov did in fact revise *In Exile* very heavily in 1901, but the essential likeness remains, despite the deletions. A young Tatar, unjustly deported to Siberia, talks with an old ferryman, himself an exile, at a crossing-point on one of the great rivers which Chekhov crossed at so great a risk on his way across Siberia. Semyon the ferryman preaches, like Ragin, total indifference and the suppression of all desires as the only way to an endurable life in Siberia. The young Tatar, like Gromov, defends human warmth and sorrows and bitterly laments what he has left behind. Moved to fury and tears, he clumsily denounces the ferryman for his inhuman defeatism; like Gromov he prefers suffering, nostalgia and hope without end to the finality and stony consolations of apathy.

Ward No. 6 closes a whole phase of Chekhov's work. Afterwards he explores one new genre and milieu after another, but *Ward No. 6* dominates with its gloom the work of 1892. Stories such as *Sosedi* (*Neighbours*) or *Strakh* (*Fear*) are minor sketches in comparison, aghast at life as at death. There is, however, in *Neighbours* a passage which Chekhov deleted when he revised the work, since it seemed to impose an interpretation; it offers the only possible footnote to his treatment of human dilemmas. The hero, who also narrates the story, rides home after visiting his sister who has eloped with the rather Layevsky-like neighbouring landowner; having failed to put his foot down, he muses, 'I had gone to settle something, but not a single one of life's questions can have a special solution; in each separate case you must say and do what you think— that is the solution to all questions.'

As in 1889, so now Chekhov's writing had reached an impasse. Not merely had ethics disintegrated and landscapes been obliterated; his characters in 1891 and 1892—Layevsky and von Koren, Ragin and Gromov, the characters in *Neighbours*, the narrator and Doctor Sobol in *Moya zhena* (*My Wife*)—were lapsing into stereotypes, too much in the typically Russian mould of Hamlets versus Don

Quixotes. In life, too, he was clearing the path for new directions. He was trying to deflect Lika Mizinova's attachment, letting the family circle close round him once more, and playing the part of the responsible landowner. Soon the pet mongoose he had kept as a memento of his journey home from Sakhalin and which he had loved and worried about for a year became too filthy an old bachelor to keep. It went to Moscow Zoo—oddly, considering Chekhov's scorn for the Zoo—and the Sakhalin period was over. The Melikhovo phase began, full of commitment and experiment.

Melikhovo

Chekhov's years on his estate of Melikhovo gave him both content-
ment and frustration, and the stories written between 1893 and 1895
are in some ways the most intense and, often, the most imperfect
of his mature work. The intensity has something to do with the
re-appearance of women among his active characters and with the
theme of the hero's bondage to his heredity, his milieu and his carnality; the imperfections can be traced to the search for a genre and
for a narrative approach, a search that does not end until the late
style of *Murder* (1895) and *The House with the Mezzanine* (or *An
Artist's Story*) (1896) fuses an objective narrative with a subjective
impressionability.

Chekhov's way of life in Melikhovo seems disassociated from his
writing. His time, especially in 1893, when he wrote very little
fiction, was almost entirely given to farming and horticulture; he
experimented with new ploughs, made a kitchen garden, planted
cherry-trees and apple-trees, built hothouses for melons and peppers,
and let loose his peasant blood. Maria, who taught in Moscow,
would come to Melikhovo every week-end laden with grafting wax,
conifer seeds, raffia and pitchforks. Friendly relations were established with Leykin on the basis of grain seeds and dachshunds, instead of literature. Chekhov would not delegate: he surveyed
ground, costed buildings, ordered timber and dug out ponds. This
manic enthusiasm is reflected only in parody: the hero of *The Black
Monk* (1894) has a father-in-law obsessed with an orchard, terrified
of frost ruining the blossom. In Chekhov's letters and the family
diary, the temperature is noted every morning as meticulously as it
is noted by the restless or idle characters of *Three Sisters* or *The
Cherry Orchard*.

This intense activity was a reaction to sickness. Chekhov grew
more ill every year. In 1893 his haemorrhoids were so painful that

family relationships became difficult and writing impossible. In spring 1894 he collapsed and had to admit to tuberculosis. In 1894 he went blind in his right eye for months. By January 1895 his 'whole chest was creaking' and it became clear that he could not stay at Melikhovo : the damp of spring and autumn was intolerable, and the winter was to drive him to the hateful spas of the Crimea and the Côte d'Azur, already the land of exile for many of his heroes and heroines. The approach of death urged him to find new means of expression. In July 1894 he wrote, truthfully or not, to Suvorin to say : 'About ten years ago I was interested in spiritualism, and Turgenev, whom I called up, replied to me : "Your life is coming to its close." ' The letter has a joke signature, Archimandrite Antonius, but the joke is hardly funny when we consider what Chekhov's ecclesiastical images of himself imply.

His relations with other people were also changing radically. Not only was he now more often alone—for his younger brothers had left to make their careers—but also death had taken away a number of his 'grand old men'. Pleshcheyev inherited a million rubles in 1890 and emigrated to the south of France, where he died in 1893; Leskov died in January 1895. Chekhov made few new friends : apart from those whom he had known at university, only a handful of men were on *ty* terms with him. One of them was Vukol Lavrov, the editor of *Russkaya Mysl'*, and friendship with Lavrov and his co-editor Gol'tsev brought Chekhov closer to the tendency towards social critique and documentary writing which distinguished this paper from *Severnyy Vestnik*. Virtually all his important work from now on was first published in *Russkaya Mysl'*.

Relations with Suvorin survived this change. Chekhov broke with *Novoye Vremya*, embarrassed and revolted by its scandalous anti-semitic attack on the sculptor Antokol'sky and by rumours of the paper's involvement in the Panama Canal frauds, but Suvorin was still the recipient of Chekhov's frankest letters and, to judge by those letters, the most stimulating of his correspondents. Suvorin's salacious gossip on the sexual mores of Petersburg and his enthusiasm for writing and financing plays acted directly on Chekhov.

In Melikhovo itself Chekhov began to show signs of the ambivalence that marked his later attitudes to other people. He constantly invited guests, as though terrified of being alone, and constantly complained of having no privacy to work in. Fame embarrassed him : he hated public meetings, speeches and introductions. For three

years he put off visiting Tolstoy, simply because there were always
intermediaries who wanted to arrange and witness the meeting. He
himself diagnosed a fear of an audience very much akin to agora-
phobia. Morbid or not, this isolation from other men seems to be
reflected in the less loving characterisations in the work of 1893 to
1895, which introduces 'the terrible volcanic women' that in December 1894 Chekhov announced he wanted to write about. Women
now play a more important part in Chekhov's life and writing than
at any time since the 'femmes fatales' of 1886 and his engagement
to Dunya Efros. His relationships were more than a friend's, but less
than a lover's. There were actresses, aspiring writers like Shchepkina-
Kupernik, Shavrova or Lidia Avilova. He was flirtatious when they
were inattentive and ironical when they responded. To all of them
he seems to have attributed the dangerous predatory instinct with
which he endows the heroines of the stories of this period. Certainly
he shared some of his heroes' suspicions that women were an atavistic reversion threatening all that the male had achieved in civilisation, and the motive for his deviousness was the preservation of his
independence and inner peace. In the case of Lika Mizinova,
Chekhov cold-bloodedly deflected her on to his new friend, the
writer and amateur singer and much-married Potapenko, who took
her to Europe and abandoned her when she was pregnant. In
autumn 1894 Chekhov secretly left Odessa with Suvorin on a tour
of Europe that circled through Vienna, Nice and Paris, but contrived not to meet Lika, who was stranded in Switzerland. In a
year or two he was friends again both with Potapenko and Lika,
but his behaviour and his letters show an iron resolve not to be
entangled.

This resolve had an intellectual basis.[1] Chekhov may have laughed
at Suvorin for writing a story about a girl who fades away after her
first sexual experience, but he himself shared the girl's fears. Writing
to Suvorin about Levitan (who was soon to attempt suicide), Chekhov wrote, 'He's been pulled to pieces by women . . . these sweet
creatures give love and take little from the man : only his youth.' For
him women were incompatible with art : 'Ecstasy is impossible
when a man has made a glutton of himself.' Chekhov's ideas of
women and sex are none the shallower for being based on observation and imagination rather than personal experience. Not only his
physical debility and the fate of his brothers and friends, but also
his own wariness and morality kept him from giving in to tempta-

tion. To Suvorin he wrote in January 1895—the nearest thing to a confession in his letters : 'Women take away youth, only not mine. In my life I have been an assistant rather than the boss, and fate has not been very kind to me. I have had few love affairs.' Chekhov's preferences are echoed by those of his heroes : he prefers comfort to debauch, the feel of silk and lace to the warmth of flesh, the attack to the conquest. It is thus not a Schopenhauerian misogyny or a neo-Darwinian belief in the male as the vanguard of evolutionary progress, so much as straitjacketed sensuality that governs the treatment of his heroines in the work of 1893 to 1895.

Chekhov's reading at this time betrays his interest in the heroine. He reread Turgenev and was amazed at the inferiority of Turgenev's sphinx-like, virago, or fateful heroines, compared with Tolstoy's Anna Karenina. And yet the heroines of *An Anonymous Story* and *Ariadna*, who bear a distinct resemblance to Turgenev's Yelena (in *On the Eve*), and Irina (in *Smoke*) are far better realised than the heroines of *Big Volodya and Little Volodya* (1893), *A Woman's Kingdom* and *Three Years* (1895), who are very Tolstoyan in their search for a life that will satisfy them morally rather than sexually. It may be that Chekhov was perfecting what he felt Turgenev had left unfinished; certainly his Turgenevian heroines are more female than his Tolstoyan ones.

The name of Turgenev[2] recurs when we look at the structure of the stories of this period. Chekhov is reverting to conventional modes : *Ariadna* not only has a heroine and a setting in Russia and Italy that could be Turgenev's; it also has a narrative framework, in which the hero tells his passionate story to a dispassionate observer, as well as generalisations on Russia and the West and even the gallery of minor characters so typical of Turgenev. There is a stronger plot-line in most of the stories of this period : *The Black Monk*, meant to be a calculated realisation of megalomania, ends with a dramatic death; *Rothschild's Violin* has a harmonious end of almost schmalzy sentimentality; *Three Years* follows the outline of Tolstoy's *Family Happiness*. Strong plotting leads to firm endings and, thus, a less Chekhovian picture of life. There is more Turgenev and Maupassant than before or after.

Each of the stories of 1893 to 1895 is highly specialised : *Rasskaz neizvestnogo cheloveka* (*An Anonymous Story*) satirises the upper crust of Petersburg; *Tri goda* (*Three Years*) is meant to be a portrait of a Muscovite merchant and Muscovite trade in the last phase of decay; *Bab'ye tsarstvo* (*A Woman's Kingdom*) gives us pictures of life in a steel foundry and of the heroine's thirst for real life; *Skripka Rotshil'da* (*Rothschild's Violin*) has a setting as Jewish as its tone is Yiddish; *Chornyy monakh* (*The Black Monk*) documents the running of an orchard as well as the course of paranoia. This specialisation answers the demands of many of Chekhov's readers and the tastes of *Russkaya Mysl'*; it also reflects Chekhov's reading of Zola, whose every novel concentrates on a particular area of society. Chekhov's interest in science was over; as *Sakhalin*, his great sociological study, came out in *Russkaya Mysl'* between October 1893 and July 1894, to be issued in book form in 1895, he realised that there was *falsh'* (falsehood, a wrong note) in the work, namely its didactic intention. His curiosity now finds its outlet in the minute accuracy and factual richness of his settings, and their variety made it more urgent for him to travel. Since his journey to Sakhalin and his trip to Europe with the Suvorins in 1891, his urge to travel had been frustrated. 1892 was a year of frantic work to pay for the journeys of 1890 and 1891; in 1893 he was too depressed and ill to move. In addition, his father's illness, Masha's typhoid and his duties in the cholera epidemic kept him in Melikhovo. Project after project was planned: he wanted to visit the Chicago exhibition with Tolstoy's son Lev; he meant to go to Madeira because of his lungs. In 1894 he was forced to spend a month in Yalta to halt his endless coughing, and in autumn that year he went to Taganrog to tend his dying uncle. This visit was followed by a whirlwind journey to Italy and France, which gave him little pleasure and little material for fresh kinds of work. It was overshadowed by his guilt towards Lika Mizinova, and he spent his time getting nettle-rash in Venice, inspecting a crematorium in Milan, and planning more tulips and peonies for the garden at Melikhovo. In 1895, except for trips to Moscow to read proofs, and to Petersburg to see Suvorin, he was confined to Melikhovo. Thus the settings of his stories show none of the excitement that Sakhalin or the steppes communicated to his work; there is artifice and coldness in his reconstruction of Petersburg, Abbazia and Venice, and of merchant life in Moscow.

His philosophy appears to take more concrete forms than hitherto, to be less concerned with general problems, such as whether the meek or the strong deserve to inherit the earth or whether evil demands active resistance or acquiescence. While Chekhov does not change radically, he focuses his hostility on two themes. One, we have seen, is sexual bondage; the other is the bourgeois way of life. For the first time the words *burzhua, burzhuaznyy* enter his vocabulary; the predatory female has her acquisitive and her philistine side—she leads to a picture of the bourgeois who accumulates and spends while remaining utterly at peace with himself. Hatred of the middle class is nothing new : it is the driving force in the novels of Flaubert and the stories of Maupassant, and in Russian literature it led critics to think that Chekhov was turning to the left. Certainly he contrasts bourgeois wealth and idleness with the peasant's poverty and enslavement, and an almost Marxist vision of capitalism ravaging Russian life is to crystallise in some of his most powerful last stories. Nevertheless, it is an aesthetic rather than a political revulsion that he feels. First the female, then images of predatoriness—polecat, cat, hawk, green eyes—and finally the predatory, bestial new class attack and destroy all that is beautiful and good. Reading Sienkiewicz, Chekhov took a particular dislike to the bourgeois love of happy endings; he wrote to Suvorin in April, 1895 : 'The bourgeoisie is very fond of so-called "positive" types . . . you can pile up capital and still keep your virginity, be a wild animal and at the same time be happy.' Like many Marxist writers, Chekhov felt that capitalism was darkening Russian life. The major difference between him and such committed writers as Korolenko is that, unlike them, he did not feel it was darkest before dawn. His observations around Melikhovo depressed him : 'A little girl with worms in her ear, diarrhoea, vomit, syphilis. Sweet sounds and poetry, where are you?' While he never refused to treat patients, he tried to give up medical practice. Everywhere he saw darkness. Even in Russia's expansion to the Pacific he saw only a future war with Japan. But he never allowed one mood to dominate him; for all the misery around him and the mediocrity that ruled in literature, he would not take refuge in despair or in idealism. Tolstoyan asceticism seemed pointless to him; his belief in the inevitability of progress never died entirely and he maintained to Suvorin (27 March 1894): 'There is more love of humanity in electricity and steam than in being chaste and abstaining from meat'; natural sciences and materialism (in the scientific sense of the word) could provide the light that art had once given. Death, solitude and degradation do not dominate him completely. Only his conviction that literature is now in a twilight zone and that life

is fundamentally meaningless and absurd is constant, but his letters
to Suvorin show that life in a senseless, unknowable cosmos is still
possible: 'All-healing nature, in killing us, at the same time in-
geniously deceives us, like a nurse taking a child away to bed from
the drawing-room' (24 August 1893). Chekhov was able to create
provisional purposes for himself; he could be aware of the uselessness of effort but still take on jury work, be a school governor, install
a fire-engine for the village and buy books for the prisoners of
Sakhalin and the citizens of Taganrog. In the same way, it is disastrous for Chekhov's characters to have no provisional purposes,
to be idealists or to be altogether without ideals: it leaves them
at the mercy either of sexual attraction masquerading as altruistic
commitment, or of bourgeois life. Two of the stories of this period,
both begun in the late 1880s, have heroes who are vulnerable because they aim too high or too low. One is *An Anonymous Story*;
the other is *The Literature Teacher*.

Rasskaz neizvestnogo cheloveka (*An Anonymous Story*) is one
of Chekhov's weakest works. It is narrated by a failed revolutionary,
and is set first in Petersburg and then in Italy. The story is wrecked
by its political overtones: the hero gets a job as a servant to the
son of the minister of the interior; Chekhov dared not be precise
about the revolutionary's aims, for fear of censorship. The story is
weakened too by its echoes of Dostoyevsky. Chekhov never set any
other work in Petersburg, a town where he was always a guest, never
an inhabitant; here he follows Dostoyevsky[3] in making it a limbo
of fevers, mists and moral miasmas, and in caricaturing its inhabitants, particularly the minister's son, Orlov, according to the cliché
which damns the Petersburg élite as satanically clever, ruthless, ice-
cold and ironical. While serving Orlov, the hero makes no progress with his political aims and, instead, falls in love with Orlov's
mistress, Zinaida, who is being cruelly mistreated and deceived.
The hero and Zinaida meet in that vindictive affection that links
the degraded and oppressed in Dostoyevsky's Petersburg novels. But
Chekhov always mistrusted Dostoyevsky's 'pretentiousness' and ex-
tremism and here, we feel, there is neither parody nor tribute, merely
an inept use of Dostoyevsky's material. The narrator's confessional
style, his self-identification as a *mechtatel'* (dreamer), his furious
loathing of the bourgeoisie, his febrile tubercular condition, his re-
bellion and his sexuality masked as platonic love all seem to belong
more to Dostoyevsky than to Chekhov. Even the ending—especi-

ally the ending—is Dostoyevskian, recalling *The Gambler* and *The Idiot*. The hero elopes with Zinaida; she finds that she is pregnant, that his ideals are only empty words, and poisons herself as she gives birth. The narrator is left with a little girl to look after, and even she has to be handed back to the Petersburg world to which she legally belongs. The melodrama and the tragic suffering of the child are Dostoyevskian, and Chekhov shows himself only in the sudden moral bankruptcy of the hero, who finds that all his grandiose philosophy is only so much twaddle about loving one's neighbour.

What Chekhov failed to do in *An Anonymous Story* he was to achieve only in 1896 with *My Life*, likewise a first-person narrative with a hero who has only a little orphaned girl to show for his ordeals; but here the rebel is a moral rebel, not just a revolutionary; the heroine is not just a torrent of silliness and self-deception; the town is quintessential Russia, not an outworn stereotype of Petersburg. The 1893 work has only incidental merit; the revolutionary is an ex-sailor and, on reaching Venice and Nice, the story is suddenly imbued with the sea and all the sense of eternity and futility that it gives to Chekhov's narratives. The sea and the Italian setting are, however, to be far better realised as beauty contrasting with human squalor in *Ariadna,* written in 1894.

Despite the obvious weaknesses of picking up threads that he had used some four years earlier, Chekhov once more returned to his work of the 1880s. His next story was *Uchitel' slovesnosti* (*The Literature Teacher*), which was made by adding a further chapter to *Obyvateli* (*The Philistines* or *The Average Man*)—the second time Chekhov had used this title—published in *Novoye Vremya* in November 1889. The first chapter shows Nikitin, a young schoolteacher, falling in love with the daughter of one of the provincial town's best families, and ends with his ecstasy at being accepted as her future husband. It is a Gogolian idyll, with the same happiness as is to be found in many of the steppe and Taganrog stories, only here there is a gentle satirical touch. Chekhov had originally described the tale as a 'lighthearted piece of nonsense from the lives of provincial guinea-pigs'. He resisted the temptation to mock his small-town characters too cruelly; he had originally intended to deal with them so that 'you'd have to scrape them off the floor (*mokrogo mesta ne ostanetsya*)', but his friends had begged him to desist. There is a good deal of personal material in the story, which might explain its gentleness. The town is very like Taganrog, with its olive trees

and *bakhchi* (market gardens) and the cemetery, brewery and
slaughterhouse on the outskirts. The naïve schoolteacher, Nikitin, is
three times humiliated when he is told or recalls that he hasn't read
Lessing's *Hamburg Dramaturgy* though he professes to be a teacher
of literature : this goes back to Chekhov's annoyance in 1889, when
the actor Svobodin visited him and was horrified that Chekhov had
written *Ivanov* without having read Lessing's great theoretical work.
Nevertheless, the element of horror and grotesquerie which fills the
story is latent in the comic touches of the first chapter. Manya, the
heroine, is a passionate horsewoman and this leads to some gruesome touches. As she rides out to the park with Nikitin, they pass
the slaughterhouse, and their ride coincides with 'a sky blood-red
with the sunset'; when their marriage is announced, the elder sister
interrupts with a yell, 'Papa, the knacker has arrived.' These touches
of horror burgeon in the second half; Nikitin's colleague, a Gogolian
caricature of a schoolteacher who even on his deathbed says only
what 'everyone had known for a long time', is given a funeral
whose ceremony recalls Nikitin's marriage. His bourgeois nest
gradually seems a hell-hole. The details are comic—his wife fills
the house with dogs and the bed with cats, saves all the milk for
cheese, feeds the servants on scraps—but the whole picture is horrific.
Nikitin realises that his 'new life' is nothing but *poshlost'*—vulgarity,
contemptibility—when he finds that the marriage is the outcome
not of love, but of the bourgeois ethic, under which any male fre-
quenter of the household must marry one of the daughters. Suddenly, the story becomes serious : Nikitin's thoughts are reflected
in the long shadows from the autumn sun, and his disillusionment
in the sunset. The seasons have run from the spring of his engagement to the autumn of his disillusionment : he is desperate to
flee.

Both the 'unknown man' and Nikitin are stripped of their illusions
because they are sexually vulnerable. Elopement disables the first
and marriage awakens the second. Sex is both a trap and, especially
for the strong, the mechanism for opening it. The tubercular revolutionary is finished, but Nikitin is one of the heroes typical of the
Melikhovo period in that, once caught, he recognises his bondage
and makes up his mind to break out. He is the prototype of heroes
in very different settings, such as Laptev in *Three Years* or Anna
Akimovna in *A Woman's Kingdom*.

For Chekhov's heroines, life is more difficult : three important stories of this period are devoted to women for whom sexuality is a prison, sometimes comfortable, sometimes hateful. *Volodya bol'shoy i Volodya malen'kiy* (*Big Volodya and Little Volodya*), of December 1893, is the first. It was published in the newspaper *Russkiye Vedomosti* (*Russian Gazette*), which excised many of the more risqué passages and made the story rather skeletal. Like *Three Sisters* and *The Kiss*, it has a military background which emphasises the isolation and helplessness of the womenfolk. The heroine has married 'Big Volodya', an officer in his fifties, *par dépit*, as she now sees, because she could not get the handsome young 'Little Volodya' to propose to her. Once the first enchantment of marriage has worn off, she tries to talk seriously and intimately to Little Volodya, but finds that he refuses to philosophise and will only make love to her. Because she is a woman, no one will treat her as a human being. The central episode in the story is a visit to a nunnery, where the heroine calls on Olya, who was brought up with her and has become a nun. The bells of the nunnery chapel and the strangely bloodless face of Olya turn a whimsical visit into a *memento mori* and make nonsense of Sofia's marriage and her impending love affair. The tolling of the nunnery bells and the roaring of the sea in *The Duel* or *An Anonymous Story* give the same impression of eternity: the rest of the world pales into meaninglessness. Like Doctor Chebutykin in *Three Sisters*, Little Volodya can only answer Sofia's pleas for help and instruction with 'tara-ra boom-de-ay'. Like Katya in *A Dreary Story* or the heroines of the late plays, Sofia demands from men what they cannot give: 'Teach me . . . if only you knew how much I want to . . . begin a new life.'

A few days later, in January 1894, *Bab'ye tsarstvo* (*A Woman's Kingdom*) was published in *Russkaya Mysl'*. It, too, has a heroine whose apparent success—she has inherited a steel foundry—masks her distress. Three times longer than *Big Volodya and Little Volodya*, it is a novel compressed into four scenes covering twenty-four hours in the heroine's life at Christmas. Chekhov has virtually identified his narrative style with the words and outlook of the heroine—the main feature of his late work; only in one phrase in the last scene does he revert to his earlier mode and comment from outside her field of thought, when he says: 'The instinct of health and youth was flattering her and lying to her.' That moment apart, the heroine's dissatisfaction—she is thirty and unmarried;

her social ambivalence—she is the daughter of a worker, ill-prepared for the standing that wealth gives; and her guilt at profiting from the hellish foundry that she hates and does not understand fill the text and create a unified atmosphere. Like *Three Years*, *A Woman's Kingdom* abridges a novel into an extended short story by using time-lapses and selecting a few moments to reveal a whole life. As in *Three Years*, compression weakens the structure; there are innumerable themes which Chekhov was later to expand into full stories : the evil of the foundry, the gap between workers and their benevolent employer, the weakness of a woman in a society run by males for males, the woman's hesitation between sexual indulgence and self-liberation are themes broached here and developed only a few years later *In the Gully*, *The New Dacha*, and *The Bride*. As in many of the stories of 1893–95, the literary models are badly digested. The first chapter, in which Anna Akimovna decides to bestow on a poor clerk the money she has won in a law-suit, is a scene of munificence greedily seized and inwardly despised that Dostoyevsky could have created far more effectively. The steel foundry and the tough workers are very reminiscent of Zola's *Germinal* (then an 'underground' work in Russia). Many of the details are to be realised more fully in the plays : the sub-plot of the desperately infatuated servant-girl and the fatuous man-servant is far more amusing and poignant in *The Cherry Orchard* than it is here. The irrational, involuntary, inarticulate noises so frequent in the mouths of Chekhov's late characters are heard : a deaf-mute girl goes 'bly-bly-bly', just as the dog in *The Literature Teacher* growls 'rrr nga' in imitation of the elder sister of the house, or the doctor in *Three Years* mutters 'ru-ru-ru'. The Dostoyevskian scene in which Anna Akimovna's charity leads to a scandal, and the Zolaesque picture of the steel foundry as a monster crushing its workers both contribute to the hell surrounding the heroine.

In the second chapter, the comic visitors, such as the aunt with breasts large enough to carry a samovar and a tray of cups, are none the less hellish for being ludicrous. The third chapter shows an intimate dinner party as another manifestation of hell. The heroine is contrasted with Lysevich, her legal adviser. Just as her relatives suggest marriage as the solution to her unhappiness, so Lysevich suggests debauch : she should have a lover for each day of the week. Lysevich himself runs true to Chekhov's belief that the intelligentsia become impotent at forty : he can only preach free love.

Nevertheless, there is a surge of poetry in his ability to tell stories and in the quite Chekhovian enthusiasm with which he recommends Maupassant to Anna. Lysevich's talk about literature has in fact some relevance to Anna Akimovna's unwanted empire : he turns away from modern literature because it can only moan, 'Ah, wretch, ah, your life can be compared to a prison . . . you have no salvation', and the only alternative to decadent despair is the decadent enjoyment, the 'bitter, sensual taste' of Maupassant's prose. Like literature, modern life offers the heroine only imprisonment in her 'kingdom' or a spending spree with her money and youth. The last chapter of the story returns her to her women friends and relatives, to the suggestions and pandering which Lysevich offered, and leaves her ashamed, bored and without hope. She cannot go back to her roots, nor cut herself off from them and join the middle classes; she cannot bear her own self nor lose it in someone else. Because she is a woman, she shows all the more vehemently the Chekhovian hero's dilemma when faced with the difference between himself and the person whom others see in him.

A Woman's Kingdom echoes throughout Chekhov's work. The 'dampness, bugs, debauchery' that are concealed in the workers' barracks at the foundry turn up again and again, in the kitchens of *The Cherry Orchard* and *The Bride*, as the filthy foundations on which bourgeois fastidiousness is built. The nervous energy that Anna Akimovna pits against the world is to drive Chekhov's later heroines into disaster or new worlds; her words, 'You can't sit around with your arms folded' are also the dangerous catch-phrase of Lida in *The House with the Mezzanine*, one of Chekhov's most cruelly active women.

Chekhov saw in women a primitive drive, more likely to end in evil than in good. Three of the stories of 1894 and 1895 show a morally irresponsible and dynamic female stripping the male first of his achievements and then of his power. To some extent these stories, *Supruga (His Wife)*, *Anna na sheye (The Order of St Anne)* and *Ariadna*, are spoilt by misogyny, as is *The Grasshopper* of 1892. In *The Grasshopper*, the conceit and self-centredness of the wife indirectly precipitate the death of her saintly doctor-husband. *His Wife* likewise has a doctor as its hero, a thoughtful, hardworking surgeon, suffering like the author from tuberculosis and, again like the author, a man who has risen from humble origins to achieve recognition; the doctor confronts his wife with a telegram from her lover. She refuses the offer of a divorce, because she still needs her husband's income and respectability. *The Order of St Anne* is not so weak, since it is comic, using a pun on Anna, the girl's name, and Anna, the award of merit that her husband covets, which Chekhov had used in 1883. A cowed young girl, married to an elderly civil servant, discovers her power to attract men at the first ball at which her husband shows her off and is then transformed into a ruthless, predatory tyrant.

Ariadna is only a more substantial elaboration of this conception of the female. It is strengthened as a work by its literary quality and by its personal tension. The title itself is literary : Ariadna, the heroine, is meant to remind us of Ariadne leading Theseus down the labyrinth to meet the Minotaur, or of the tragic sister of Racine's Phèdre,

> Ariane, ma soeur, de quel amour blessée
> Vous mourûtes aux bords où vous fûtes laissée.

The story, set first in the Russian countryside, then in Abbazia and Florence, and related to the casual narrator on the boat home, is Turgenevian. Its study of sexuality and the blows that each revelation deals to the somewhat prim hero bear some resemblance to Maupassant's work (which Chekhov knew almost in its entirety). The personal tension derives from its link with Chekhov's relationship to Lika Mizinova; the story was written at the end of 1894, after Chekhov's lightning European tour. Ariadna's rejection by the thoughtful Shamokhin and her trip to Europe with Lubkov, a married man, witty, resourceful, shallow and penniless, have more than a casual resemblance to Lika's elopement with Potapenko. Ariadna, unlike Lika, does not end up pregnant, but Shamokhin when he joins her in Europe feels that she is. It must be emphasised that Chekhov used the Potapenko-Lika episode both in this story and in *The Seagull*, but that neither Lubkov nor Trigorin is modelled cosely on Potapenko, and neither Ariadna nor Nina bears much resemblance to Lika Mizinova. The real Potapenko was a kind and honest man : it was he who sorted out Chekhov's financial affairs with Suvorin's accountants; to judge by his memoir of Chekhov, the only piece of his prose to survive him, he understood Chekhov well and was liked well in return. Lika Mizinova was strong-willed, perhaps passionate and unlucky, but she was later successful as a teacher, then as a milliner, and finally as a married woman. *Ariadna* uses personal material, but not in confession or revenge.

The opening narrative and the close of the story show Shamokhin talking to a narrator who is a spectral Chekhov. Shamokhin, however, also reflects what Chekhov had thought about woman ever since his plan for a dissertation on the history of sexual dominance. Woman, Shamokhin begins, is in a particularly difficult position because of man's, Russian man's, idealism, which makes a goddess out of a slave. Every love-affair must thus be a disillusionment; this is a moral which the story sets out to illustrate. At the end, another moral is drawn, which seems a little more scientific. Woman, especially bourgeois woman, has been isolated from cultural progress and is in fact a throwback; with her primitive thirst for dominance, she threatens everything that the struggle for existence has given to humanity. The conclusion that Shamokhin reaches is not unlike Chekhov's own : women must be given co-education, so that they can find interests that will weaken their drive to prey on man. Once the steam leaves the story and Ariadna appears only as an illustration of a moral, Chekhov can release his hero from bondage and give a comic ending : Ariadna turns out to be plotting marriage to a prince, and Shamokhin is free.

Ariadna is not so much the story of a woman as the charting of a man's changing reaction to her. She bursts in on Shamokhin's quiet country life as a vital force : her impulses and her selfishness are charming. Only when Shamokhin is summoned to join her and Lubkov in Europe for a *ménage à trois* in which he is at first the only platonic member, does he begin to reflect. Ariadna's sensuality, Shamokhin realises, is inseparable from emotional coldness, from idleness and squalor. The same details dominate this story as the description of Nadezhda in *The Duel* : Ariadna's bedroom has a half-eaten bun, eggshells and a suffocating perfume to symbolise her carnality. She herself, for all her veneer of culture, is a primitive : like Chekhov's 'progressive' women in *My Life* she cannot mask her superstitious fear of the thirteenth, or of three candles. *Ariadna* rationalises Chekhov's distrust of the female through Shamokhin's apologia for puritanism. A desire for more than flesh in sexual relations is, for him, a natural process of evolution :

Revulsion for animal instinct has been nurtured for centuries in hundreds of generations, it has been inherited by me with my blood and constitutes a part of my being, and if I now poeticise love, is this not just as natural and indispensable in our time as the fact that my ears are immovable and that I am not covered in hair?

By arguing for prudery, by identifying the fight against lust with the fight for wholeness and progress, Chekhov rationalises the misogynistic outburst.

The names of other writers have been mentioned more often in this chapter than in any other. The fact is that 1893–95 is a period in which Chekhov most clearly reflects his reading. Only here can we see Dostoyevsky as well as Tolstoy, Turgenev and Maupassant, Zola as well as Garshin and Leskov. The taut plots and methodical backgrounds do not always match Chekhov's innate tendency to isolate moments of time and background objects, but nonetheless, by reverting to traditional and contemporary models, he was eventually to give fresh life to his own work. It should be remembered that 1895 was also the year in which he wrote *The Seagull* and that this is the most literary and at the same time the most innovatory of all his works. In 1893–95, authors, discovered or rediscovered, gave him more new ideas than did his journeys, for nothing in Western Europe or the Crimea could impress him as deeply as the steppes or Sakhalin. In fact, the Western Europe of *An Anonymous Story* and *Ariadna*, with its tourist circuit and the sad resorts of the Côte d'Azur where the tubercular come to die, owes rather more to such works as Maupassant's *Sur l'eau*, than to Chekhov's own reactions. *Sur l'eau* is quoted in *The Seagull*, where it plays an important part in the intrigue; here too, this loose travelogue with its digressions and evocations shows a remarkable affinity with Chekhov. The misery that the glitter of the Côte d'Azur conceals was pointed out to Chekhov in Maupassant's definition: 'Ce pays ravissant et tiède, c'est aussi l'hôpital du monde et le cimetière fleuri de l'Europe.' In many cases, Chekhov found, as did the professor of *A Dreary Story* and Lysevich in *A Woman's Kingdom*, that Maupassant could say freely what he himself could only hint. It is not merely that Maupassant was sophisticated politically and sexually uninhibited, but that his *amour-propre* and self-assured role of artist made him less afraid of his contradictions than was the modest, much censored Chekhov. *Sur l'eau* is to provide the characterisation of the artist Trigorin, unprecedented in Chekhov's work; it also contains many more clear-cut, if not more cogent, expressions of a philosophical duality common to the two writers :

Certes, en certains jours, j'éprouve l'horreur de ce qui est jusqu'à désirer la mort. Je sens jusqu'à la souffrance suraigüe la monotonie invariable des paysages, des figures et des pensées. La médiocrité de l'univers m'étonne et me révolte, la petitesse de toutes choses m'emplit de dégoût . . . La caresse de l'eau sur le sable des rives ou sur le granit des roches m'émeut et m'attendrit, et la joie qui m'envahit, quand je me sens poussé par le vent et porté par la vague, naît de ce que je me livre aux forces brutales et naturelles.

Less original, less sensitive to sight and sound, Maupassant was better able than Chekhov to come to terms with his own inconsistencies, and the clarity and the acceptance of two opposite reactions to the universe, so typical of Chekhov's late prose, might not have come without Maupassant as a catalyst. The horror of *Ward No. 6* and the ecstasy of *Steppe* interact in 1893–95.

The interaction is most spectacular in *Chornyy monakh (The Black Monk)*. In this story, Chekhov meant to combine his medical expertise and his imagination by making use of a black monk, who had entered one of his dreams, and the textbook symptoms of *mania grandiosa*. His hero, Kovrin, is a young academic who cannot sleep for mental and emotional excitement. A vision of a black monk tells him that he is one of the world's elect and it is only when he marries and his wife forces him to take treatment for his delusions that the madness begins to destroy him. He leaves his wife and ends up with a mistress in the Crimea, where a last vision of the monk comes to him as he dies of a haemorrhage. He is the third tubercular hero of the Melikhovo period and, as with the 'unknown man' and the doctor married to the predatory 'spouse', his fatal disease introduces a melodramatic note into the story. It is only in Chekhov's very last stories that he copes with death with the same conviction and sensuousness as he infuses into nature and life. The inevitable course of insanity and tuberculosis makes *The Black Monk*, in fact, a rather inferior version of Garshin's *Red Flower*, for Garshin's own madness carries more conviction than Chekhov's clinical expertise.

If Kovrin's madness and illness render the horror of life, the background to the story gives us a correspondingly powerful beauty. Kovrin is staying with his future wife and her father, Russia's greatest gardener. His orchard, like *The Cherry Orchard*, is like no

real orchard: it is a dream to which his whole existence is dedicated. Into the gardener, Pesotsky, Chekhov has put all his own
preoccupations with frosts, blossom, harvests and workers. The
garden is a paradise, and when Kovrin leaves his wife and Pesotsky dies of grief the paradise is destroyed as mercilessly as the cherry
orchard. Like the cherry orchard, Pesotsky's orchard provokes the
action that is to undo it. In the first chapter we enter the orchard
on a frosty night: fires are burning to keep the frost off the trees:
'Black, thick corrosive smoke spread over the earth . . . now and
again they met workers wandering like shadows in the smoke.' The
smoke and the shadows conjure up the black monk, corrode and
destroy the characters' lives. Whatever the weaknesses of *The Black
Monk* as a plausible story, it does incorporate beauty and horror
in a new way, which is to be the fundamental method of Chekhov's
prose and drama from 1896. Beauty and horror are now latent in
the same images—the blossoming orchard with its ghosts—and not
in opposite images like those of town and country.

Chekhov did not settle on any direction for his prose until *The
Seagull* was finished. Most of the Melikhovo stories are 'one-off'
prototypes. By far the most ambitious is one of the last of these
exploratory works, *Tri goda (Three Years)*. Like *A Woman's Kingdom*, it is a complex picture of a man trapped in an empire he
does not wish to rule. Laptev, the young merchant who has been
educated out of his class, is a victim of transition and of his own
sexuality, very like Anna Akimovna. The title, *Three Years*, tells us
that Chekhov should have written it, as he originally planned, as a
novel. He knew that something had gone wrong: 'The intention
was one thing, but something different, rather jaded came out, not
silk as I wanted, but satin.' The time-scale is matched by the range
of the setting. The first four of its seventeen chapters are set in a
provincial town where Laptev makes a proposal of marriage to the
daughter of the doctor who is tending his dying and deserted sister.
The proposal succeeds, although Laptev knows that Yulia, his
bride, does not love him: at this point Chekhov has arrived at a
generalisation that is very important for the story and for his plays.
Laptev knows his declaration of love has something false about it:
'Why had he lied, saying that he had grown up in an environment
where everyone without exception worked? Why did he talk in a
didactic tone about a pure, joyful life? It was stupid, boring, false
—false in a Muscovite way.' Laptev is meant to be a typical Musco-

vite, torn apart by Asiatic falsehood and European honesty: his phrases about work and joy are in fact the Muscovite camouflage which is to hide from others and themselves the true personalities of so many Chekhov characters. His story is meant to show a liberation from second-hand and hypocritical phrases, but the falsehood of love gives way to the falseness of work: four of the story's chapters are devoted to a picture of Laptev and Co., wholesale haberdashers, in their magnificent decay. The business, founded on cheating and exploitation, and the overpowering atmosphere of religious service, dirt and sycophancy show Chekhov attempting a monumental sociological picture that Zola would have done more successfully. Laptev and Co., like Chekhov's orchards, is too awesome to be credible: as it declines, run by a senile old man and his grotesque son Fyodor, trade still grows until Laptev finds he is a millionaire six times over. The description of the company incorporates much material from Chekhov's own background. It is a little like Gavrilov and Co. which first employed Chekhov's father in Moscow. Laptev's boyhood memories of forced service as a chorister, of thrashings, of serving in the shop after school are precisely those that were most deeply etched on the minds of Aleksandr and Anton Chekhov.

The course of *Three Years* is a rather ambling process of renunciation. Laptev accepts that sexual love can bring him nothing; he and his frigid Yulia grow estranged by sex and by the death of their child and, finally, are reconciled by time and by their insight into others' unhappiness—that of Laptev's orphaned nieces and of his old father. The renunciation and conciliation strongly recall the unpalatable ending of Tolstoy's *Family Happiness*.

Three Years is tedious as a whole; the minor characters, however, whose hostility or indifference helps jerk Laptev along his development, come to life. His former mistress, ugly, hysterical and eccentric, is drawn with an affection that makes one suspect that Chekhov based her on a woman friend, Kundasova, the 'astronomer' whom he and Suvorin supported surreptitiously so as not to offend her immense pride. Yartsev, who is the university friend who liberated Laptev from the mental slumber of the haberdashers and who takes over his mistress and at one point nearly becomes Yulia's lover, puts forward that composite philosophy, half optimistic and idealist, half materialist and despairing, that is latent in Chekhov's last works. Laptev's progress is, to a certain extent, humanity's:

Differences of climate, energy, taste, age make equality of men physically impossible. But educated man can make this inequality harmless,
as he has done with marshes and bears . . . there will come a time
when, for instance, the present state of the workers will seem just as
much an absurdity as serfdom, when they swapped girls for dogs.

There is something of Lopakhin's dreams in Yartsev's naïvety : it
is not quite as optimistic as it seems, for the struggle for existence
and the impotence of good will always be the same in Yartsev's
and, perhaps, Chekhov's view. This is not the 'new life' of
dreamers and revolutionaries, so much as the continuum of the
future. Forms change, but the essence of humanity remains the same.
　　A welter of ideas and characters, a hurried tying up of loose ends,
make *Three Years* a failed novel. Its lyrical side is its best side.
Laptev is a Muscovite and the story is a poem about Moscow, Chekhov's second home. The parks at Sokolniki have sunsets, and
Moscow's history hatches hallucinations in these sunsets, which go
against the rather rational narrative tone of the novel. The lyrically
conceived sunset in chapter 13 and Yartsev's dream of barbarian
Polovtsian tribes suddenly introduce sights and sounds quite unlike
the dull impressions that run through Laptev's mind : 'A terrible
roar, clanging, shouts in an incomprehensible language, quite possibly Kalmyk; and some village, all engulfed in flames, and the
nearby forests, covered in frost and soft-pink with the fire, can be
seen all around, and so clearly that every pine-tree can be distinguished.' Out of a lyrical interlude arises a mystical vision, just as
prophetic of Russia's future as Yartsev's ideas of progress; it undoes
all the calm resignation of the story's central characters.
　　The mystic side of Chekhov—his irrational intuition that there is
meaning and beauty in the cosmos, which aligns him more to
Leskov than to Tolstoy in the Russian literary tradition—is very
nearly suppressed in the Melikhovo phase, preoccupied as it is with
the objective and concrete. But there is one work of 1894, *The
Student*, which Chekhov insisted to Bunin was his favourite and
most optimistic piece. It is the only story of the Melikhovo period
which links the lyricism of *Steppe* with the late prose of *The Bishop*,
and almost the only story of Chekhov's which can be read as a
parable about art. Lyrical praise of nature brings about fusion
of love and reflection. For the first time Chekhov shows that he
has found out what makes art of crucial importance to humanity,

and, as always when dealing with poetry or music, he sees it at its purest in an ecclesiastical setting. A seminary student is walking home on a wintry day just before Easter; the wind and the desolate landscape arouse the romantic thought that this cold and wind are something perpetual that Ivan the Terrible and Christ too experienced. Misery and oppression are the essence of human life and will always be so. Debilitated by this insight, the student stops to talk to two peasant widows and finds himself clumsily retelling the story of Peter's betrayal of Christ, mixing half-intelligible Church-Slavonisms with the utmost simplification of the story. To his amazement, the women burst into tears, and the student discovers the inexplicable magic of narrative that has nothing to do with the person of the narrator, and the affinity that the suffering and oppressed have with all the suffering and oppression in history. Time and space are bridged in an instant. The story ends with the student filled with a joy at this sudden collapse of time and space as powerful as the depression which the oneness of the world evoked in the beginning. He has touched 'both ends of a chain'. This is Chekhov's only image for describing what art does. The student understands that the misery and horror of life engender truth and beauty in those who suffer from it. His joy may be conditional, for Chekhov breaks in as a narrator when he says 'he was only twenty-two', but faith in human response to a hostile universe is to be the strongest strand in the late prose.

The Student is an oddity among the Melikhovo works, but technically it is among the most representative in Chekhov's *oeuvre*. At the outset Chekhov very precisely establishes time and place, the visual and auditory impressions on the hero, and leaves vague all the traditional details of his face and gait. Nature is given predominance. Even in such a brief work, changes of mood are initiated by nature : the weather suddenly becomes wintry, thrushes and snipe call, something croaks in the marshes, slivers of ice appear in the river. These images lead to a series of apparently unrelated phenomena : a shot, a sound like someone blowing over an empty bottle, all bring a sense of desolation and hollowness to the hero, whose name, like all those in late Chekhov, is perfectly convincing and yet also links him with the open countryside through which he is passing : he is Velikopol'sky, 'great fields'. The fragmentary background given—the coughing father, the bare-footed mother, the student's hunger—integrates him all the more closely into the scene.

As he approaches the two widows to whom he is to tell the story of Peter's betrayal, the verbs of the narrative already prefigure tension, conflict: the verb *dulo, dul* (blew) shows the disturbance in nature and in the hero; the paradox of the hero's fingers frozen stiff (*zakocheneli*) while his face is burnt (*razgorelos'*) by the wind anticipates the strange mixture of misery and joy in his story and the reaction to it.

The most striking element of the structure is its cyclic shape: all the details of the scene are mirrored in the story of Peter's betrayal, which in turn is mirrored in the final page of narrative. The workmen on the other side of the river correspond to the workmen warming themselves by the fire in the story of Peter: the calling of the birds in the opening phrases corresponds to the triple crowing of the cock; the description of the younger widow as *zabitaya* (beaten down) corresponds to the description of Christ, beaten and tormented (*bili, zamuchennyy*); the weeping of Peter (*zaplakal* and the Church Slavonic *plakasya*) leads to the weeping of Vasilisa. The campfire in the story of Peter is echoed by a campfire in the background of the last scene; the dawn of Peter's betrayal corresponds to the sunset into which the student walks. On one level, this structure merely shows how a natural scene—desolate spring, a campfire, two widows—provokes a narrative which embodies its mood and its details. But two paragraphs, at the beginning and the end of the story, show us how Velikopol'sky's thoughts make more of the connection. The word *dul* (blew) inspires the student with the thought that 'now' is part of eternity, that this scene of poverty is, like the wind, timeless. From that idea of dejection spring the narrative and the final joy of the whole story: if want and wind are timeless, so are the great moments of human suffering. And if these moments are meaningful to later generations, then art, the narration of suffering, like religion, is meaningful. Rarely was Chekhov's integrated imagery so economically effective. The final paragraph of the story is typical in its symbolism of his ecclesiastical works. The overjoyed student crosses the river by the ferry: as in *On Easter Night* of 1886 and elsewhere, the river symbolises the division of two worlds. He climbs a hill and looks down on his village—a moment of transfiguration, of escape from the prison of environment, again to be seen in *In the Gully* when Lipa walks on the hillside above her village. The images of sunset and daybreak, with their blood-red colouring, remain ominous, but in *The Student* the association of Peter and the present day makes the 'coldness' insignificant: the final impressions are of truth, beauty and happiness.

The rhythm of the language brings out the joy of the student's narration. The first part of the story is harsh and laconic; when the student begins to speak, the style becomes rich and gentle. Some of his language is childlike: his double adjectives, *tikhiy-tikhiy*, *tyomnyy-tyomnyy*, *gor'ko-gor'ko* (quiet, dark, bitter). Some is exotic, his Church Slavonic *petel* (cock), *vecherya* (last supper), *plakasya* (he wept), mingling the past with the present in the very texture of the prose. The last part of the story has a verbal rhythm that follows the movement of the characters. 'Vasilisa suddenly sobbed [*vskhlipnula*], tears, big, copious' is punctuated to show the convulsions of tears. The third paragraph from the end of the story is cast as a Tolstoyan series of syllogisms, slow, firm and dry: 'If Vasilisa cried . . . then clearly, what he had just been relating . . . was relevant to the present . . . and probably to this empty village, to himself, to everyone. If . . . then not because . . . but because . . . and because . . . in what had been happening.' Almost without concrete imagery, with a stringent syntax unlike that of the rest of the story, this paragraph mimics the tortuous, even clumsy cerebral reaction in Velikopol'sky. If we compare this 'cerebral' passage, with its conjunctions and its parallel constructions, with the last paragraph, we can see the difference between thought and intuition. The last paragraph is one long sentence of a hundred words, one flow of images concrete and abstract, moving from 'the ferry . . . river . . . hill . . . village . . . sunset' to 'truth . . . beauty . . . youth . . . health . . . strength . . . joy . . . sense'. There is no 'because': the construction is parenthetic, not logical, and is made with 'when', 'where', 'he thought about how'; with dashes, with 'and's, leading not to an elucidation, but to a climax. The third paragraph from the close explains what has happened; the last paragraph is a subjective ending. For Chekhov the illusion of an imminent breakthrough of happiness was in his last works more important than the verifiable observations on the present. *The Student* is a perfect example in miniature of Chekhov's art, and it bridges the gap between the ecstatic mood of the ecclesiastical and steppe stories of 1886 and 1887 and the lyricism of the prose of the 1900s.

F

1896

Early in 1896 Chekhov concentrated his physical strength and creative energies. This was the last year in which he was able to spend most of his time at Melikhovo: two-thirds of the year was devoted to building a school for the villagers at Talezh and to improving local communications, as if he were determined to set his mark on Melikhovo before he left. In literature, he brought all his talent to bear on just two stories, *Dom s mezaninom—rasskaz khudozhnika* (*The House with the Mezzanine—An Artist's Story*) and *Moya zhizn'* (*My Life*). Though superficially different, they both establish the late Chekhovian style, with its sensitivity to the misery that isolates the gentle hero, and a narrative tone that expresses his personality, looks at the world through his eyes, and yet still communicates the moral philosophy of the author. Both works draw heavily on Chekhov's experiences in 1896. The building of the school, for instance, gave him a mass of detail and an insight into manual labour without which *My Life* would have been inconceivable. The school was planned in January, and the building went on in step with the writing of *My Life*. Chekhov had to organise the finance, attend to all the details of quantity surveying, buy nails, cement and iron, inspect and reject timber, supervise labour, help with the painting and decorating: all the material of chapter 12 of *My Life*. In July, the school was consecrated at a ceremony very like that described in chapter 15. Chekhov was as proud of having deserted literature for architecture and subcontracting as his hero Misail was at becoming an ordinary workman. After the school was built, he had a bell-tower constructed by the peasants; he agitated for a paved road to be built through Melikhovo; he had a post-office established at the station of Lopasnya, and took an interest in bridge construction. Much of this contributes to the technical expertise of *My Life*. He devoted immense time and trouble to buying books for Taganrog's new library, which a fellow-doctor, Iordanov, was building up. Like the school at Talezh, this was work which Chekhov demanded should remain anonymous, in case the press got wind of it. The books he chose and bought for Taganrog give an extremely interesting picture of what he himself was reading: *The Seagull* and the later plays show how relevant is his reading of Norwegian drama and of decadents such as Merezhkovsky and Gippius.

The estate of Melikhovo continued to drain Chekhov's strength. Every detail, from the insurance policy on the cows to the rebuilding of a store that had caught fire, was personally attended to. In the garden, he switched his attention from vegetables to roses, an interest that gives new images to his prose. The weather, however, made it clear that his tenure of Melikhovo would be short. The exceptionally cold spring of 1896 weakened him; the wet autumn drove him south to the Caucasus. His heightened sensitivity to the seasons creates some of the most intense scenes of autumnal despair in *My Life*, but he himself refused to acknowledge the hostility of the north until he collapsed in spring 1897.

His main literary connections were now in Petersburg, where Potapenko was taking *The Seagull* through the tortuous labyrinth of the censorship and where Chekhov had been approached by the publisher Marks and his popular illustrated monthly, *Niva*. Marks paid exceptionally well—at something like twice the rate of *Russkaya Mysl'*—but his contracts, as Chekhov was later to find out, were in fact indentures. The year 1896 was one in which the censorship was particularly oppressive, partly because of the political reaction that followed the new tsar Nikolas's declaration that he remained faithful to autocracy, and partly because of the moral laxity of the characters of *The Seagull* and the filial disrespect and rebelliousness of the hero of *My Life*, which, the censor clearly felt, were especially dangerous in a magazine as widely circulated as *Niva*.

The Seagull gave Chekhov little but worry. First the censorship, then the difficult assignment of roles to the actors of the Aleksandrinsky theatre, and finally the poor and belated rehearsals made him anxious. The first performance on 17 October was a disaster which led to his first public loss of self-control. Its effect on his work was decisive. Resolved to write no more plays, he concentrated more than ever on prose: 'Plots have been wasted, wasted wantonly, scandalously, unproductively', he wrote after the five Petersburg performances of *The Seagull*. *My Life* shows a prodigality of material that is unrivalled except in the plays : Chekhov had sacrificed wealth of character and plot to his stories.

Both *The House with the Mezzanine* and *My Life* show a philosophical breakthrough. They no longer set pessimism against optimism : all isms are delusions, and good and evil exist only in courageous action or cowardly acquiescence. The 'mortal anguish' which Chekhov mentioned on a two-day visit to Taganrog on his way to the Caucasus is an anguish at the invincible provincial deadness that we see in *My Life*. There is no longer any question of enlivening it or conquering it : Chekhov's heroes now determine to create an inner life that will isolate them from the outside world. The hero of *My Life* refuses to run away to Petersburg or Moscow : he is made of a different material from that of the literature teacher.

We can only guess at Chekhov's own inner life in 1896; his letters are more secretive, ironical and terse than before. Once his correspondence with Suvorin dries up, a year or two later, almost nothing is given away. To many of his correspondents he was now an awe-inspiring maestro or an influential protector; to all of them he tried to belittle his own illness. Frankness was becoming more and more difficult. *The Seagull* and the stories of 1896 show a radical change in his attitude to women : it may be that Lidia Avilova's declaration of love in Petersburg in January 1896 initiated the change, but Chekhov rejected her as firmly as he rejected his illness. He urged fellow-consumptives to go and drink fermented milk; he himself stayed where he was.

The House with the Mezzanine has some features in common with the Melikhovo period; it has a strongly Turgenevian manner —the story is told by N., and set in the province of T. six or seven years earlier. It has a theme of unhappy first love, caricatured minor characters, and an intense prose poetry of Russian nature. The intensity and the imagery are peculiarly Chekhovian. The discussions about what must be done to alleviate the peasants' misery may sound like a Turgenevian device to let the hero and his beloved come together, but their futility and self-deception are Chekhovian. The imagery of predation, in the last sentence that the hero hears as he leaves the house, 'God sent the crow a piece of cheese', carries over the predatory images of Melikhovo stories such as *Supruga*

(*His Wife*)—where the 'spouse's' family are 'polecats . . . bigger beasts . . . a company of predators'—into Chekhov's late prose.

Despite the anonymous hero's view of humanity as degenerating 'predatory animals', he is, like Chekhov's late heroes, a gentle and reticent character. *The House with the Mezzanine* shows a love of life all the stronger for the sense that it is slipping away. The hero, N., is a landscape painter[1] and he blames his dissatisfaction not on the world but on his own character. What happens to him is typical of what happens to the artist who tries to find happiness in life as well as in landscapes. Even in the first chapter, filled with scents of summer, there is a valedictory feeling of decay. N., idly wandering, stumbles on the estate of the Volchaninovs, the 'house with the mezzanine'; immediately he is overwhelmed by the slippery needles of the avenue of pines, and the description is full of images that are slightly ominous : the light in the treetops is 'a rainbow in a spider's web'; the smell of pine needles is 'suffocatingly strong' (a suffocating perfume always heralds love or sexual confrontation in Chekhov); the bird singing in the trees is an oriole, but an 'old woman of an oriole'; the church cross burning in the light of the setting sun— one of the images common to the late prose of both Chekhov and Turgenev—adds to the elegiac mood.

The two girls in *The House with the Mezzanine* show that Chekhov has altered not so much in his characterisation of women as in his reaction to them. The elder sister, Lida, is strong, aggressive and, in the outcome, predatory; the seventeen-year-old Misyus' is passive and vulnerable. But there is no suggestion of atavistic female instinct or of Schopenhauerian traps. N. is attracted by both girls and falls in love with the younger, for he senses the elder sister's hatred. Lida,[2] the indisputable mistress of the household, ruling her mother and her sister, is drawn as the villain : she has an obstinate mouth, carries a riding-crop, talks loudly and a lot, and is engaged in a political fight on the local council. But much of her work—treating the sick, opening libraries, collecting for victims of fire, campaigning against the clique that runs the *zemstvo*—is exactly that of Chekhov in Melikhovo and the town of Serpukhov. It is not so much her activity as her certitude that is wrong.

The hero clearly has no views at all in the beginning and at the end of the story. Only in reaction to Lida does he start to formulate a philosophy, and thus we begin to grasp that Lida's views and the narrator's counter-arguments are nothing in themselves : they are weapons in a war for domination over the gentle, malleable Misyus'. Spurred by Lida's contemptuous 'all this bores you', the narrator begins to play with ideas. In the second section he finds Misyus' alone and courts her with his worship of the incomprehensible, with mystical declarations that man is immortal, above nature. To attract attention, the artist has to stop painting landscapes and become a soothsayer and this, eventually, is his undoing. In the third section, Lida's repetition of the phrase 'this bores you' forces him to prove her wrong: he argues that her libraries and medical improvements only add new burdens to the peasant's life, that she is not breaking the chains that bind him, but adding new links. N. lets his words generate a 'positive' dream; instead of trying to change a peasant existence that has stayed unchanged since Rurik's times, we should share his manual labour and thus give him freedom to develop spiritually. These ideas were already latent in *The Student* of 1894, with its intuition of the sameness of peasant life and toil since pre-history, and they are carried over into the quest of Misail Poloznev and the speculations of Doctor Blagovo in *My Life*. They are not in themselves wrong or right, but N. is wrong in his insincerity and unconscious manoeuvring.

Much of *The House with the Mezzanine* can be placed in time and space. Mikhail Chekhov places it at Bogimovo, where Chekhov spent part of the summer of 1891. Reminiscing about Chekhov in Turkestan in 1910, Vukol Lavrov asserted that N.'s phrase about the peasant's helpless bondage to physical labour and the futility of all attempts to relieve him by education and medicine recapitulate Chekhov's own words of the summer of 1895, when he was staying with Lavrov. Thus N. and Lida may both embody Chekhov's own thoughts, one the scepticism and idealism, the other the pragmatic self-sacrifice. They make a contrast not unlike the contrast between passive and active in *Ward No. 6* of 1892, but here the idleness of N. is infinitely preferable to the quietism of Doctor Ragin. Even though we may feel a discrepancy between N.'s talk of men sharing out physical labour until it disappears and they become like gods and his later despair as he talks to Misyus' in the garden about man being a predatory animal that has degenerated, his passivity and gentleness leave room for the outside world. His passivity loses him his love, for Lida has Misyus' and her mother despatched to the wilds of Penza province, but it gains him the reader's sympathy. He emerges as a hero in contrast not only to Lida but also to the man whose house he is sharing. N.'s host Belokurov is idleness incarnate, talking about work while his mistress controls him like a puppet. Comic though he is, he brings out the freedom of movement and thought that is N.'s salvation. Belokurov is a prisoner as much of clichés as of his mistress: he talks of pessimism as the curse of the times and thus allows N. to make the point of the story when he says that the important thing is not pessimism or optimism but the fact that ninety-nine people out of a hundred have no brains. Chekhov is anticipating the existentialists in attaching so much value to acts of choice made by individuals in rejecting preconceptions, and in letting the dilemma decide the line of thought.

Chekhov's readers naturally took *The House with the Mezzanine* to be not a love story, or an evocation of a decaying paradise, but a dispute between practical quasi-socialism and quasi-religious quietism. They were puzzled that Lida should be seen as a destroyer when she typified all they thought best in the new generation of Russian women. They could not accept that the pain she causes in killing the love of N. and Misyus' outweighs the possible good of her social work. Even less could they accept that the point of the story was not so much in its weighing-up of pragmatism and idealism as in its evocation of fleeting time, of happiness almost grasped and lost.

The dying imagery of the first section intensifies as the story progresses. The smell of pine needles gives way to the scent of mignonette and oleander as N. falls in love. As the argument rages, rain begins to spatter and, in the last chapter, falling stars hint at the inauspiciousness of N.'s love. As he watches the house, while Misyus' goes inside, never to reappear, he sees the light turn green (the shade is put over it) and the moon fuse all the colours of the garden. The green light and the moonlight are images of which the significance is familiar from *Gusev*, *The Duel* and *Ward No. 6*. The final images take us back to the pine-trees and the rye, now harvested, and subtly show summer turned to autumn. Chekhov has mastered an elegiac mood without sentimentality, merely letting his images suggest loss and death.

The original title of *The House with the Mezzanine* was *Moya nevesta* (*My Fiancée*) and it shows how closely related the story is to *My Life*, whose provisional title was *My Marriage*. (Their subtitles, in the final versions, also link them: 'An Artist's Story' and 'A

Provincial's Story'. Both are tales of a hero who loses, the first his fiancée, the second his wife, his sister and his social standing, only to preserve something more valuable. But while *My Life* has a hero who speaks for the humanity of the future, *The House with the Mezzanine* is narrower in its scope. The essential quality of N. as an artist is his apartness which not only justifies his idleness and explains his unhappiness but also determines his position as an outsider. Wanting only to paint, he is forced to take sides, and, even worse, he is put into a position which writers long after Chekhov, in particular Aleksandr Blok, were to see as the procrustean bed of the Russian intellectual : his sympathies are with the land and the peasant, but his art is dedicated to serving the needs of the exploiters and predators. His way out of the dilemma is to paint less and less. It is a dilemma that *My Life* is to set out on a broader plane and to solve by a radical decision.

My Life needs a cautious approach. It is Chekhov's longest work since *The Duel* (apart from *The Island of Sakhalin*); it is by far his richest in ideas and human material; it is the first of his works with strong political implications. The words *soslovnyy antagonizm* (class antagonism) had entered his vocabulary some years earlier; now the idea plays a part in his work.

My Life took all spring and summer to write and grew to three times its intended length, sapping Chekhov's energies, so that he referred to it as a 'big, wearying tale, I'm hellishly fed up with it'. He felt more unhappy about the title than he had ever felt about any other. *My Marriage* gave way to *My Life*; but the word *'My'* embarrassed Chekhov, and he kept it only when the editor of *Niva* rejected *In the Nineties* as too pretentious.

The story contains autobiographical material, but it is not autobiographical. The town has many of the characteristics of Taganrog; the hero, Misail Poloznev, like the author, catches wild birds as a boy, hates Greek classes and is beaten by his father; his nickname 'Little Profit' is in fact a nickname given to Aleksandr Chekhov. Many minor characters, such as Prokofy the butcher and Red'ka the painter and decorator, belong to Taganrog. But Chekhov is still distilling the essence of the Russian provinces and their bourgeoisie, untouched by principles or real civilisation; he is not writing about his childhood.

My Life has a narrative style unique in Chekhov's work. It is the first time that he uses the first-person technique with a hero who is not particularly eloquent. Misail Poloznev broadens his vocabulary and softens his syntax only as he is matured by his experiences. The achievement of the story is all the greater for its being told by the abrupt, impulsive and half-educated Misail.

The story as we have it, in book form, has recovered from the censor's attention: scenes such as Misail's reprimand by the provincial governor, his final confrontation with his father, and his indictment of the town were mutilated. But the editor of *Niva* took it upon himself to make some changes and it is not clear whether Chekhov restored all of his text when he revised the story for publication by Suvorin.

My Life met with an extraordinary critical reaction: total silence, followed a year later by inane attempts to link it with Tolstoyanism. Chekhov himself seems to have been exhausted by the work. Writing, with obvious reluctance, to Nemirovich-Danchenko, he shares Misail's dismay at society, with little of Misail's verve: 'What can we talk about? We have no politics, we have no life in society, in circles, even on the streets, our urban existence is poor, monotonous, wearisome, uninteresting.' Literature does not lift the oppression:

We have got stuck in our profession up to the ears, like it or not it has isolated us from the outer world and as a result we have little free time, little money, few books, we read little and unwillingly, we hear little, we rarely travel . . . conversations on more general, broader themes never get going, because there are only tundra and Eskimos around one, and general ideas, being inapplicable to the present, become vapid and elusive, like thoughts of eternal bliss.

For Chekhov the Eskimos of the literary world, who vulgarise and demean art, were only another incarnation of the bourgeoisie of *My Life*, living in houses with magnificent façades and filthy kitchens.

Like a number of Chekhov's late works, particularly *In the Gully*, *My Life* plunges us with a bad joke into the middle of the story. Misail is being sacked from his ninth job and, told he'll be out on his neck, replies that his boss is mistaken if he thinks he can fly. It is still comic when the twenty-five-year-old Misail is scolded by his father; not until his father starts to beat him does comedy become horrible and the hero become sympathetic. Here we have the first conflict of father and son since *Difficult People* of 1886; once again, the clash is made worse by the obstinacy passed down from father to son. But in this case, there are many more universal overtones. The father is the town architect and the hideous buildings he has created turn him into a god, the Jehovah of his bourgeois world. To all his talk of the 'divine fire' that the genteel Poloznev family has passed on through the generations, Misail can as yet only clumsily oppose a Christian and Marxist condemnation of the power of capital. But at the end of the story there is to be a final confrontation between father and son, and in this, Misail's picaresque journey through life and death will give him an unanswerable eloquence. He is one of the first 'drop-outs'[3] in literature. Though he loves his father, he identifies his father's self-deceit and empty phrases with the dead bourgeois society of the town. It is not the town that Misail hates, but its people: like the other nameless southern provincial towns in *The Bride* or *Ionych*, it has 'not a single decent person'. There is no park, no theatre, no clean drinking-water, and its self-respecting inhabitants sleep in filthy beds, eat filthy food and calmly take bribes as tributes to their spiritual qualities.

Misail is found a job on the railway that is being built to link the town with civilisation. The railway, as always in Chekhov, symbolises the straight onward thrust of ruthless modernity: the engineer, Dolzhikov, cuts through the countryside, a sort of Peter the Great, turning old family estates into offices. As he repeatedly boasts, he has worked as a simple greaser in Belgium—just as Peter the Great worked as a shipwright in Holland. But the railway no longer has the beauty that it had in *Lights* of 1888; the construction work suggests neither the camps of the Philistines nor man's journey into the future. Amiably unpretentious, Dolzhikov is just as grasping as the bourgeois, and his railway brings with it not civilisation but rough gangs of navvies. Misail stays in his job for two weeks, before he drops a little further and at last finds his own level. He begins to work as a roof-painter and decorator with a contractor, Red'ka. The town ostracises him, his friends disown him, but his fellow-workers accept him as some sort of sectarian. Exhausted and satisfied by his work, Misail is content. Red'ka is a Tolstoyan figure, loving his craft, imbued with a simple Christian outlook on life, which he expresses again and again in the phrase that might be the moral of all Chekhov's work: 'Mildew eats grass, rust—iron, and lies—the soul.' At this point, Tolstoy might well have ended the story, but for Chekhov Misail's troubles are in fact only beginning. He is summoned to the governor, in a scene of Gogolian ludicrousness, and told to return to his proper class. At this point a gruesome undertone of blood and death enters the story. Just before going to see the governor, Misail has gone with Prokofy the butcher, with whom he lodges, to fetch meat from the slaughter-house. He then goes on to the governor stinking of blood and dung. The governor reacts only subconsciously, asking out of the blue, 'Are you a vegetarian?': a comic touch that marks the essentially carnivorous nature of the town's society. Viciousness appears in in-numerable details—the town's dogs are insane from the tortures that the market traders inflict on them. This is part of Misail's own boyhood: he suffers from memories of the dying birds that he trapped for sale in the market.

Women, too, will not allow him to find himself. Three women affect him. One is Kleopatra, his sister, like him afflicted by their father with a pretentious Christian name. At first she calls on Misail to repent and only when she falls in love does she rebel. The second is Anyuta Blagovo, who loves Misail but is too horrified by his anti-social behaviour to dare to come near him. When work runs short, she sends anonymous gifts of food and clothing; right at the end, she meets Misail at his sister's grave. The third woman is the most important in the story: the engineer's daughter, Masha Dol-zhikov. In the Melikhovo stories, Masha would have been another 'terrible volcanic woman', undoing with her atavism all that Misail had achieved, but here her energy and her inconstancy are natural. She is the engineer's daughter, a coachdriver's grand-daughter, and if she rides rough-shod over Misail, it is her heredity not her sex that is to blame. In this provincial limbo, Misail is the only man she can fall in love with, and in doing so she has to fit him into her scheme. She persuades him that painting roofs is only another form of service to the bourgeoisie and that for real self-fulfilment he must work the land with the peasants. Their marriage and their life on the estate of Dubechnya form the central third of the tale. Begin-ning in May and ending in autumn, progressing from hope to dis-illusionment, it is a Chekhovian story in itself. Vain attempts to integrate with the alien life of the peasants are, in fact, to be the theme of Chekhov's later stories, for instance *The New Dacha*. Dubechnya has been bought by Dolzhikov from the Cheprakovs, grotesque remnants of the landed gentry. The mother has taken to

usury and a peasant lover; the son is reduced to working as a guard
on the trains.

The marriage and the tilling of the soil are ill-fated. The first kiss
Misail gives Masha draws blood, as her hat-pin scratches his face.
The labour of ploughing, with its prehistoric brutality, is hateful to
him. In the peasantry, this 'coarse, wild force' is fearsome. True
to their Tolstoyan principles, Masha and Misail decide to build a
school for the peasants. The peasants agree and then cheat them
of materials, prevaricate and sabotage until Masha's idealism is
totally defeated. She calls them 'savages, Pechenegs' and with-
draws. Only Misail, whose slowness is his virtue, cannot condemn
them : their drinking and thieving are to him innocent compared
with the frauds and drunkenness of the bourgeoisie or the engineer.
The school is eventually built and consecrated. The peasants' gratitude brings even Masha to tears. But the experiment, and with it
the marriage, is over. Physical labour has not left any mark big
enough for her to notice : she wants to make political or aesthetic
gestures. After their last night together, sleepless because of the
brawling outside, Masha leaves, at first for the town, then for Petersburg and a career as an opera singer in America. Passive and
tolerant, Misail lets her slip away; we see his mind focusing on her
gloves, her pen, her scissors, as she disappears out of his life. With
that gentle altruism which is plausible only because Chekhov does
not force it on us, he realises that he is merely an episode in her
life.

The difference between the reactions of Misail and Masha to the
peasantry is crucial. Misail, like N. in *The House with the Mezzanine*, sees physical labour as the peasants' sole bondage. But in *My
Life* N.'s vacuous idea of man progressing to godhood is attributed
not to Misail but to Doctor Blagovo, the brother of Anyuta and the
lover of Kleopatra. Blagovo sees physical toil as something 'unworthy
of a free man' that the future will leave to animals and machines.
For him, culture has yet to come to Russia and, when eventually it
does, the peasantry will be automatically transformed. But we sense,
even more than with N., that Blagovo's words are not real self-
expression so much as a technique of seduction. Kleopatra is so
enthralled by his vision of the future and his optimism that she
breaks with her father. But Blagovo is as disastrous for her as Masha
Dolzhikov is for Misail : he leaves for Petersburg (where he has
a wife and children) to follow his medical career, just as Masha

leaves Misail to take up the stage. Science and art give them both
an excuse for betraying people.

Misail is at his most alone when he realises that he is the only
one of the group to love the peasants. All Masha's projects, Blagovo's
speculation and Kleopatra's independence cannot disguise their
hatred. Near Misail's Dubechnya is a mill. The miller, Stepan, will
not let his peasant wife near him because she is not clean enough.
Gradually, Masha, Blagovo and Kleopatra take to talking with
Stepan, enjoying his pompous discourses on the ineradicable squalor
of the peasantry. Only Misail feels that the peasants have a 'strong,
healthy measure' and instinct for justice which the bourgeois and
the intellectual rebel have lost.

His marriage having failed, Misail returns to Red'ka and the
town; after all he has seen and done, he can accept the town as
spiritually incurable and can satisfy himself with Red'ka's primitive
morality: 'Mildew eats grass, rust—iron, and lies—the soul', 'toil,
grieve and bear sickness'. His ordeals are not over: pregnant, Kleopatra is dying of tuberculosis, and again the imagery of death enters
the story: Misail has a waking dream that takes him back to the
day he visited the slaughterhouse and the governor.

With Kleopatra's pregnancy, we can see signs of Chekhov's new
morality. Blagovo visits her, pronounces her doomed, but gives no
sign of repentance. What he and Kleopatra have done is not to be
regretted: 'Anyone afraid of love or who avoids it, is not free.'
Red'ka tells him that he is damned, but Misail lets Blagovo depart
without blame, as he lets Masha. There is only one fundamental
difference between himself and people like Masha and Blagovo.
Masha writes to tell him she has had a ring made as a talisman
with the words inscribed in Hebrew, 'Everything passes', to console
her. Misail's reaction is that, if he had a ring, he would inscribe it,
'Nothing passes.' He is made up of every grain of his experience:
nothing is purged, transformed or superseded. Everything has to be
accepted, neither forgiven nor avenged.

Grown out of his tutelage, Misail can bring his narrative to an
end with a second confrontation with his father who is unchanged,
still believing in his 'divine fire', in providence and in reaping as
one sows. Misail catches him as he is designing a house with Gothic
windows and towers: there is no hope of re-educating a Jehovah,
and Misail can only deliver an indictment of the town, phrased
like the indictment delivered by Sasha in *The Bride*: 'You have

suffocated anything alive and bright in the embryo! A town of shopkeepers, innkeepers, office-workers, priests, a futile, useless town, which not a soul would feel sorry for if it suddenly was swallowed up by the earth.'

Like the 'unknown man' of 1893 and like Laptev and Yulia in *Three Years*, Chekhov's hero is left with an orphaned girl—Kleopatra's baby—to live for. It may seem an old-fashioned, sentimental stroke, but there is a gentle irony in Misail's visit to his sister's grave, followed by Anyuta Blagovo who still does not dare to speak to him in public. Misail is one of the natural Christians, the meek whom Chekhov would like to inherit the earth; he is to be followed by characters from the peasantry. Ol'ga in *Peasants* and Lipa in *In the Gully*. These later works expand the theme of indictment. Misail still loves his father and his town; it is Red'ka who looks at the dying Kleopatra and utters the other half of the Christian message, 'Woe, woe to the well-fed, woe to the strong, woe to the rich, woe to the moneylenders' which we hear more loudly in Chekhov's works on peasant life.

Thus Misail ends his story by justifying his nickname 'Little Profit'. It is one of Chekhov's barest narratives since *Ward No. 6*; it is concerned almost entirely with the fufilment of a human personality as it detaches itself from its heredity and its environment. Nature obtrudes less than anywhere else in Chekhov's work. In the town, the cherry-trees, the acacias and the lilacs of 'Great Gentry Street' (Bol'shaya Dvoryanskaya) are only a mask. In the countryside, the thrust of the railway line puts the winter corn and the Scythian burial mounds out of our mind. Misail loves working with his hands, not watching nature. The garden at Dubechnya has no poetry : it is nothing but an orchard and shrubbery overgrown with weeds and wrecked by cattle. The seasons affect Misail only through his work. Autumn and spring rains make him chafe; winter and summer set him free. It is Stepan, the miller, who can contemplate nature in his mill-pool : Misail has to work with it. Yet *My Life* overflows with detail : thousands of objects, the techniques of scaffolding and painting, the smells and sounds which make first the father's house and then Dubechnya uninhabitable, show a remarkable economy. Every casually mentioned object plays a part in the story, like a stage property in a play. Prokofy's meat, the painter's oils, the creosote that Kleopatra has to drink as medicine—all suggest contamination. The roses (of which Chekhov was then so

fond) lead to a comparison of Masha as a delicate cultivar with
Anyuta as a wild briar. The buildings of the town, with their pretentious exteriors and their squalid basements, are a reflection of the
citizens' minds. Every object in *My Life* is a symbol.

Some of its material is exploited in later stories. The Azhogins,
mother and three daughters, who put on amateur theatrical produc-
tions and who claim to be modern by the inverted superstitiousness
of using three candles and beginning plays on the thirteenth, and
who then hound Kleopatra out of the room, are to lead to the
Turkin family of *Ionych*. The well-meaning benefactors of the
peasantry who end by hating them are to be found in *The New
Dacha*. But the most important feature of *My Life* is its objective
approach to the peasantry. Neither shunning them nor idealising
them, Misail points out that we 'see the stains on the glass, but not
the glass itself', and this penetration into a people more alien than
many foreign nations to the Russian intelligentsia is one of the most
important pursuits of Chekhov's late prose. Unlike Tolstoy, he does
not try to identify with the peasant, nor to extract from him some
patriarchal, religious authority which he then obeys. Chekhov's
peasants are leaderless and all but broken. Only their love of
righteousness raises them above the bourgeoisie. Chekhov is not advo-
cating Tolstoy's 'simplification' or return to roots. It is Masha who
first uses the Tolstoyan word *oproshcheniye* in *My Life*; when
discussion began, most critics assumed that the work was Tolstoyan.
But if anything, Misail is a man who complicates and thus enriches,
rather than simplifies. Certainly, like Tolstoy he comes to see pro-
fundity in the working man's phrase, 'they've forgotten God', to
describe the cheating bourgeois. But the work is in fact very un-
Tolstoyan. Misail has found his own life, not salvation for humanity.
His asceticism—he does not smoke, drinks only to be polite and is
revolted by the smell of meat—is a matter of taste, not of principle.
Like his ascetic nature, his Christianity is instinctive; there is
no concern for the soul or for divinity. He rejects the great 'X'
which Blagovo postulates as the goal for man, and lives in the
present. Chekhov was not interested in resurrection, only in a 'little
profit'.

The political overtones in *My Life* strike a new chord in Chekhov's work. Misail's scepticism about progress comes out in a remark
that once we had serfdom, now we have capitalism. Chekhov is
responding to a controversy of the 1890s, when people first began

to question whether economic bondage and spoliation by banks and industry did not hurt the peasant even more than the moral and legal servitude of the old days—a political problem that Chekhov raises to a philosophical level in the following year.

12

Peasants

> If thou seest the oppression of the poor, and violent
> perverting of judgment and justice in a province, marvel
> not at the matter: for he that is higher than the highest
> regardeth . . .
>
> Ecclesiastes 5.8

The House with the Mezzanine and *My Life* both have narrators
persuaded that civilisation in Russia will be worthless until the
peasant has been liberated from want and can grow spiritually.
This is a topic that was more important to many of Chekhov's
readers than personal salvation or the hero's love-life. In his late
prose they were grateful for and moved by stories such as *Peasants*
and *In the Gully*, from which the hero, the intellectual and his
private life had vanished.

Muzhiki (Peasants, 1897) is not the first of this new type of story.
Ubiystvo (Murder), printed in *Russkaya Mysl'* in November 1895,
is Chekhov's first study of the miseries of country life, dominated
by penury and the *traktir* (inn) where the peasantry drink, get into
debt and sell what they have stolen, and of the undermining of their
moral being by poverty and tyranny. The objectivity of *Murder* is to be found only in *Ostrov Sakhalin (The Island of Sakhalin)*,
which had just been published in book form; the last scene of
Murder, set in a stormy Sakhalin night, shows the link between
Chekhov's sociological study and this new type of documentary
fiction.

The picture of life in *Murder*, *Peasants* and *V ovrage (In the
Gully*, written in December 1899) grows darker and darker, as if
the Russian peasantry were sinking too fast for Chekhov to keep
up with it. Certainly, his last years in Melikhovo, building three
schools one after the other, collecting statistics, dispensing medicine,

gave him a more and more depressing vision of disease, distress and disintegration.

Murder is based on Chekhov's reconstruction of a crime, by taking it back through his imagination from the prisoner in Sakhalin to the murder in a lonely Russian *traktir*. It is an evocation of the north, with its sectarians and its loneliness. The later peasant stories, however, are grounded very firmly in life around Melikhovo : Chekhov felt he could not have written *Peasants* without his years of intimate contact with them, so that, when he left Melikhovo for good in 1898, he said that 'in the literary sense, after *Peasants*, Melikhovo has now been exhausted.'

After the building of the first school in Talezh in 1896, Chekhov began a second. He also started 1897 by supervising the collection of data for the census of 1897. This brought him into the same relationship with the peasants as with the prisoners of Sakhalin. The figures, such as an infant mortality rate of sixty per cent, transfixed him with horror : in 1897 we find him still apolitical, but now filled with an evangelical hatred of exploitation and injustice. He observed the peasants' natural reaction to the census : they suspected that the authorities were planning genocide to make more room for the gentry. Circumstances conspired to involve him yet more deeply in social problems. The poor who were discharged from the Moscow hospitals were dying for lack of after-care : Chekhov wrote to his friend Yezhov (a feature-writer for *Novoye Vremya*) to point out that the rich got money by making people into drunks and whores and ought to contribute to the cost of their cure.

At the end of 1897 Chekhov was forced to recognise the change in himself. In April he had collapsed in Moscow and was taken to a clinic for a fortnight. His illness was now public knowledge and he could no longer evade treatment. In September he left Russia to spend the winter in France, first at Biarritz, then Nice; his arrival coincided with Dreyfus's second trial, and Chekhov, hastily improving his French, followed the transcripts of the trial and Zola's entry into the affair. He became convinced, as were most of the French intelligentsia, that Dreyfus was the victim of a frame-up by the state. The more he wrote to Suvorin, arguing in favour of Dreyfus and in praise of Zola, the more radically his sympathies developed. Suvorin's *Novoye Vremya* was now on the brink of disgrace : Suvorin maintained that Dreyfus, as a Jew, was probably a traitor and, even if innocent, should be kept on Devil's Island because there was a Jewish conspiracy to undermine Europe. Chekhov wrote politely, joking that he too had had a hundred francs from the syndicate, but his hostility to Suvorin's campaign began to kill his fondness for the 'old man'. In Chekhov's eyes Zola had atoned by his brave defence for all his earlier sensationalism, and Russia's intelligentsia, ignorant and hypocritical, seemed inferior to that of France. Chekhov began to feel that literature should go hand in hand with the defence of the innocent. He was particularly upset by Suvorin's refusal to print the despatches of his own correspondent and by the pirating of Zola's *Paris* in the supplement to *Novoye Vremya*, while he poured venomous slander on Zola in his leaders. In vain Suvorin tried to excuse his behaviour: he declared that Zola was no Voltaire, that he (Suvorin) was anti-Dreyfus because he loved the military. By spring 1898, Chekhov was committed: he had begun to read Voltaire (whose defence of the executed protestant, Colas, was analogous to Zola's defence of Dreyfus) and even gave an interview on Dreyfus to the French press. He felt that writers must always be for the defence, be Pauls, not Sauls, and that they should steer clear of authority: 'Great writers . . . must interest themselves in politics just so much as is necessary to defend themselves from politics.' In May 1898 he returned to Russia with every publication and transcript he could buy on the Dreyfus affair, and a complete set of Voltaire[1] for Taganrog's library.

No longer could he resist the pull away from Suvorin. He found *Novoye Vremya* 'foul to read', 'floundering in mud'. By February 1899, the journal seemed a 'pack of hungry jackals, biting each other by the tail'. In one thing only did he defend Suvorin: a student strike had been broken up by police with whips and Suvorin had praised the authorities for their restraint. The Union of Writers (to which Suvorin and Chekhov were elected) then summoned Suvorin to a 'trial of honour', which greatly distressed him. Chekhov was furious that the literary world should imitate the bullying procedures of the State: his despair at authority spread to include the intelligentsia of Russia:

In an Asiatic country, where there is no freedom of the press or of conscience, where the government and nine-tenths of society regard the journalist as an enemy, where people live so close-packed and badly and there is so little hope for better times, such amusements as throwing slops at each other, trials of honour etc. put writers in the ridiculous and pathetic position of little animals which bite off each other's tails when they are caged.

There is an energy in Chekhov's disgust which springs from the same 'stepped-up pulse' he noticed in his emotional life of 1898 and 1899 : he finds the courage to step out on his own: 'I don't trust our hypocritical, false, hysterical, badly brought-up, lazy intelligentsia, I don't trust it when it is suffering, complaining, for its oppressors come from its own loins.' The diagnosis is very like that of the peasants' ills in *Peasants*, where the peasant, next to the authorities, is his own worst oppressor. For Chekhov, the intelligentsia was a class, like the officials and the peasants, and he saw in classes only the vicious selfishness of the herd. In his letter to Doctor Orlov of Serpukhov, he showed where his faith lay now: 'I believe in individual people, I see salvation in separate personalities, scattered here and there all over Russia—whether intellectuals or peasants— theirs is the power, though they are few.' The hero of *My Life* is one of these few, a 'prophet despised in his own country'. And in Chekhov's study of the peasantry, the gloom is lightened only by individuals of natural goodness, meek but firm, whether Ol'ga in *Peasants* or Lipa and 'Crutch' in *In the Gully*.

The reader should not fall into the trap of linking too closely Chekhov's apocalyptic picture of the peasantry with his own life. His peasants at Melikhovo liked him and felt none of the hatred shown in the fictional villages of Zhukovo and Ukleyevo. When he wrote to Lidia Avilova, who was thinking of buying a country estate, he tried to calm her fears: 'I live peaceably with the peasants, I've never had anything stolen.' He thought his easy relationship came from his own politeness (for he never shouted and he used the polite *vy* form of address), and from medicine. 'The peasants treat all newcomers in the beginning by being harsh and insincere', was the worst he could find to say.

Reading *Murder*, one is struck by the central role which Chekhov gives to the peasant's religious beliefs. Even when his faith is destroyed, his whole life is governed by fasts and feasts, by the liturgy and the pageantry of the church. *Murder* owes much not only to Chekhov's *Sakhalin*, but also to Leskov, who was fascinated by the depth and poetry of the peasant's understanding of Christianity. *Murder* was, in fact, written shortly after Leskov's death and although Chekhov was annoyed with Leskov for his will, in which he asked to be autopsied so as to prove the doctors' diagnosis wrong, he owed much to him and uses here both the horror of *Lady Macbeth of Mtsensk* and the intense sense of religion of the schismatic in *The Sealed Angel* to create that curious amalgam of violent amorality and submissive devotion which is common to the peasants of both Leskov and Chekhov.

Chekhov's notebooks (which survive for 1891 to 1904) contain phrases of *Murder* interwoven with material used in many other stories of 1895 and in *The Seagull*, dating perhaps from the dark days of 1892 (*Ward No. 6*). Like *Ward No. 6*, *Murder* is overhung with an aura of prison, of an ironic fate that destroys a man by his own maxims. It is set in a *traktir* by an isolated railway station; all the action takes place in winter and, to judge by the language, in the desolate country near the northern bend of the Volga,[2] where religious dissent and poverty were at their sharpest. The victim of the murder, Matvey Terekhov, is almost a conventional Chekhov character in one thing: like the hero of *Ivanov* he has 'overstrained himself' (*nadorvalsya*), and can only wonder at his past energy and past illusions. But in every other respect this is a type of character that Chekhov had not touched since his steppe stories of 1887. A former chorister, Matvey has had to retire, sick; his religious life has also changed. Once a sectarian with virtually a church of his own, a church of fasting and of dancing to the point of ecstasy, he has repented and returned to orthodoxy. Now he lives with his cousin, Yakov Terekhov, who shares the same hereditary inclination to religious excess; Matvey interrupts Yakov's prayers until Yakov and his sister Aglaya in fury batter him to death with an iron.

Religion is the Terekhovs' emotional and sensual outlet; their life, however, is run on economic principles. Yakov owns the *traktir* which, as in *Peasants* and *In the Gully*, is the source of corruption in the village. The rusty-roofed, half-gutted building, full of drunkenness, quarrels and misery, shelters the peasant's real life, while its little rooms with icons and candles and constant praying are his dream-world. The two are incompatible: Yakov himself is upset by the constrast between his trade and his faith, more and more depressed by the gospel's message that a rich man can have little hope of entering the kingdom of God. The conflict can be resolved only in violence. Yakov can only pray or hit out. The seething violence corresponds to the blizzards, the bare trees and wild animals outside; when Yakov himself goes out into the snowstorm, 'it seemed to him that it was not him walking, but some beast, an enormous, terrible beast, and that if he were to cry out, his voice would be a roaring that resounded through the fields and forests and frightened everybody.' The murder itself is nightmarish : Chekhov's eye follows Yakov Terekhov's, so that the violent bashing shakes everything out of focus : the ironing-board collapses, the murderer nearly falls in his desperate movement not to tread on a blood-stained potato. In the background are the amazed reaction to the crime and the inarticulate noises of Yakov's half-idiot daughter, Dashutka.

The passion of the murder is beautifully contrasted with the cool methodical entry of the police and their mechanical, slow investigation. The bare factual narrative details of the eleven-month wait in prison and the sentences on all the participants in the crime make the authorities in their indifference seem even more brutal than the intolerant, grasping Terekhov. The setting of the murder is full of omens : the 'wild, dark force' of the peasants, the men digging ditches, the women carting bricks, the 'blood-red fire' of the goods-train that holds up Terekhov's disposal of the body, the noise of the cricket—all make violence seem natural. The judicial murder by the authorities, interested solely in legal facts, has a cold barrenness that becomes concrete in the last chapter, where we meet Yakov Terekhov imprisoned for life on Sakhalin, waiting with a gang that is to load a ship in the pitch dark of the gulf of Tartary.

Chekhov's belief in the 'strong healthy measure' of the peasant is as strong here as in *My Life*. In Sakhalin Yakov Terekhov recovers his normal faith. Sakhalin, with its Jews, Russians, Georgians, Ukrainians, Tatars, is a melting-pot of humanity, so that Terekhov grasps that the essence, not the form, of faith is important and manages to 'raise himself up to God'. This is not a Tolstoyan ending : Chekhov himself remains an agnostic and Terekhov's faith is just a recovery of an innate force within the peasant. The questions are still unanswerable : like the hero of *My Life*, Yakov Terekhov has to buy wisdom at enormous cost, to be content with a 'little profit'. Purged, he can only wish to save others.

The ending of *Murder* is perhaps not so powerful as the substance of the story, and Yakov the penitent not quite so convincing as his broken victim, Matvey, whose unconscious stealthy goodness and strange, shy language anticipate Misail Poloznev's dogged honesty. But the story was highly praised. Bunin, who was then entering the literary scene, admired it for its detachment and its impact : the reduction of the narrator to an eye and an ear, letting his alien characters come through directly, is in fact the feature that makes *Murder* the first of Chekhov's late stories. Other critics were struck by the strangeness of his first serious venture into peasant life. Without preconceptions, without stylising or idealising it, without making it a text for a sermon, Chekhov had managed to use fiction in an electrolytic separation, as it were, of the elements of peasant life.

The documentary impact of *Peasants*, written eighteen months later, so struck the censor that in his reports he referred to the story as an article. He was alerted by the last chapter, in which, through the mind of his heroine, Chekhov says goodbye to the life of the peasants and realises that the casual cruelty of the authorities is as brutalising as the peasants' own self-corruption through drink, self-pity and exploitation. *Peasants* reduces the element of plot to a minimum; only on reflection do we realise that it has a heroine through whom we see, hear and smell life.

The censor removed a whole page from the offending final chapter; later in the year Chekhov managed to restore the excerpt for book publication, but an entire chapter which, apparently, linked the authorities and their taxes and confiscations with the priests (who were also a financial burden on the villagers) was thrown out, and this chapter Chekhov did not restore. When the translator Roche asked for a copy of the original so that the French edition should be complete, Chekhov refused. (It is interesting that he could see no point in having *Peasants* translated into French at all, let alone with the missing chapter. His winter in Nice had convinced him that his treatment of Russian quandaries, whether in *Ward No. 6* or *Peasants*, would be as meaningless to the Frenchman as the Dreyfus affair was to the average Russian. The lamentable result was that he took no interest in who translated his works or how badly. Unlike Tolstoy, he felt that Europeans would only sneer at the Asiatic side of Russian life. *Peasants* is meant to show Russia, not the human condition.)

To make the familiar look strange, Chekhov views a year in the life of the peasants through the eyes of his heroine, Ol'ga, who is a stranger to the village. Her husband Nikolay has lost his Moscow job through illness and must go back to his village : the dirt, the crowding and the deprivation strike him all the harder for being quite unlike his childhood memories. However, not very much is made of the plot. The clash of the villagers with the newcomers is subdued; Nikolay dies and Ol'ga and her daughter leave for Moscow to seek work. Even the seasonal structure is hardly noticeable: there are flashbacks from winter to summer, a steady state of misery, and the overall picture is more static than in any other of Chekhov's late works. Certain words develop the story. The first shock to Nikolay, Ol'ga and Sasha comes out in the recurrent word *bit'*, to hit. The cat is deaf because it has been beaten; the slopes leading down to the river are littered with smashed (*bityy*) crockery, and when the men come home, the drunken Kiryak beats his wife. Imagery of sunset and redness begins with the setting sun reflected in the river and culminates in the set-piece of chapter 5, when fire breaks out and in the darkness everything goes red—the sheep are red, the doves are pink.

Two themes pervade the work. One is that the village is a potential paradise: its trees, its views, its clean 'inexpressibly pure' air make its misery seem absurd. 'What a beautiful life there would be in this world, were it not for want, horrible, inescapable want.' The details of the picture show us the cause of want: the *traktir* lends money and turns every festival into a drunken spree. The effects of want are to turn every peasant into a creature incapable of real happiness, always oppressed by a 'relentless, persistent something'—pain, worry, vindictiveness, fear, scabies or hunger. The other theme is the incursion of alien worlds into that of the peasant. The authorities enter only as police and tax-collectors. The village is permanently in debt, so that peasants have their samovars taken away, or their chickens and sheep confiscated and left to die. The authorities contribute nothing: instead of an icon, a portrait of Battenberg, ex-prince of Bulgaria, hangs in the elder's hut. When the old peasant Osip, Nikolay's father, comes in and crosses himself before Battenberg, there is a hint at the lost authority of Christianity and the new, completely incomprehensible hierarchy of the civil authorities. The peasants cannot grasp a word of the legal regulations that govern their lives, whereas the language of the New Testament rivets their attention and moves them to tears. But the church enters their lives only to tell them when they must fast and when they may feast. They are too beset with misery ever to concentrate on thought or prayer. Only once, when the icon is brought from hut to hut in pageantry, does light break through, and this last glimmer means that 'they understood there was more than emptiness between heaven

and earth, that the rich and powerful had not yet grabbed everything', that they themselves have a shred of defence from their
oppressors. Twice in the story, the gentry enter; first, in a church
service two young ladies pass through the crowd, then at the fire
they and their student brother come to watch and supervise. Only
for the religious, sentimental Ol'ga are the gentry beautiful; for
her sisters-in-law they are loathsome. The beaten-down Mar'ya
shudders at the two girls as if they were monsters threatening to
crush her. The brazen, wanton Fyokla wishes them 'ripped limb
from limb'. Only Ol'ga calls them 'little cherubim'. Ol'ga is not
merely an intermediary between the reader and this new, cruel
world. She is the bearer of an underlying Christian theme : deeply
religious, she and her daughter are passionately fond of the New
Testament, as much for its half-unintelligible language as for its
ethical message. She consoles Mar'ya by quoting Christ's words,
'Come unto me, all ye labouring and burdened.' More often her
words affect the peasants unconsciously. Making Sasha read out the
passage on the flight into Egypt, 'Arise, take the boy and his mother',
Ol'ga touches on the peasants' longing for protection and refuge.
She herself has poetic sensibility : it is the non-Russian slavonisms
of the text, *ashche, dondezhe*, that move her to tears. Chekhov sees
the peasant's Christianity not as a stern belief that life on earth is a
preparation for eternity, nor as an ethic of self-denial, but as an
identification with the fate of Mary and Joseph, their gratitude for
God's protection from Caesar. The New Testament vindicates the
simple carpenter and fisherman and damns the rabbis, the Roman
governor and Herod.

This underlying Christianity is the last note of *Peasants* : Ol'ga
leaves the village, begging for alms. There is an illusory sense of joy :
the cranes are flying, the last impressions of the village are, like the
first, of sunlight, colour and beauty. As in *Gusev*, nature is so beautiful that human language has no adequate epithets for it; the greenery
suggests happiness, despite the horse skeleton that reminds one of
death. The last words are Sasha's 'Give for the sake of Christ, what
you can, kingdom of heaven.' The kingdom of heaven is the peasant's
dream here, as at the end of *In the Gully*, of which the last words,
'they crossed themselves', also emphasise the Christianity of the
Russian peasant. If he cannot see the kingdom of heaven around
him or in the future, he sees it in the past. The miseries of emancipation, when every peasant was effectively mortgaged to the govern-

ment to the third generation, tied more tightly by debt and collective responsibility than ever by any serfdom, seemed in the 1890s worse than the miseries of the old days. In fact, in the hungry years of the early 1890s, the peasantry ate less and died younger than at any time since the 1840s. Alcoholism, venereal disease and epidemics were arguably worse; in many areas literacy and income were hardly greater. The old men of the village, like Firs in *The Cherry Orchard*, can rightly look on emancipation as a disaster. The idealised past has convoys of game to be eaten, cooked meals twice a day, the personal care of the gentry, complete shelter from the police, the taxman and the industrialist. It is all the more amazing that only the old men believe in this Land of Cockaigne. In her sleep, Mar'ya insists, 'No, freedom is better.'

Treated like lower animals by the officials, ruined by drink, Chekhov's peasants are mere remnants of natural man. They have none of the moral grandeur of Tolstoy's peasantry, and they have lost even the poetry that Chekhov saw in the steppe peasants of, for example, *Fortune* (1887), who dream of buried treasure. Their sense of mystery is gone : they do not dream, but blame. They cannot understand who is oppressing them : they take a lead from the rich peasants who have become their exploiters, and blame the *zemstvo*, the rural council, for their ills. They still have no fear or inhibitions about death, but, unlike Tolstoy's peasants, they are terrified by illness to the point of savage superstition. Only a vestige of their morality is left : the division into those who believe in God and those who do not. The collective spirit, the patriarchal order have rotted away.

Tolstoy disliked *Peasants*. It proved, he said, that Chekhov did not know the people; it was 'a sin before the people'. But *Peasants* brought Chekhov more praise than all his other works put together. It doubled his income for 1897; it reconciled the radical critics to his objectivity. Peter Struve, then a 'legal' Marxist, saw *Peasants* as a blow to idealist populist thought, as the first revelation of the abyss separating the classes of Russia.

Chekhov wisely left *Peasants* as a complete picture of a typical village. His manuscript, however, took the story on a further two chapters; Ol'ga and Sasha return to Moscow, staying with Ol'ga's sister, Klavd'ya, a prostitute. Presumably Chekhov intended a second half of the story to show the city destroying what was left of peasant innocence.

As we have seen, Chekhov became much more vehement in his

reactions to the society around him in 1898 and 1899. *In the Gully* shows far more of a clash than *Peasants*: industry, crude and poisonous, transforms the village, dividing peasants into proletariat and a new bourgeoisie. The process was observable around Melik- hovo, as cottage industries farmed out by factories gave way to brickworks, small textile mills, tanneries, and, torn from the land, family life fell apart. *In the Gully* was written some time after Chek- hov left Melikhovo. To a certain extent, all his prose recalls past impressions rather than present experience: he wrote to the critic and editor Batyushkov in December 1897, explaining why he could not write about Nice while he lived there: 'I can write only by memory, I have never written direct from nature. I need to have my memory sieve through the subject-matter so that, as on a filter, only what is important or typical should remain.' Thus *In the Gully*, written in Yalta, recalls Melikhovo eighteen months earlier.

Yalta gave Chekhov many incitements to be more radical. Desperate consumptives flocked there, penniless; there was no charity or sanatorium to house them. In Yalta Chekhov met Gor'ky, with whom he had been exchanging letters since late 1898. Chekhov thought more highly of Gor'ky than of any other younger writer (except perhaps Bunin) and, while he tried to teach Gor'ky to pay attention to the sound of the language and the ear of the reader, seems to have been drawn, if not influenced, by him towards a more protesting note and more topical themes than ever before. In Chekhov's work, factories polluting the countryside had long symbolised the spoliation by man of nature. *In the Gully* gives this encroachment of capitalism a more apocalyptic overtone. It was Gor'ky who put Chekhov in touch with the magazine *Zhizn'* (*Life*), a radical journal for which Gor'ky ran the literary section. Chekhov published *In the Gully* here, determined, as he told his friend Doctor Rossolimo, that this was to be the 'last tale from the life of the people'. Certainly, the indictment of the new factors in the Russian countryside is radical to the point of being revolutionary: Chekhov could have gone no further, despite the loosening of the censorship in the early 1900s. Only the stress on the individual and on the Christian outlook of his heroine stops the story from being a Marxist work.

If *Peasants* is constructed on images of breaking and of fire, *In the Gully* has an undercurrent of contamination in its imagery. The village, Ukleyevo, suggests stickiness (*kley*, glue); its river is polluted with acetic acid, its fields poisoned by effluent from the tannery. Even the telephone which links the factories to the administration building is rotten with bugs and cockroaches. The officials 'are saturated with untruth' until their skin seems changed. A moral contamination spreads through the Tsybukin family whose destruction makes the story : 'Sin, it seemed, had condensed and stood like a mist in the air.' As in *Peasants*, predatory images create terror. *Peasants* has only a hawk sailing through the air, a crow after the chicks, and the bleached skeleton of a horse at the end, to convey a deadly sense of evil. *In the Gully* is horrible : at the wedding of Tsybukin's son, a peasant woman suddenly cries out, 'You've sucked all our blood, Herods.' The village clerk's wife grabs at the food 'like a bird of prey'. Tsybukin's senior daughter-in-law, Aksin'ya, the main predator, has eyes that 'burn green, like a wolf's in a sheepfold'; her neck is like a 'young viper's'; her deadly greenness is emphasised by a green dress with a yellow front that, with her unwinking eyes, makes her snake-like. (Much of the imagery may derive from a green snake, a figurine, which Ol'ga Knipper had just given to Chekhov.)

Unlike *Peasants*, *In the Gully* is firmly plotted. It has a conflict of sisters-in-law, married to men who cannot control them, very like the situation in *Peasant Women* of 1891. At the opening of the story the old man Tsybukin, who runs the village trading-post, is surrounded with prosperity and happiness. His idiotic younger son has married a simple peasant girl, Aksin'ya, who shows herself to be a business-woman of incredible strength. He himself has remarried and in Varvara has an efficient and good-natured wife. His elder son, Anisim, a detective, is now to be married to Lipa, a penniless beauty, all but a child. Gradually, everything falls apart. Anisim turns out to be a counterfeiter and his counterfeit coins are for Tsybukin indistinguishable from genuine money. Aksin'ya starts to go into business on her own account, building a brick-factory in league with one of the factory-owners. Lipa has a baby, which threatens to be the heir to the Tsybukin business; Aksin'ya scalds the baby to death. Lipa leaves to become a simple peasant worker and, three years later, we see Tsybukin himself ousted from the house, unfed, uncared-for, while Askin'ya has transformed herself into the leading capitalist of Ukleyevo. The gentle, oppressed Lipa finds herself giving Tsybukin charity. The meek have inherited at least some of the earth : the first have become last.

Like Zhukovo, Ukleyevo ought to be a paradise. Seen from the hillside, only the factory roofs are ugly, and the permanent mud and endemic fevers are invisible. With Lipa, as she walks on pilgrimage in chapter 5 or trudges home from the hospital with the corpse of her baby in chapter 8, we escape the heavy atmosphere of the village. The miasma that hangs over Ukleyevo, the 'condensed sin' of the first chapter, appears as a real fog hanging over the valley when Lipa looks down on it. The countryside is still pure; only in the village are there felt 'so many sins that you can't free yourself'. The contamination is not only in the effluents, but in the rotten meat and polluted cooking-oil that Tsybukin sells, the counterfeit coins that Anisim brings home. Humanity is enslaved by it : the seamstresses work for Lipa's wedding and are paid only in shop-soiled goods, the reapers are paid in false money. The natural life of the peasant is undone : as one peasant says, confusing the words *krest'-yanin* (peasant) and *khristianin* (Christian), 'I've been taken off *khrest'yanin* work, I can't do anything.'

The more Lipa is oppressed and downtrodden, the more her strength is concentrated. She is befriended by the one workman in Ukleyevo with any spirit left, the carpenter 'Crutch'. 'Crutch' maintains that he, a simple carpenter, is higher than any boss, because Joseph, father of Christ, was a carpenter; his work is thus sanctified, and he persuades Lipa that those who labour and endure are superior to their oppressors. Like Red'ka in *My Life* he shows the meek their place in the Christian scale of things. This confidence and the beauty of nature are the sole signs of natural justice left, as in Ecclesiastes.

But it seemed to them someone was watching from the heights in the sky, the blue, where the stars are, could see all that was happening in Ukleyevo, was guarding them. And however great evil may be, the night is still quiet and beautiful and, all the same, truth is and shall be in God's world, just as quiet and beautiful, and everything in the world is only waiting to be merged with truth, as the moonlight merges with the night.

The hope of justice—for *pravda* implies both truth and justice— is qualified like almost every impression in Chekhov's late prose by 'it seemed'. If there is to be any hope, then Lipa and 'Crutch' are among those few people in whom Chekhov saw the first signs of salvation.

At the end it is a sense of nature's energy rather than God that redeems *In the Gully* from utter darkness. Exhausted by carrying her dead baby, Lipa gets a lift from two carters. One consoles her by telling her how much he has gone through in life, wandering over Siberia, losing his wife, and yet still wanting to live. He is content that there should be no answer to 'Why?', that man must take his ignorance of divine purpose as his lot. Resignation, vitality and Christianity keep Lipa alive. Just as, in *Peasants*, the larks and corncrakes sing as Ol'ga and Sasha leave the village, so Lipa listens to the invisible birds—bitterns, nightingales and cuckoos—and hears the message of nature, that 'you only live once.' The Tsybukins have only their ruthless maxim of 'each man to his trade' and the pursuit of wealth to help them face life : Lipa still has the instinctive golden rule of the peasantry. It does not matter how illusory her intuitions of eventual justice may be : she is uncontaminated, natural, vital.

The gentry are as incidental to *In the Gully* as to *Peasants*. Only at the end does Aksin'ya's prosperity make her as indistinguishable from the rich factory owners as George Orwell's pigs are from their erstwhile masters : the gentry have disappeared from the scene. But there are two stories of 1899 which do juxtapose the world of the peasant with that of the gentry. *Po delam sluzhby (On Official Business)* shows a young legal official sent out to a remote village to investigate a suicide. He is put up for the night by the local gentry, happy, surrounded with luxury. But an evening in the elder's hut, where the corpse is lying, leads to a nightmare. The two worlds are incompatible and, in the night, it is impossible to tell which is the dream—the warmth and gaiety of the big house or the nightmare vision of some peasant upheaval. After quadrilles, champagne, four beautiful daughters, he dreams of a much more real world, the corpse and the elder marching through the snow, singing, 'We're coming, we're coming . . . We take all the weight of life on ourselves, yours and ours.' He awakes, but his mind cannot find the link that joins the island of genteel happiness to the sea of misery outside. Lyzhin, the lawyer, is disturbed by his nightmare, while the doctor with him calmly accepts the miseries of Russian life as the result of geography and climate. *On Official Business* uses a set of characters, of whom Chekhov had once been fond, to show the contrast of two natures, the sensitive and the imperturbable; here the formula shows the whimsical absurdity of any reflection, when the impressions of life are too horrible to contemplate. The moral impotence of Lyzhin and the doctor when, on official business, they meet death and injustice is one of the characteristics of the Chekhovian hero in his sentimental life, one of the themes of the other stories of Chekhov's last years.

It is also the downfall of the engineer in *Novaya dacha* (*The New Dacha*). He comes to the country to build a bridge. His wife likes the view and persuades him to build a cottage, a *dacha*. They settle in, and try to understand and help the peasants, only to be embittered by their enmity. The peasants had no need of the bridge and they distrust the engineer. Even their language is unable to cross the chasm that separates gentry from peasant. Reproaching the peasants for stealing from him, the engineer tells them that they are repaying good with evil, and the peasants immediately assume that he is demanding compensation, and grow even more wary. The engineer and his wife, frightened by their hostility, and blind even to the well-wishers among the villagers, desert their dacha, selling it to new owners. The larks and nightingales sing and turn the whole episode into something like a mad dream for the peasants: only the iron bridge remains. The gentry have melted away.

In the Gully shows a Russia in which the peasantry are the only real force; Chekhov's last stories, written in Yalta, are obsessed with a much more personal life. Society vanishes from his hero's eyes, leaving only a desperate sense of time passing and old age encroaching, and with it a crisis of identity. We can see this crisis in the love-stories which are Chekhov's most important work in the late 1890s, and it is one of the dynamic motifs in the late plays. It is as if the Christian peasantry have a destiny utterly separate from that of Chekhov's intelligentsia, who live under different, pagan gods.

13

Love

Peasants showed how radical Chekhov's reaction to the outside world had become by the mid-1890s. *The House with the Mezzanine* and the stories of love, requited or not, consummated or not, of 1898 and 1899 reveal a radical change in his attitude to woman and sexuality. Suddenly the unhappiness that arises from indifference, rationalisation or cold calculating self-interest makes the consequences of sensuality or impulsiveness seem good, natural and salutary. His women do not alter in themselves: they deceive themselves, they age, they ensnare. But they no longer seem predatory.

The changes in Chekhov's private life can be traced to his own passionate desire to live—that of the consumptive—his growing distrust of all authoritarianism, and his attachment to individual freedom, or to the fact that he was now revising his earlier work for his Collected Works and was brought back to the romantic situations and the heroines of his work for *Novoye Vremya* in 1886. Certainly the abnegation of sensual enjoyment which tinges *Three Years* has entirely gone by 1897. Lying on his back in Ward No. 14 of the clinic in Moscow in spring 1897, the author of *Ward No. 6* had much to reflect on. Tolstoy visited him; their arguments led to a severe haemorrhage, but Chekhov managed to make Tolstoy define his ideas of divinity and immortality. Tolstoy said he looked on the after-life as an embodiment of pure reason and pure love into which human souls would merge. To Tolstoy's amazement, Chekhov was repelled and perplexed by this Kantian transcendence of the individual. Suddenly, in Chekhov's world death is no longer fearsome: just as the peasant Lipa is to realise that 'you only live once', so Chekhov's doctors, lawyers, bankers and teachers are to stumble on the truth that happiness lies in grasping opportunities, in acting on desire, in letting the individual blossom to the full be-

fore it has to fade. The 'new, beautiful life' of the future goes on
luring and bewitching the hero, but it no longer matters whether
the 'new life' is real or illusory, so long as it works as a myth in
which the hero can act. The first thing we notice in Chekhov's
last stories is the proliferation of verbs such as 'it seemed to him', 'he
calmed himself with the thought', 'he was thinking'. The narrator's
viewpoint has collapsed; once there is no certainty of right and
wrong, the hero is free to let his instincts and impulses lead him
on.

Undoubtedly, Chekhov's stay in France, with the boredom of the
Pension Russe in Nice and the fresh, stimulating atmosphere of
French intellectual life, must have changed him. Like Pushkin before him, he became a follower of Voltaire. Zola's defence of Dreyfus led him first to Voltaire's defence of Colas, and then to read
further. The cultivation of one's garden, the nurturing of private life
in a public hell—which is the morality of Voltaire's *Candide*, the
idea that it is impossible to predict good or evil from good or evil
intentions, the conclusion of Voltaire's *Zadig*, are carried over into
On Love and *The Lady with the Little Dog*. All the spell of Tolstoy was dissipated : reading his tract *What is Art?*, Chekhov could
dismiss it as an old man's natural belief that the end of the world
was coming. Chekhov begins to describe himself in a new way. He
praises idleness (*prazdnost'*) as a prerequisite of happiness, dis-
tinguishing it from laziness (*len'*); while conceding that 'my disease
is going crescendo—it's incurable', he could say to Avilova that
he was 'a man who enjoyed life'. Later, at Yalta, he could ironically
welcome 'classlessness in the face of the bacilli', the ease that he
felt when society's rules no longer mattered much.

The Dreyfus affair had cut Chekhov off from Suvorin. Chekhov's
father died; for much of his time in Yalta, Maria worked in Moscow : he was now almost without dependents and without tutelage.
The shock of leaving Melikhovo was considerable; although he
bought land and had a house built in Yalta, planting hundreds of
trees and shrubs, Chekhov knew that his tenure in the Crimea was
short, and his husbandry there never absorbed him as had the
estate of Melikhovo. For the first time in his life he was idling,
and nothing disciplined or cut short his impulses. In 1898 he sold
his complete works to the Petersburg publisher Adolf Marks, who
had printed *My Life* in his magazine *Niva*. Marks printed his
authors at greater cost and far more beautifully than Suvorin. He

offered Chekhov in effect 75,000 rubles in three annual instalments for the rights to all Chekhov's prose, past and future. The money, in fact, soon proved inadequate. Marks covered his investment in his first year and Chekhov, recklessly generous, soon spent his first 25,000 rubles on charities, on his home town and on his new property in Yalta. But this large capital sum gave a feeling of freedom such as Chekhov had never known before. He realised, of course, that this freedom to travel, to do nothing, to write what he pleased, to fall in love, had come too late. This gives poignancy to his late stories where, more often than not, the hero fails to act, or acts too late. It comes out in Chekhov's letters: to Lidia Avilova whom, like most of his would-be loves, he kept on as a useful friend and correspondent, he wrote, 'God doesn't give horns to a butting cow' —enlarging on the picturesque reference to the money coming too late to be enjoyed with the regretful 'I was free and I didn't know freedom.'

Like many men at the end of their lives, Chekhov had returned to his youth. It is remarkable how many of those who were now close to him had been classmates at Taganrog—the lawyer Konovitser (whom Dunya Efros had married), the Tolstoyan Sergeyenko, the Moscow Arts Theatre actor Vishnevsky, the Paris correspondent of *Novoye Vremya*, for instance. The cold and ghastly provincial boredom of Taganrog made living there out of the question, but Chekhov devoted more and more time and money to his town. Not only did he personally buy most of the books in the library: he also commissioned from the sculptor Antokol'sky a statue of Peter the Great, the founder of the town, and contributed to the local museum.

Chekhov's two important new friendships were with Gor'ky and Bunin,[1] both naturally good and warm in character. Gor'ky's 'coarse, rudimentary but still enormous talent' and Bunin's gentle disposition may well have contributed to Chekhov as much as they derived from his company.

Marks had not in fact liberated Chekhov, who soon discovered that his worries were only increased. 'Now I'm a Marxist,' he said ironically. Preparing the earlier volumes of his Collected Works took more of his time than the writing of new original works. Up to 1885, his work was difficult to trace and often had to be copied from newspaper files. A million words had to be reread, stories sorted, retitled and rewritten. His work for Suvorin, with very few exceptions, was transferred *in toto* to Marks; but here, too, Chekhov could not bear to let stories of the 1880s be reprinted without applying to them all the intensity and terseness, the self-sufficiency of characterisation and purity of language which he had learnt in the 1890s. This Herculean task explains why he wrote so little in 1898 and later years. In 1899, for instance, *In the Gully* and *The Lady with the Little Dog* were almost his only new work. There were, however, important results. Looking at his early writing Chekhov was flooded with material that he had not used to the full. Innumerable incidents—some of which already have been pointed out—phrases, scenes, characters such as the gauche young doctor, young heroines thirsting for life such as those of 1887, all stuck in his mind and develop out of all recognition in his later work. Doctor Toporkov of his first serious story, *Tardy Flowers*, is a prototype of Doctor Startsev in *Ionych*; Verochka leads to the lady with the little dog, and to Yekaterina in *Ionych*.

The very process of rewriting forced Chekhov to look at his own style. With each work of 1898 and 1899 a still greater density of imagery is to be noticed, more terseness, the repression of adjectives and adverbs and recourse to rhythms, to assonance and alliteration, to elaborate cadences as a counterpoint to the sense. The adjectives begin to fit into a pattern of images, so that the overall effect has the unity and intensity of *pointilliste* or *fauve* painting. The accelerated fruition of Chekhov's style is due not only to his own revisions, but also to his teaching of others. All his life he had to put up with the mediocre novels and stories of his friends; only now was he able to help real talent. His criticism of Gor'ky makes him more stringent towards himself. He writes in September 1899 :

'A man sat on the grass' is intelligible, because it's clear and doesn't hold up one's attention. On the other hand, it is hard to understand and rather heavy for the brain if I write : 'A tall, narrow-chested man of medium height with a red beard sat on the green grass that passers-by had now trampled down, sat noiselessly, looking around shyly and timidly.' That takes some time for the brain to take in and literature must be taken in at once, in a second.

Chekhov's notebooks reflect the change in his work : the later the work, the more closely its text corresponds with the extremely laconic phrases and synopses of which his notes consist. This terseness is also due to a quickening of the pulse. In 1898, when Chekhov became

involved with the Moscow Arts Theatre, his links were emotional
as well as literary, despite the disappointments and arguments. The
idea of a new type of theatre implied for him a new type of audience
and response; in his private life, it meant his first unrepressed love,
for the actress Ol'ga Knipper. 'The older I get, the faster and
harder the pulse of life beats in me,' he wrote to Lika Mizinova
in September 1898, enthusing over the 'little actresses' of the
theatre.

The novelty of Chekhov's late style can best be seen in a trilogy
of stories, *Chelovek v futlyare* (*The Man in a Case*), *Kryzhovnik*
(*Gooseberries*) and *O lyubvi* (*On Love*) (*Russkaya Mysl'*, July and
August 1898). They are linked by a trio of narrators—Ivan Ivanych,
a veterinary surgeon; Burkin, a science teacher; and Alekhin, a
gentleman turned miller—and they were to begin a series of further
stories, which Chekhov never wrote. In some ways, they revert to
his earlier technique of setting a story in a 'frame narrative', just as
Ariadna has its passionate events framed by a casual discussion of
woman. But this is now a very economical device. The landscapes
of the south, Chekhov's poetic nocturnes of moonlight, the symbolism
of rain and water, are taken out of the story and form a contrast to
the enclosed, dead world of the tales that the narrators tell. They
themselves appear as the 'new individuals', free, sensual, open and
unpretentious, in contrast to the senseless characters of the stories,
prisoners of ugliness, dreams and inhibitions. Each story is opened
and closed by descriptions of shifting weather and light, of sun and
water, so that nature's life contrasts with the characters' deadness.

The first story of the series is told by Burkin, the schoolteacher;
it flows casually out of an incident as Burkin and Ivan Ivanych settle
down for the night in a shed (they are out shooting) and notice
the peasant girl who has never left her own world for the town.
Burkin tells the story of *The Man in a Case*, his colleague the Greek
teacher, Belikov. It is a Gogolian tale. Like Gogol's landowners,
Belikov's characteristics envelop his possessions, so that animate and
inanimate are the same. He himself (like Professor Serebryakov in
Uncle Vanya and like Chekhov's brother Ivan) never goes out without galoshes and an umbrella.[2] There is cotton-wool in his ears,
there are covers on his chairs and, in the end, heavy clouds over
his graveside. When he goes out it is as if he 'has been pulled out
with pincers'. Like Gogol's heroes, Belikov is destroyed by the

prospect of marriage. The headmaster's wife plans to marry him off to a lively Ukrainian woman and when, after Belikov's hesitant courtship, a caricature appears of the 'anthropos in love', he takes to his bed and dies of humiliation. His death is an occasion for rejoicing : life has triumphed. But this most grotesque of Chekhov's schoolteachers, the precursor of the decadent schoolteacher of Sologub's symbolist novel, *The Petty Demon*, is more than a Gogolian joke. He is the spirit of tyranny : he preys by repressing and denouncing. His motto is that of authority : 'If it is not expressly authorised, it is forbidden.' His eyes are 'like a ferret's'; to the Ukrainian who is faced by the prospect of having him for a brother-in-law, he is a voracious spider. His green colouring is, in Chekhov's work, ominous. Puny though he is, his fears of 'something happening' terrorise the whole school. When they have buried him in his last case, their joy is short-lived : there are plenty more Belikovs to bury.

Before the second story begins, there is an interlude. It is a nocturne, in which the moonlight transforms the world, so that all signs of misery and ugliness disappear and beauty and love seem likely again. *Gooseberries* is then begun, but before Ivan Ivanych tells the story of his brother's life, the ramblers take refuge from the rain with their friend Alekhin. Alekhin is washing in his millpool and there is a warm sensuality in his bathing, his dressing again, his beautiful servant girl, and his soft carpets, which is to contrast with the aridity and harshness of the imagery in Ivan Ivanych's story. This, too, owes much to *Dead Souls*. Ivan Ivanych's brother, burdened like him with the ludicrous name of Chimsha-Gimalaysky,[3] has an ambition to own an estate on which he can grow his own gooseberries. To get the money together, he leads a life of privation, marries a widow for her money and starves her to death. At last his dream comes true. The irony of the story emerges when the narrator visits his brother. The estate's name, *Chumbaroklova Pustosh'* (wilderness), has been enlarged by the addition of the rhyming *Gimalayskoye tozh* (Gimalayskoye as well). The river that flows through it is brown with the pollution of a brickworks and a bone-processor—those symbols in Chekhov's work of corrupted nature. The gooseberries are sour, but the dreamer finds them sweet. The nightmare which was meant to be an idyll is sheer Gogol'; just as Gogolian is the pig-like fatness of the new landowner—'any moment now he'd hoink into the blanket'—spreading to his dog 'as fat as a

pig' and his sow-like kitchenmaid. The narrator quotes Pushkin's
lines to draw a moral :

> Dearer than ten thousand truths
> Is deceit that can uplift us,

lines which Chekhov had quoted on two occasions in his earliest
prose.[4]

When the story of *Gooseberries* is ended, the narrators interpret
it. Happiness, they conclude, must be founded on others' misery, as
the gooseberries are grown on a lifetime of suffering and oppression. Happiness disguises the 'brazenness and idleness of the strong
and the ignorance and bestiality of the weak'; it is a hypnotic state
which could not exist without the crowding, degeneration and
drunkenness of the masses. Here we see how Chekhov related the
genteel world to that of the peasants. Prosperity is based on pain,
so that every happy man should have someone standing by him
with a hammer to batter a sense of pain into him.

Interpreting family happiness as the summit of a pyramid of
suffering, we are prepared for the next day's story. During the night
the rain bangs all night against the window and the next story, *On
Love*, is given its aura of closeness and turbulence in advance. One
of the shortest of Chekhov's late works, it is most typical. Alekhin
looks back at the one love of his life, which he let slip. He refuses
to generalise, saying, as did Chekhov, that a narrator should, like
a doctor, 'individualise each separate case'. But the conclusion is
clear. As the story opens, we meet again the beautiful servant girl
and the good food which Alekhin is accustomed to indulge in, and
see the contrast with his pained and puritanical past life. He is upset
by the cerebral element in his love. Just as his mistress always
thought about the price of beef while in his arms, so he, faced with
the chance of love, thinks about duty, happiness, right and wrong.
He tells how he started to relax from hard work, went to town to
work as a magistrate and met the Luganoviches. Luganovich is
middle-aged and complacent, his wife young and active. Alekhin
takes issue with Luganovich over a trial with anti-semitic overtones,
but still remains friendly. With the wife Yelena he grows closer
and closer, but fails to speak up, while she becomes more and more
soured and ill. Eventually, she has to leave to convalesce in the
Crimea. Alekhin kisses her, but won't take any irrevocable step. His
situation is not unlike that of Gurov in *The Lady with the Little*

Dog.[5] Like Belikov and Chimsha-Gimalaysky, however, he has refused the wide world and stands firm on his own patch of ground.
Now, too late, he realises that he should have acted as Gurov is to
act. He realises that in times of crisis happiness and unhappiness are
too low a basis for reasoning.

The three narrators have had their say. Their philosophy is clear :
man needs not a plot of ground but the whole globe, not a set of
principles but moral courage, to explore not to consolidate, to build
his happiness purely on his own efforts and not on other people's.
The ending of *On Love* is positive—the sun clears the rain, the pool
and garden appear cleansed, and Alekhin's self-examination, 'like a
squirrel in a wheel', gives the sensation of tremendous nervous energy
about to be released. Chekhov had no need to continue his series,
the only set of stories in his entire work.

Alekhin's squirrel-like wiriness finds its outlet in his manual labour :
he is now healthy, saved, as much as Misail Poloznev in *My Life*.
But his past failure to take the bull by the horns is the theme of other
stories of this period. The first is *U znakomykh (A Visit to Friends)*,
which Chekhov wrote in Nice for the four-language magazine
Cosmopolis, run by Batyushkov. Perhaps because he wrote it in
France and had considerable annoyance over proof-reading and
editorial mistakes, Chekhov took a dislike to this piece. It is the
only one of his late stories that he excluded from his Collected
Works. Possibly, he was embarrassed by certain parallels between
the characters and the Kiselev family, now facing ruin, of Babkino :
whatever his reasons, there are no grounds for regarding *A Visit
to Friends* as inferior to the other tales.[6] The story takes up the
theme of *Verochka* of 1887. A loving, beautiful girl attracts the
hero, yet he cannot find in him the response that the girl and the
scene ought to arouse, and he packs his bags and flees. This theme
is to be elaborated further in *Ionych* at the end of the year, and
scenes of *Ionych*, especially the wait in the cemetery at night, follow
on from *A Visit to Friends*. The hero, Podgorin, reluctantly
accepts an invitation to stay with the Losevs, whom he has avoided
for some time. He is a lawyer and knows he is expected to help
them out of their impossible financial mess and to propose to
Tat'yana Losev's sister, Nadezhda.

The bankruptcy of Losev and the auction arranged for the
summer, in which the entire estate will be sold, make the background far less simple than that of *Verochka*, linking the story in-

stead with the irresponsibility and doom that overhang *The Cherry Orchard*. Knowing that he is expected to give money and advice, Podgorin is even more inhibited. The mood of love is spoilt not only by the ill-concealed imminence of disaster; another guest, Varya, once close to Podgorin, casually recites poems she used to know. Quotation is as common in Chekhov's last works as in his very first; here, the poetry is disturbing. Varya speaks Nekrasov's lines about the railway, for Nekrasov and Chekhov a double-edged symbol of linking and breaking, of progress and oppression :[7]

> Straight is the track : the embankments are narrow,
> There are poles and rails and bridges,
> And by the sides, nothing but Russian bones . . .
> The Russian people have borne enough,
> They've borne this iron road as well—
> They'll bear the lot—and lay out for themselves
> A broad clear road with their chests . . .

Thus the marching workers of *On Official Business*, the oppressed of *In the Gully*, burst into the gentry's private world. Podgorin cannot respond to the allurements of Nadezhda. There is a nocturnal scene in the garden, one of Chekhov's most unforgettable evocations of moonlight, as Nadezhda waits. The black shadow of a statue contrasts with her white figure and creates an illusion of peace and melancholy. The birds—corncrakes, quail and cuckoo—make the same call to life as they do in *Peasants* and *In the Gully*. But Podgorin can only see that poetry is as stale as prose to him, realise his 'inability to take'—the weakness of the Chekhovian hero—and long for a woman who will fit in with the ideas of the Nekrasov poem, offering not love but 'new, high, rational forms of life', promising something of the dream-world 'on the eve of which we are perhaps now living and of which we sometimes have a premonition'. The dream of the future, which captivates Podgorin as it does Trofimov in *The Cherry Orchard*, blinds the hero to the present and makes him impotent. He is not saved by his prescience of 'new forms'; he is damned by his 'inability to take'.

Using a doctor as his hero instead of a lawyer, Chekhov writes a parallel story at the end of 1898, the brief *Sluchay iz praktiki (An Incident in Practice)*. The doctor arrives to treat the factory-owner's daughter. The house is all-female, all unhappy. The sacrifices and misery of the workers do not even bring happiness for the few, whose dinners of sturgeon and madeira are the only purpose of the hell over which they rule. The girl is not ill but frustrated. Doctor Korolev half responds, by telling her that her incapacity to endure her life is a hopeful sign, but he has not the courage to tell her to abandon her wealth and family. Like Podgorin, he leaves as soon as he can and puts the meeting out of his mind. *An Incident in Practice* is paralysed by the horror of the factory as effectively as Podgorin is paralysed by the image of the railway and the Russian people. The factory is so monstrous that the workers can only turn to alcohol to 'sober themselves from this nightmare'. Looking at the miseries of the house, Korolev can only assume that there is a devil in the universe enslaving rich and poor. The devil appears in the red light reflected by two windows, and the oppression of the house spills out in the smell of paint and the weird, inexplicable noises 'der . . . der . . . der . . . dryn . . . dryn . . . dryn . . . zhak . . . zhak . . . zhak' that fill the atmosphere and mark the passing of the hours. Only outside the factory, as he leaves, does Korolev emerge like an Orpheus without Eurydice, finding peace in thoughts of the 'brightness and joy' of the life to come, a daydream to mask his nightmare and his inability to take what was offered.

Korolev, Podgorin and Alekhin are melted down into Doctor Startsev of *Ionych*. The story covers a wider time-scale than any other. It begins with the newly qualified Startsev, idealistic and vulnerable, starting practice near the town of S., and ends with him, now known by his strange patronymic Ionych, grasping and alone. Each chapter sees him a little fatter and less responsive. Turned away in love, he takes refuge in food and money. First his emotions, then his body, and finally his mind atrophy. The setting is particularly important. The town of S.—in which the lady with the little dog also lives—is the first of Chekhov's quintessential provincial backwaters after *My Life*. Like the town of *My Life* it has a library which is kept open only by the young Jews, and it is inhabited by philistines, *obyvateli*, whose vacuous, easy-going temperament overlays a vicious intolerance. Startsev is an innocent who falls bit by bit into the clutches of the town. Like many Chekhovian doctors, he has humble clerical origins and finds his feet in society too late. He is introduced to the most interesting family in town, the Turkins. Ivan Turkin, like Losev in *A Visit to Friends*, can only talk in the catch-phrases of some long-forgotten vaudeville; his wife, a cruel caricature of Chekhov's women friends, amuses herself writing novels about a beautiful young countess who builds

schools for the grateful peasantry and falls in love with a wandering
artist; the daughter, Kotik, plays the piano; the servant is trained
to pose, declaiming, 'Die, you wretch.' Startsev is bewildered by
this household; only later is he to wonder what the rest of the
town is like, if this is its most cultured section. He can sense that
the folksong he can hear outside is more talented than anything
in the Turkins' world; he can feel with Chekhov that Kotik's piano-
playing is interesting for its technique, not its sound : but he falls
hopelessly in love. Like all the late Chekhov heroes, he utters
thoughts and feels impressions that really belong to the author.
The description of Kotik's playing is too original to belong entirely
to Startsev's mind. 'Startsev . . . pictured stones rolling down a moun-
tain, rolling on and on' is the hero's impression; the detached 'her
shoulders and breasts quivered, she obstinately struck at one place,
and it seemed she would not stop until she had bashed the keys
into the body of the piano. The drawing-room was filled with
thunder; everything roared : the floor, the ceiling, the furniture' is
too ironic for the naïve young doctor.

Startsev reaches his apogee in Chekhov's most extended 'nocturne'.
Kotik tells him to wait for her in the cemetery. With only faint
hopes, Startsev goes—a trick that Chekhov had once used in a
comic story. Idly he wanders about the tombstones and is gradually
overcome by the atmosphere. For the first time he has an intuition
of beauty :

a world, unlike anything else—a world where the moon's light is so
good and soft, as if its cradle were here, where there is no life, not a
bit, but in each dark poplar, in each grave you can sense the presence
of a secret, promising peaceful, beautiful eternal life. The gravestones
and the faded flowers, together with the autumnal smell of the leaves,
waft forgiveness, melancholy and peace.

Moonlight in Chekhov's work is always a sign of the presence of
death; only in his late stories does a symbol of death revitalise the
hero, as if making life more urgent by emphasising its uniqueness.
The effect of passages like these would be lost were it not for their
hypnotic structure, giving a more than elegiac cadence. There is the
alliteration of *proshcheniye, pechal' i pokoy* (forgiveness, melancholy and peace), the internal rhymes of *svet, net . . . net i net* (light,
not, not a bit), the assonance of *u*-sounds in *chuvstvuyetsya prisutstviye
. . . tikhuyu, prekrasnuyu, vechnuyu* (you can feel the presence . . .
peaceful, beautiful, eternal). The triads of nouns or adjectives that

end the last sentences, and the arc-like structure of the sentences themselves, all contribute to a lyrical climax that exceeds anything that Startsev's mind is capable of. The scene is almost animated by the statues in the moonlight. When clouds obscure the moon, the curtain comes down and Startsev's emotional awakening is cut short.

He is rejected by Kotik. He retreats to his practice, while she follows her ambition to be a concert pianist. They meet again four years later. Kotik's illusions about art are shattered and Startsev has found only horror of the town's *obyvateli* and the prosperity of a rich practice to console him. There is a second nocturne in the garden, but Startsev has atrophied and is 'unable to take'. He can feel only a spark of response and, when Kotik begins to talk about the nobility of a doctor's calling, that spark dies. In the epilogue Startsev has degenerated into the town's bully and Kotik leaves for the Crimea. Ambition and illusions have ruined them both: Kotik has faded away, Startsev is 'bloated with fat'. Only the Turkin parents are the same as before. The town of S. triumphs over youth and love; its triumph was already symbolised in the cemetery, whose most notable monument is the grave of an Italian singer who passed through S. and died there.

The same town of S., with its grey dust and grey fences, tries to ruin the heroine of *Dama s sobachkoy* (*The Lady with the Little Dog*). But this, the best-known and most affirmative of Chekhov's works, has a freedom of movement from S. and from Moscow to Yalta, in which the hero and heroine can get away from the prison of their marriages and their towns. *The Lady with the Little Dog* is the only one of Chekhov's stories set in Yalta, where the combination of nature at its most awe-inspiring and the town at its most provincial is more extreme than anywhere else in his experience.

A series of accidents turns a casual affair into a liberation: a candle, a grey fence, dew on the grass, an accidental glance in a mirror alter Gurov's view of Anna Sergeyevna and of himself, weaken his cynicism and change his outlook. He and Anna follow their impulses and thus free themselves. There is no suggestion of a happy ending: the worthwhile result is that there is no ending in sight, only complications and a mirage of 'a new life' to keep them fully stretched and alive.

Gurov, particularly in the magazine version of 1899, arrives in

Yalta as a cold-blooded sensualist, skilfully seducing Anna Sergeyevna, with his light talk and predatory patience. We meet him
as a type : the womaniser, embittered by each affair, but never able
to remember the bitterness. In a way, he is a victim. Chekhov phrases
'he was married' as *'yego zhenili'* (they married him)—a terse hint
at Gurov's vulnerability to outside pressures. Gurov's wife is made
repulsive by a few subtle strokes : she calls him Dimitri, not Dmitri,
calls herself a 'thinking woman', and uses advanced spelling. Once
Gurov has picked up Anna, the sexual conquest turns bit by bit
into something less easy. Yalta, with its anonymity, makes them
'free people'; the sea predisposes them to sensuality with its 'soft,
warm, lilac colour'. Neither Yalta nor Anna fits into Gurov's categories. He divides women into sensualists, intellectuals and predators. Each category repels him as easily as it attracts him : the
first by its gratitude, the second by its conceit, and the last by its
coldness so that, in Chekhov's unforgettable image, 'the lace of
their underwear seemed like fish-scales'. Thus he can plan the
beginning of his affair, but not its end.

The second section shows Anna reacting to her fall with a remorse
that Gurov cannot believe : only the poetry of the single candle
stops him from showing his irritation with her. A seduction that
begins with the conventional suffocating smell of flowers and perfume ends with an austerity that Gurov cannot yet understand. Up
to this point he is remarkable only in his Chekhovian hypersensi-
tivity : his image of fish-scales, his smelling flowers on Anna's face
after she has sniffed them, indicate his sensuality. Once there is a
sense of mystery in the penitent Anna, Gurov begins to show unsuspected depths. Together they ride up to the mountains at Oreanda
(as Chekhov rode with Ol'ga Knipper to Ay-Petri) and stare at the
sea. The effect of this nocturnal scene is the same as the cemetery's
spell on Doctor Startsev. The sea's roar suggests peace and eternal
sleep, and in that suggestion Gurov feels a sense of salvation, an
affirmation of beauty, a stimulus to act. All his reactions are conditional : Chekhov says 'it seemed to him', and the absolute beauty
of nature leads to an endless chain of qualifications. What man
thinks and does seems, to Gurov, to detract from beauty; then he
qualifies this by adding 'when we forget about higher aims of being',
though at no point in the story do any higher aims of existence become clear. Dawn breaks and shatters the dream, but from this
point Chekhov turns an adventure story into a love story. The idle-

ness, *prazdnost'*, of Yalta life transforms Gurov from a mature Don
Juan into a naïve lover.

Then the lovers are parted, each in a separate prison. Chekhov's
portrayal of Gurov's married life is a remarkable picture of unspoken irritation. In a letter to Meyerkhol'd, advising him how to
play the part of Johannes, the unhappily married hero of Gerhardt
Hauptmann's *Lonely People (Einsame Menschen)*, Chekhov points
out Johannes' *nervnost'* (highly-strung temperament), as something
normal : 'Every educated man feels most irritation at home, for the
clash of the present and the past is most palpable in the family.'
The irritation grows : Gurov needs to talk and no one will listen.
His poetic reminiscences evoke from his friends only the remark
'The sturgeon was a bit off.' Feeling as if he is in 'a madhouse or a
prison', Gurov leaves for S.—the apotheosis of greyness, grey car-
pet in the hotel room, grey dust on the streets, a grey fence opposite
Anna's home. After a long interval, he finds Anna in the local
theatre and she agrees to visit him in Moscow.

The story ends where earlier novelists would have felt it was
just beginning. Gurov now has two lives, a real secret life and a
false public life. There are symbols of trouble everywhere. He tells
his little daughter why snow can fall when temperatures are above
freezing, why thunder occurs only in summer, hinting at the turbulence in his mental atmosphere. Anna is wearing a grey dress, the
colour of S. But the affair will not end. Gurov's scepticism suddenly
falters when he catches sight of his grey hair in the mirror, and his
love is strengthened as much by self-pity as by pity. Love promises
a 'new, beautiful life' as undefinable as the salvation that the sea's
roar seems to promise. It does not matter that Gurov and Anna
find no answer to the questions they have raised. The complexity
and difficulty of the questions, the tangle of deceit and pain, are
evidence enough that they are alive, not fossilised. All Chekhov's
imagery in the last chapter—'two migratory birds . . . male and
female', the snow and the thunder, 'real life under the cover of
mystery'—brings out the primitive vitality of love.

Gurov is the last of the few active heroes in Chekhov's work. The
final stories and plays show a world in which the men are dying
and only the women are prepared to fight on. But the message of
The Bride or *Three Sisters* is the natural consequence of *The Lady
with the Little Dog* : routine is death, and turbulence—the unknown
—is life. The distinction is so important that the happiness or un-

happiness that the future may hold for humanity can no longer matter. For Gurov 'this little woman, in no way remarkable . . . now filled his entire life, was his misery and his joy': for Chekhov misery was as good an expression of life as was joy.

14

Chekhov's Last Plays

Much, perhaps too much, has been written on Chekhov's last plays. Everything in his letters and in the memoirs of his contemporaries has been collated to help directors, producers and actors approach an authorised version. But the nature of the theatre, subject as it is to the demands of the State, its audience and its own workers, is such that an authorised version of Chekhov's plays is no more possible and perhaps no more desirable than an authorised version of Shakespeare's. Television and cinema have given Chekhov—as they have given Shakespeare—new possibilities, a subtlety of sound effects and detail, a naturalism of speech and gesture of which Chekhov might well have approved. As long as audiences and directors are free to choose what interpretations they will watch and create, it is far better to let natural selection take care of Chekhov's plays than to impose an interpretation. Stanislavsky's production notes bring us little closer to a definitive version, for Chekhov took issue with Stanislavsky on many points, generally on his over-enthusiastic attempts to put on *trompe-l'oeil* effects and to shock and rivet attention. In the case of *The Cherry Orchard* something is to be gained from looking at Meyerkhol'd's more symbolist or expressionist interpretation of masks and horror, but here, too, a great director cannot but distort his author.

In appreciating what—apart from accidents of history—made Chekhov's plays of such importance to European theatre, it is necessary to look at developments in a European context. Chekhov's reading was unexpectedly varied. He was familiar not only with Hauptmann and Ibsen, but also with Strindberg (*Miss Julie* in a manuscript translation by Shavrova) and with Maeterlinck (during his 1897–98 stay in Nice). Scandinavian contemporaries such as Bjørnson and Marholm are other dramatists whose work, one day, may have to be more thoroughly explored in comparison with Chekhov's drama. Within the scope of this book, it is possible to venture only partly into the field of the new drama that began to fill Europe's theatres as melodrama and opera deserted them.

In chapter eight, Chekhov's first three plays and *Uncle Vanya* were linked by their construction around one male hero. *Chayka* (*The Seagull*, written in 1895), *Tri sestry* (*Three Sisters*, written in 1900) and *Vishnyovyy sad* (*The Cherry Orchard*, written in 1903) may be linked by their 'polyphonic' construction around several characters, usually heroines. But they all share certain fundamental features : all the plays are set far from Moscow and Petersburg and, except for *Three Sisters* which is set in a stylised Perm' (one of the remotest towns of Russia in the northern foothills of the Urals), they are all set on country estates somewhere south of Moscow. In all the plays, imminent bankruptcy threatens the world in which the characters live; in all of them trees are cut down to clear the way for the new tenants. All have a firearm involved—offstage in *Three Sisters*, not fired in *The Cherry Orchard*. All, even *The Seagull*, have a musical accompaniment. On to all the weather encroaches. In all the plays characters eat and drink on stage.

The Seagull, though a 'comedy' like *The Cherry Orchard*, is notably different in more than paucity of music. It is Chekhov's most heterogeneous work and, in some ways, his most literary. Written after a vow not to work for the theatre again, it is an act of vengeance. It not only breaks the theatre's traditional canons; it also attacks the profession through its heroine and her son, and it argues out the two possible approaches, conservative and experimental, to literature (including drama) through its two male antagonists, Trigorin and Treplev. Some of the intensity of *The Seagull* is undoubtedly due to its extraordinary wealth of autobiographical detail. Chekhov was to say, 'I have a disease—autobiographobia' (a letter to Doctor Rossolimo in October 1899), but on this occasion he was free of it.

The origins of *The Seagull* are mysterious. Much of the phraseology, especially Trigorin's derogatory comparisons of himself with Turgenev and Tolstoy, would date the idea to 1893, and in fact three years was the usual period of gestation for Chekhov's plays. But conscious preparation for the play came later. There were rumours, that Chekhov denied, of a play about life in Siberia : some of this play may survive in *Three Sisters*. In February 1894 Chekhov was interested in Ludwig Börne's *Letters from Paris* and intended to create a play around a character called Ginselt, loved by women and ill at ease with men—a forerunner of Trigorin. *The Seagull—Chayka*—was the title of a literary magazine that Suvorin and Chekhov considered in 1893. (There is also a fragment of a love-letter with the phrase 'to two white seagulls', which may have some link with the yearning sensuality of the play.)

The play was written in autumn 1895. Its immediate impulse may have been in April, when Chekhov sorted out his correspondence and was struck by the liveliness and interest of his letters to and from Suvorin in 1889, when both were busy with plays. But *The Seagull* was written immediately after Chekhov's first contact with the new drama. He had read Hauptmann's *Lonely People* and Ibsen's *Little Eyolf*, and the morality of *The Seagull* shows the same crumbling of family ties and convention as real antipathies and bonds are revealed.

The personal element in *The Seagull*, which makes it so eccentric, should first be disentangled. The *belle-lettriste* Trigorin, the lover of the heroine, is not, of course, Chekhov, but he shares many essentials of Chekhov as a writer, and caricatures a number of personal traits. First of all, he is obsessed with his rank as a major writer, but one worse than Turgenev or Tolstoy. Others—for instance, his rival Treplev, Arkadina's son—find his writings talented, but inferior to those of Tolstoy or Zola. Trigorin's epitaph for himself, 'He was a good writer, but he wrote worse than Turgenev', reflects Chekhov's self-assessment in his letters to Suvorin of 1892 and 1893. But there are closer parallels, particularly in the compulsive urge to continue writing. In his first long talk with Nina, the young girl-friend of Treplev who is now falling in love with Trigorin, he tells her : 'Day and night I'm in the grip of a thought that I can't get rid of : I must write, I must write, I must . . .' In March 1894 Chekhov complained to Lika Mizinova (whose relationship to him overshadows the play) : 'I'm miserable . . . because not for a minute am I free of the thought that I must, am obliged to write, write, write.'

Other parallels are well known. Treplev in an envious monologue complains that Trigorin has a set of tricks which make his writing easy : 'He has the neck of a broken bottle shining on a weir and the dark shadow of a mill-wheel—and there you have a moonlit night'—a passage from Chekhov's *Wolf* of 1886. In January 1896, Lidia Avilova gave Chekhov a medal inscribed with a page number and a line number from his last book : Chekhov consulted the book and found the lines in his *Neighbours* of 1891, 'If you should need my life, come and take it.' He gave the same line to Trigorin's book, *Days and Nights*, to which Nina refers on a medallion, giving page and line numbers. Chekhov lent Avilova's medal to the great actress Komissarzhevskaya for use in the Petersburg production.

There are many other links. Nina and Arkadina are both amazed that Trigorin should derive more pleasure from fishing than writing. 'His portraits are sold, he's translated into foreign languages, and he spends all day fishing and is glad he's caught two bullheads.' This reproduces the reactions of the Kiselevs and Lintvarevs to Chekhov's summer days and nights with a fishing-rod. Trigorin is shy and taciturn, except tête-à-tête, and disarmingly polite—like Chekhov.[1]

Yet the reasons for making Trigorin so autobiographical are not confessional. Trigorin seduces Nina and abandons her when she is pregnant : this outlines Potapenko's behaviour with Lika Mizinova, not Chekhov's. (Chekhov was worried enough by the resemblance to be afraid that Potapenko and Mizinova would appear in adjacent boxes on the first night.) Trigorin, however, is the epitome of 'belles-lettres' reaching the end of their development, the end of the literature which analyses reality, the emotions and the senses, and which long ago reached its apogee with Tolstoy and Turgenev. His sexual literary rival is Treplev, the young 'decadent'. It is a great mistake to laugh at Treplev's playlet, which is presented to the other characters in Act 1 and which Nina, who performs it, recalls almost in its entirety in Act 4. Treplev's mother, Arkadina, is contemptuous; Nina is disappointed by its coldness; Trigorin understands nothing. Nevertheless, when the Petersburg production of *The Seagull* adopted Arkadina's tone, the play was doomed to failure. Chekhov wanted the smell of sulphur and the imagery of cold and satanic spirits to linger over the rest of Act 1. Treplev's play may be a failure, even untalented, but it is meant as a serious attempt to find new forms of art, and new realms to operate in. Its neo-Platonic idea of all creation reverting to the spiritual state of the Soul of the World—every living thing from the fish to Alexander the Great—and then fighting the spirit of evil is, in fact, one of the main themes of Russian symbolism. But Chekhov is anticipating, not parodying, this. Ideas of Treplev's kind are not to be found until, ten years later, Blok's ominous 'marsh' poems of his 'second book' recreate Treplev's atmosphere. Treplev's play has its stylistic origins, its myth-making tone, in Maeterlinck, but Chekhov is not sneering at him. The play is a pastiche of a style which Chekhov neither liked nor disliked: he was to assure Bunin that his own art would not survive him for more than a few years; he felt that new forms must be found. If these new forms seem more impoverished and inflexible than the old, that is posterity's business.

To a small extent, Treplev's playlet also catches some of the lyricism of Chekhov's mystical feeling for nature. The passing of life into a lonely battle of good and evil, the development of the piece from a catalogue of creatures to a cosmic vision of the universe passing away reminds us of passages in *Panpipes* of 1887 or the thoughts of Ragin in *Ward No. 6*.

The Seagull is a play about literature as well as about writers. Konstantin's decadence is his personal undoing: he cannot sufficiently detach himself from life to endure it. But it is Trigorin who is obsessed with his epitaph: Konstantin has a future. The most objective figure in the play, Doctor Dorn, appreciates the playlet best, when he sees that its fault is not its anti-materialism but its lack of direction.[2]

Unique in its discussion of literature, *The Seagull* is outstanding for its allusions to many other writers. The first, obviously, is Ibsen. By the Theatrical-Literary Committee that reluctantly passed the play for the Alexandrinsky Theatre in Petersburg, the title was assumed to be an alignment with Ibsen's *Wild Duck*. In the gratuitous way in which a dead seagull is picked up and Nina is associated with it we can see not just a parody of Ibsen, but a parody of Trigorin's way of poeticising the ugliness of reality. By casting Nina as a 'seagull', a victim, he soothes any guilt he may feel at having hurt a human being. The Petersburg committee, however, saw only 'preconceived and unnecessary Ibsenism'.

Hamlet is the play that figures most in *The Seagull*, even though Treplev's and Hamlet's deaths are not similar. Konstantin Treplev's resentment of his mother's lover and of her whole attitude to life, mingled with his touching dependence when Arkadina bandages his head for him, recall *Hamlet*. The device of provoking his mother to rage and guilt by a play, and the lines from *Hamlet* that he and Arkadina exchange before the play begins, all show how crucial was the influence of Shakespearean material. Most of Chekhov's prose up to 1895 quotes and ponders *Hamlet*. Time and time again, he uses Hamlet's line of bewilderment, when faced with the mystery of an actor merging with his role, 'What's Hecuba to him and he to Hecuba?' It is not just the Hamlet role of the Russian intellectual, torn between the State he hates and the people he stands above; it is Hamlet, bemused by art, tormented by sexuality, the lover of the sea, who is so close to Chekhov. *Hamlet* is not quite purged in *The Seagull*; Lopakhin parodies it in *The Cherry Orchard*, but it disappears from Chekhov's late prose. On a more general level, the complexity of *The Seagull*'s situations, with its network of unrequited love, like the extravagant plotting of *Three Sisters* (which has overtones of *Macbeth*) points to a Shakespearean influence. The influence is all the more remarkable when we consider how different are Shakespeare's and Chekhov's doctrines of nature.

The third of the avowed influences in the play is that of Maupassant. In Act 1 Treplev relates his horror at his mother's vulgar ideas of art to Maupassant's mad flight away from the Eiffel Tower that 'threatened to crush him with its vulgarity'. But Maupassant gets more than an affectionate tribute in *The Seagull*. In Act 2, Doctor Dorn is reading aloud to Arkadina and Masha, the daughter of the estate manager Shamrayev, but in the first version of the play the natural daughter of Doctor Dorn: the book he is reading turns out to be Maupassant's *On the Water*, a natural enough choice, being an account of a sailing trip along the Côte d'Azur, Arkadina's spiritual homeland, like Ranevskaya's in *The Cherry Orchard*. But suddenly Maupassant's comments begin to strike home and hit at the relationship between the ageing actress and her acquiescent lover, the writer. Arkadina, as always, is alert to danger and takes over the reading: 'and of course for people in society to cherish and attract novelists is just as dangerous as it is for a cornmerchant to raise rats in his stores. And yet they love them. Thus when a woman has set her mind on a writer she wants to adopt, she besieges him with compliments, kindnesses and treats.' Arkadina cannot let this pass: she argues that Russian women are different and fall in love themselves, as she has with Trigorin. But when Nina enters, Arkadina reads a few lines to herself and refuses to go on, changing the subject. The rest of Maupassant's paragraph is the truth that Arkadina cannot face. Perversely, Chekhov's point is in an excerpt at which he himself stops short.

Like water piercing the hardest rock drop by drop, praise falls word by word on the sensitive heart of the man of letters. Then, as soon as she sees him softened, moved, won over by this constant flattery, she isolates him, cuts bit by bit all his links that he might have elsewhere and, without his feeling it, gets him used to coming to her, to being at home there, installing his thoughts there.

For Chekhov this passage from Maupassant was a horrible warning. All his life, unlike Trigorin, he had cut short his love-life in order to avoid becoming the prisoner of a salon, or, as Maupassant puts it, 'the God of a church' whose priestess is his mistress. This is the fundamental difference between Trigorin and Chekhov.[3]

The weight of literary themes explains why Chekhov said, after writing *The Seagull*, 'the result is a story.' But it is theatrical in a very literal sense. Arkadina represents everything Chekhov felt was wrong in the old theatre. She is worshipped above all by her estate manager, Shamrayev, who can tyrannise over the estate while enthusing over the second-rate farces and melodrama in which Arkadina made her name. She loves the life of fame, of peregrination from hotel room to hotel room; her main characteristic, apart from her self-centredness, is her avarice. Her son is reduced to rags; her brother Sorin, whose estate is the play's setting, is too poor to pay for medical treatment, while Arkadina hoards her takings in an Odessa bank. Applause and money motivate the old theatre. But the new theatre, in the shape of Konstantin Treplev's amateur stage-effects (a remarkable anticipation of Stanislavsky's interest in evoking total atmosphere), does not win. Nina, abandoned by Trigorin, becomes an actress of the same kind as Arkadina. Full of stamina, intoxicated by the joy of acting, travelling third class from one provincial backwater to another, she is just as much a victim of the theatre as Katya in *A Dreary Story*. Only the carpentry of Konstantin Treplev's stage survives : the provincial theatre swallows up all the human talent.

All this points to the uniqueness of *The Seagull* in Chekhov's work. It seemed to the audience at the first night that this uniqueness was a sign of his hostility. The actors and producer were only partly to blame. They themselves were more Arkadinas than Ninas : they were used to farce, not to the indeterminate genre of Chekhovian comedy. They did not know their parts and they ruined the final effect of Konstantin's suicide : Doctor Dorn said that a bottle had been drunk (*lopnula*) instead of a phial of ether bursting (also *lopnula*) and the horrible anticipation of the news of the fatal shot was lost in general laughter. October 17, 1896 was one of the worst nights in Chekhov's life : he had sensed a conspiracy of reviewers who, at the end of the first act, were shouting out their contempt in the bar. But by showing a play so outspoken in its discontent with the theatre, so close to parody, so perverse in what it left unsaid, so obviously aimed at Petersburg's most conservative theatre, Chekhov must subconsciously have been asking for a showdown. He resolved never to write for the theatre again. He even held up the printing of *The Seagull* and *Uncle Vanya*. It was not until 1898 that the Moscow Arts Theatre, or rather those people in it, Nemirovich-Danchenko and Vishnevsky, whom Chekhov had known and trusted for nearly twenty years, persuaded him that the new theatre which could feel for and realise his work had arrived.

The Chekhovian peculiarities of *The Seagull* are present in its structure, its non-verbal effects, its characterisation, and its language. They are common to *Three Sisters* and *The Cherry Orchard*, and to *Uncle Vanya* as far as its deviations from *The Wood-demon* are concerned. The most obvious feature is the continuity. Scenes are abolished and acts flow on uninterrupted. The first act carries the bulk of the material and the climax is reached in the third act, in which Trigorin quarrels with Arkadina and gives Nina an assignation. *The Seagull* is still, however, more primitive than *Uncle Vanya*. The opening of Act 4 has a rather clumsy exposition to explain Nina's seduction and her return and, though it is muted, the act ends with a bang, rather than a whimper. Treplev's suicide is subtly plotted beforehand; it breaks inevitably into the final game of cards, but it is nonetheless conventional.

The non-verbal effects of *The Seagull* are less extreme than those of the later plays, where a town on fire or forty thousand cherry-trees create an almost cosmic, symbolic mood. But the lake, which separates Sorin's estate from Nina's house, and is the background of Treplev's play, has much of the poetry of the cherry-orchard, the same interconnection with the rising moon which tenses the atmosphere of Act 1 of *The Seagull* and Act 2 of *The Cherry Orchard*. The effects of Konstantin's play, the horn, the sulphur and the glowing red eyes, are effects that belong to Chekhov's prose. They recall the panpipes of 1887 and they anticipate the devil's eyes reflected in the windows of *An Incident in Practice*.

The sound-effects are fewer. Music in *The Seagull* is limited to a melancholy waltz in Act 4, and the incursion of time comes out only in the banging of the night-watchman. But the stage-properties are remarkable: all of them are Chekhov's possessions. A visitor to the Chekhov museum in Yalta will find the game of *loto* (bingo), the rifle, the revolver, the fishing-rods that play such a part in *The Seagull* among the very small collection of objects that Chekhov hung on to in his wanderings. These mundane properties, like the game of *loto*, are meant to create not just the illusion of normal trivial life, as people eat, drink and smoke their way through disaster, but a sort of counterpoint in which the line of action is set against the line of small talk and absurd incident, arousing that bemused, bewildered reaction, as quick as comedy and as long-lasting as tragedy, which is the intention of Chekhov's plays.

The characterisation of *The Seagull* provides material for the two last plays. Arkadina, in her indestructible love of life and her sexuality, anticipates Ranevskaya (though there are substantial differences). Her brother Sorin is, like Ranevskaya's brother Gayev, derided as 'an old woman', unable to control his estate. Though very different in their nature, Konstantin Treplev and Nina fill the same place in the scheme of the characters as do Trofimov and Anya in *The Cherry Orchard*: hopeful youth pitted against hopeless middle age. Doctor Dorn, who believes in no treatments and who hides his affections behind a screen of indifference, anticipates Doctor Chebutykin in *Three Sisters* in his cool, casual handling of death. His inventive 'a phial of ether has burst' is only a little less pathetic in its forced gaiety than Chebutykin's 'tarara-boom-de-ay'. Medvedenko, the schoolteacher in love with Masha, has all the stupidity and persistence of the teacher Kulygin, married to Masha of *Three Sisters*. Masha the daughter of Shamrayev, dressed in black with extravagant self-parody, anticipates Masha, also in black, of *Three Sisters*. Shamrayev, the employee who has somehow become the master, unaccountable, irrelevant and evil, looks ahead to Yepikhodov of *The Cherry Orchard*. The 'two hundredweight' of love, that Chekhov enjoyed loading the play with, makes *The Seagull*, in fact, more stylised than the later plays. A situation in which Arkadina loves Trigorin who fancies Nina (whom Treplev loves) while Masha loves Treplev, Medvedenko loves Masha, Polina Shamrayev loves Dorn (who admires Nina), stretches to absurdity the use of unrequited love as a generator of intrigue and comedy. The perversity of love, on the classical formula of A's love for B being in inverse proportion to B's love for A, is the comedy of *The Seagull*, a comedy which otherwise only flares up at individual moments. The individual comic moments are in fact as classical as they are in Molière : Arkadina giving a ruble to be divided among three servants, Nina's refusal to answer Treplev's questions, the sudden transitions in Treplev from infantile affection to proud hostility, the revelation of Trigorin's conceit when he cuts the pages of a magazine to read his own work, but not Treplev's—these are all moments when the mask of generosity, love or deference slips to reveal the miser, the infatuated lover, the child, or the egocentric monster.

If *The Seagull* is an experimental work, sometimes too aggressive, sometimes too timid, it is none the less one of the first great modern dramas. It is the first 'comedy' to take death in its stride : Nina's survival makes Treplev's death an accepted loss. The moral freedom of Ibsen and Hauptmann has found a new form that solves none of the questions, makes no divisions between good and evil, but leaves us with a feeling for the complexity and absurdity of life. For Chekhov's contemporaries, the Ibsenian morality was shocking enough. The censor found it intolerable that Sorin and Treplev should view Arkadina's affair with Trigorin with so much equanimity; that Nina recovers, and does not end as a stuffed monument to sin and love, like the seagull, also seemed to lack a sense of retribution. The flabby will of old Sorin, who prides himself on being *l'homme qui a voulu*, and lets his manager Shamrayev reverse the roles of ruler and servant, seemed to be a comment on the decline of the gentry which Chekhov had failed to follow up : critics felt it therefore lacked 'dramatic consequentiality'. Only Nemirovich-Danchenko in the Moscow Arts Theatre could see that the morality of love and social position was not the point of the play, which defended life against symbols, rules and explanations, humanity against divisions into major and minor characters, and the theatre against routine.

In 1898 the Moscow Arts Theatre made its name and Chekhov's reputation with *The Seagull*. It is a symbiosis unusual in the history of the theatre. The very name of the theatre, known by its capital letters of MKhAT, caught on as a synonym for the theatre as art dedicated to life. (*MKhAT* is also the Georgian stem for *mkhatvari* meaning 'artist', which helped to fix the name.) The dominance of director over actors, the idea that the part should project out of the play so that the actor entered into his role as a new personality to be lived from birth to death in every trivial action, the stress on realistic stage effects, largely—but not altogether—fell in with what Chekhov was trying to do.

The association of Chekhov with MKhAT was closest in the preparation and staging of *Three Sisters*, which was specifically conceived for the theatre early in 1899, and written with great care and difficulty in summer and autumn 1900. Detail after detail of its complex plot and language was settled in consultation with the actors and with Nemirovich-Danchenko. For the first time in his life, Chekhov could be sure of a sympathetic interpretation: he had known Nemirovich-Danchenko for nearly twenty years, the actor Vishnevsky who played the school-teacher Kulygin was a Taganrog class-mate, and Ol'ga Knipper, who played Masha, was soon to be his wife. The resulting production mystified the critics: the very complexity of the play, in which each character expresses a self-sufficient philosophy of life, and its relationship to *The Seagull* and *Uncle Vanya*, left them bereft of reactions. But the audiences greeted the play with enthusiasm: while it is one of Chekhov's most symbolic and complex works, it is also his most direct and most emotional treatment of life. It gave MKhAT an ascendancy it still has not lost, and, in a variety of appalling translations, made Chekhov a progenitor of modern European drama.

Unlike *The Seagull* or *The Cherry Orchard*, but like *Ivanov*, *Three Sisters* is a drama, not a comedy. Chekhov felt that his subtitles were important, though he did not enlarge on them; nevertheless, drama implies compassion: the sisters are, like all comic villains, superfluous. Death in *Three Sisters* is a blow struck by evil against good; in the comedies it is absurd, supererogatory. There is much comedy and more absurdity in *Three Sisters*, but its lyricism, its complaints and its finale lack the irony and self-deceit which are integral to comedy.

The basic material of *Three Sisters* is comic. Three young women, stranded in the provinces, dreaming of Moscow, the metropolis, seizing on anyone they can take to be an emissary of Moscow, yet act by act receding from their dream—this is the basis of a *Précieuses ridicules*. Kulygin, the Latin teacher, and Natasha, the predatory bourgeoise, are likewise comic characters who would be at home in *Les Femmes savantes*. But lyricism, the natural goodness which, as nowhere else in Chekhov, imbues so many characters and the author's compassion differentiate *Three Sisters* from the comedies (*The Seagull* and *The Cherry Orchard*). Comedy is a question not so much of material or even themes, but of tone : in comedy 'common sense' satirises eccentricity. *Three Sisters* has none of the common sense of *The Seagull*'s Doctor Dorn or *Uncle Vanya*'s Astrov. All its characters are eccentric; none is wholly comic.

A quarter longer than the other late plays, *Three Sisters* is in its structure the most complex of Chekhov's works. The characters make for a multiple structure, in which Muscovites—the three sisters, the artillery officers Vershinin and Tuzenbakh—are opposed to the provincials of the remote northern town—Natasha, Kulygin and, off-stage, Protopopov. Brought to the town by their father, the sisters are stranded there when he dies, a year before Act 1. Act by act, the provincial reality triumphs over the dream of returning to Moscow. The eldest sister Ol'ga is more and more embroiled with her career in school-teaching; Masha, the middle sister, is married to the provincial pedant, Kulygin; in the final act, Irina's suitor Tuzenbakh, who was to take her to a new life, is killed in a duel. For a while their brother Andrey hovers between the two worlds; by Act 2 he has married Natasha and given up his ambition of being a Moscow professor and his love of the violin in favour of a job on the town council and playing cards. Act 1 brings into the lives of the characters Lieutenant-Colonel Vershinin, who knew them as children in Moscow, and appears as an emissary from another world. But in the final act, the battery is posted elsewhere and all contact with Moscow is broken. The provinces triumph : Natasha has reduced Andrey to a dummy and has ousted the sisters room by room from the house, filling it with her babies and her vile and vicious presence. The tree imagery that played such a part in the opening lines of the play is resumed in Natasha's last lines, 'I'll have that fir avenue chopped down and then this maple . . . It's so ugly in the evenings.' Philistinism has destroyed beauty. The revenge is subtly underlined in the play's symmetry. In Act 1, Ol'ga tells Natasha that she is wrong to wear a green belt with a pink dress; in Act 4 Natasha tells Irina that her belt is 'in bad taste'.

The play not only contrasts beautiful Muscovite life with the ugly life of the provinces, it is also a contrast of male and female and of civilian and military. All three sisters, differentiated by age and temperament as they are, have a feminine strength and persistence : they make a myth out of Moscow, to give their life purpose.

None of them can tolerate the idea that life may be meaningless, love hopeless, or people inhuman : to keep reality at bay, they are prepared to lie to themselves. Ol'ga persists in thinking she will not become headmistress (but she does); Masha has a bitter-sweet affair with Vershinin (who leaves with the army); Irina accepts Tuzenbakh, whom she does not love, in the perennial hope of 'a new life'. The men, however, propound philosophies which, though varying, all admit defeat. Tuzenbakh worships work as an opiate, a preparation for posterity's happiness; Vershinin preaches stoicism. But for both of them, we realise, the philosophy itself is less important than its effect on the woman to whom they are appealing for sympathy. In other characters, philosophy becomes horrific : Solyony, who operates on a human plane as a shy misfit and on a symbolic plane as death incarnate, propounds nothing but idiocy, cruelty and irony. Doctor Chebutykin, the father-figure to the three sisters and the god of the play on a symbolic plane, wills himself to believe that all reality is an illusion and by Act 4 is so successful that he can officiate at the killing of Tuzenbakh and sing 'tarara-boom-de-ay' when he breaks the news to Irina, of whom he is so fond. The women affirm life—poetically, like the sisters, or brutally, like Natasha; the men reject it, like Vershinin, who talks of his unhappy mad wife and little girls only to make himself more poetic, or Solyony, who mocks and kills.

It is the military who bring poetry into the play; not since *The Kiss* of 1887 or *The Duel* of 1891 had Chekhov used the army in this way. Their uniform and their self-confidence give them an illusory vitality : they dance, joke and respond in such a way that much of the play, particularly the first half of Act 2, has a ballet-like choreography. In the words of Kulygin's Latin tags—which provide epigraphs for the acts—*omnia mea mecum porto* : the military have a world of their own that they carry with them. The fire that dominates Act 3 destroys them : Rode and Fedotik have their camera and guitar burnt, Vershinin's hands are blackened, and the news of the soldiers' departure is broached. Act 4, as in *Uncle Vanya* and *The Cherry Orchard*, is a prolonged farewell : the military depart leaving the town to the colourless desolation of the civilians. The three sisters are left to the tender mercies of Natasha and the good-natured stupidity of Kulygin, both glad to see the army leave.

Over these scenes of desertion, betrayal and disillusion, Chebutykin reigns like a god. We learn that he was in love with the three sisters' mother : his affection for Irina, the youngest, is almost that of a putative father. (In this, he resembles Dorn of *The Seagull* who, it is hinted, is Masha's father.) Chebutykin sees everything that comes to hurt the sisters, presides over it, and does not intervene. He is a god who is obsessed by absurdity, a collector of irrelevant information, an accidental killer of his only patient : his love is cruel and useless.

The only one of Chekhov's plays to be set in a town, *Three Sisters* uses much of Chekhov's provincial-town material. Kulygin, the Latin teacher, in his sycophancy, 'in case anything might happen', is a transposition of Belikov in *The Man in a Case*. The contrast between Natasha and the three sisters is the contrast between the predator and her prey so common in Chekhov's late prose. Even her green belt links her with the imagery of green that connotes death, for example the green dress and eyes of the killer Aksin'ya in *In the Gully*. The avenue of firs and the maple that are doomed in Act 4, like the birches in Act 1, are to give way to Natasha's flowerbeds : a contrast of noble trees and ignoble flowerbeds that we can see in *The House with the Mezzanine* and the unfinished *Ruin of the Compensation*. Like Startsev in *Ionych*, Andrey degenerates scene by scene, getting fatter and more ill-tempered as the bourgeois world envelops him; like Chekhov's late heroines, the three sisters lose their accomplishments : Masha stops playing the piano, Irina forgets her Italian : schoolteaching or marriage degrades the heroine. The philosophising of Vershinin and Tuzenbakh takes over the arguments of N. and Lida in *The House with the Mezzanine* and of Misail and Blagovo in *My Life*. Tuzenbakh's thirst for manual work, his 'dropping-out' from his barony and his army career, his naïve, slow-witted goodness are Misail's; Vershinin's brief affair with Masha and his desertion of her for his career, his indifference to the present and speculations about the future are Blagovo's.

The situation and characterisation of *Three Sisters* make it a bridge from *The Seagull* and *Uncle Vanya* to *The Cherry Orchard*. Doctor Chebutykin is the main span of the bridge : he abjures medicine, as does Dorn and, to a lesser extent, Astrov; he presides over Tuzenbakh's death like Dorn over Treplev's suicide. His paternal involvement, like Dorn's, is useless. It is inevitable that the doctor-figure should fail to appear in *The Cherry Orchard*, when he persuades himself that he does not exist in *Three Sisters*. Like Astrov, Chebutykin drinks. But while Astrov watches time pass, Chebutykin smashes it : in Act 3, the most destructive of all Chekhov's third acts, Chebutykin breaks the porcelain clock and with it the sisters' hopes that time is not yet past.

Of the three sisters, Ol'ga belongs to the strong women of Chekhov's prose. Masha, however, dressed in black, is the same desperate, forward woman as the Masha of *The Seagull*, whose black dress opens the play. In *The Cherry Orchard*, with its sterility, the black-dressed Varya is to inherit only the tearfulness and the alternation between dream and protest that Masha Prozorova exhibits. Irina develops the poetry of aspiration and the stamina of Nina in *The Seagull*; *The Cherry Orchard* reduces her to Anya, whose white dress and dependence on Trofimov's rhetoric are but a shadow of Irina's beauty and yearning.

Like the sisters, the men of *The Cherry Orchard* become hollow echoes : Trofimov is Tuzenbakh minus love and dignity, Yepikhodov is Solyony reduced from a devil to a petty demon. Uniform gives the men of *Three Sisters* a strength unique in Chekhov's late heroes : Treplev becomes Tuzenbakh and, minus the bandages, plus a uniform or a Homburg hat, is made tragic, rather than pathetic.

The servants, the old nurse Anfisa and the senile messenger Ferapont, take the material of *Uncle Vanya* (in which Chekhov introduced the old nurse Marina as an image of stability) half-way to *The Cherry Orchard*, in which the elderly Firs and the young man-servant Yasha parody the old and new aspects of their masters' world. Like Firs, Anfisa is a victim of the new bourgeois : but unlike *The Cherry Orchard*, *Three Sisters* does not use the servants' world as a sub-plot.

In structure, *Three Sisters* encompasses a greater span in time and setting than any other of Chekhov's plays. Time plays a more important part in its themes and symbolism : it operates not over seasons, as in *Uncle Vanya* and *The Cherry Orchard*, which take us from early summer to autumn, but over years. Anniversaries as well as clocks, successive children as well as changing foliage, remind us of the time. Act 1 in itself gives us the sense of time past : we know the exact date, 5 May, Irina's birthday, a year after the death of father Prozorov and eleven years after the 'fall', the departure from Moscow. The trees still in bud so late tell us the latitude of the town. At the very beginning the clock strikes twelve,

to set the hour and end the spell cast over the sisters. Time flows
so strongly that it has to be arrested. In the last part of Act 1, Rode
and Fedotik, two junior officers, hold it up : they 'freeze' the
characters on stage by photographing them.

Act 2 has the same scene—the hall and dining-room of the Prozorov house—so that the changes we see can do nothing but remind
us of time moving. The fact that it is *maslenitsa* (the Russian equiva-
lent of *mardi gras*) and that Natasha has married, given birth and
started an affair with Andrey's boss Protopopov, in the shortest
physically possible time, gives a sense of calamity. All the events of
one act are mirrored in the next, distorted only by time : Andrey's
violin gives way to cards; Vershinin's wife, mentioned in Act 1,
takes poison in Act 2. Irina is deprived of her bedroom by Natasha's
first baby in Act 2. In Act 3, a year later, Ol'ga and Irina are
asked to move yet again for the next baby; in Act 4 Ol'ga has had
to take a flat of her own. Each act shows us a succession of couples :
Andrey and Natasha followed by Masha and Vershinin, then by
Irina and Tuzenbakh. The symmetry and spacing show us time
altering and breaking the couples. Andrey and Natasha move from
love to domesticity to disillusion and finally to total ruination; Masha
and Vershinin from temptation to happiness and heartbreak; Irina
and Tuzenbakh from enthusiasm to unequal love and death.

As Chekhov stated in 1889, Act 3 is the lynch-pin : it is dominated by a fire burning in the town, which destroys not only the
stage properties—the guitar and camera of Acts 1 and 2, the porcelain clock—but the last illusions. Set by firelight and at early dawn,
at three in the morning, stage-time runs methodically at exactly twice
real time : at every moment of *Three Sisters* we know the hour. Act
4, an aftermath to the 'restless night', is also timed at twice real
time : taking thirty minutes to act, it begins at noon (like Act 1),
notes the death of Tuzenbakh by an off-stage shot at 12.30 and
ends at 1 p.m. Chebutykin's last remnant of godhood is his counting of time : while Vershinin and Tuzenbakh talk of life in two or
three hundred years, Rode and Fedotik of life in ten or fifteen
years, Chebutykin watches the minutes to death and departure.
Time creates the tension and the pathos, without which the tragic
element would be impossible. The essence of tragic drama is that
we are held not by the question *whether*, but by the question *when*
the sacrificial victim will die.

It is not just the situation which is mirrored from act to act.

Three Sisters has an elaborate system of images that operates with the symmetry and self-sufficiency of a set of symbols. The image of trees that opens and closes the play is part of this symbolic plane: the trees that symbolise regeneration, the natural cycle, are to be chopped down. Likewise, the image of migratory birds runs through the play. Tuzenbakh dwells on the image in Act 2, and at the end of Act 4 Masha repeats it with the romantic image 'the cranes are flying', as does Chebutykin, who calls himself a migratory bird too old to fly. It is an image first of transient generations in the history of man and then of stranded humanity in a hostile world.

'To Moscow' is the most memorable refrain in *Three Sisters*. Uttered by Irina, echoed by the others, it is a dream which becomes more remote and intense with each act. It becomes an image of human aspirations for the Eden of their childhood, the Kingdom of God. Vershinin is loved because he is a Messiah, albeit false. Moscow is the measure of all : when the birches are in bud, Moscow, Ol'ga recalls, is in blossom. As the town overcomes the sisters, Moscow becomes more absurd : the dream breaks up into an argument between Andrey and Solyony on how many universities Moscow has, into Ferapont's senile talk of a rope stretched over Moscow, or a frost that killed thousands there.

Much of the symbolic and non-verbal plane is common to Chekhov's other works : the contrast of Irina in white and Masha in black is to be repeated in *The Cherry Orchard* with Varya and Anya. The howling of the stove that Masha hears as an omen of disaster is a folklore superstition in many works; in Act 1, there are thirteen at table, with Solyony as a Judas—a superstition that plays its part in *My Life*.

The guitar that runs as a counterpoint to so many of Chekhov's speeches is, in *Three Sisters*, burnt up. Music takes other, more serious, forms : if Ol'ga's and Irina's final laments seem more moving, it is because they are accompanied by a military band. They become an operatic *Sprachgesang*, instead of pathetic speeches broken up by Telegin's guitar-strumming (in *Uncle Vanya*) or the discordant jangling of an intimidated Jewish orchestra (Act 3 of *The Cherry Orchard*). *Three Sisters* reverberates with music : Masha whistles, Andrey plays the violin in Act 1; Act 2 has a harmonica, a guitar and Anfisa's songs. Only in the fire of Act 3 is there silence. Act 4, with 'The Maiden's Prayer' on the piano, the wandering

minstrels' harp and violin, and the band playing the army out of
town, uses music as much as speech to convey pathos.

Language, too, functions musically. At one extreme we have
the prose-poetry of the dreaming sisters, full of imagery of trees and
birds; at the other extreme we have isolated words and phrases
void of relevance or meaning. One example is the argument between Chebutykin and Solyony on *cheremsha* (wild garlic) and
chekhartma (a Georgian soup). It is not only a traditional *non
sequitur* comic joke: the words themselves are on the periphery
of the audience's vocabulary. Then Kulygin tells his story of a pupil
who read *chepukha* (nonsense) as if in Latin script, *renixa*: a meaningless word that reverberates in Chebutykin's mind, making him
mutter 'nonsense, *renixa*' as a commentary. Solyony's mocking, hen-
like 'cheep, cheep, cheep' is yet another example of language re-
fusing to work, turning against its users. Much of the language is
collage: *Three Sisters* is full of quotation. Some of it comes from
Chebutykin's newspapers—recipes for restoring hair, sentences such
as 'smallpox is raging in Tsitsivkar' and 'Balzac was married in
Berdichev.' This extends the technique of Uncle Vanya's map of
Africa: what is apparently absurd takes on a symbolic relevance.
The African heat mirrors the hell of Vanya's life: Balzac in Berdichev mirrors the sisters in Perm'; the smallpox raging in Tsitsivkar
symbolises the anguish raging among the Prozorovs.

Quotations come from literature, too. It is one of Pushkin's most
magical passages, the opening of *Ruslan and Lyudmila*, that Masha
uses like a rosary in extreme anguish. Solyony alludes to Pushkin's
Gypsies, the hero of which is, like him, a murderer, and models himself on Lermontov's fatal hero, Pechorin. Popular song runs through
the play: Vershinin and Chebutykin sing snatches of love-song:
Masha and Vershinin express their love in a wordless refrain, 'tram-
tam-tam', 'ta-ta-ta'. Chebutykin composes one of Chekhov's rare
rhyming verses, 'Tara-ra-bum-di-ya/Sizhu na tumbe ya' ('Ta-ra-ra
boom-deay/I'm sitting on a flowerbed') at the death of Tuzenbakh.
Articulate language cannot cope.

There are, despite the play's originality, still Shakespearean allu-
sions: Solyony sprinkles his cadaverous hands with perfume like
Lady Macbeth, and Natasha walks by during the fire like Lady
Macbeth. But the literary echoes are far more subdued than in
The Seagull: *Three Sisters* is not experimental, but self-sufficient
in its composition.

The use of stage properties is extended. Knowing Stanislavsky's love of elaborate effects, Chekhov provides for especially complicated sets: the living-rooms of the Prozorov house, followed by a bedroom from which the town can be seen burning, and a finale set in a garden with terrace, access to the house, a river, trees, the military in the background. The stage is cluttered with objects, each of which contributes to the symbolism: the gifts of flowers, penknives, a humming-top, samovar, sweets, show the compassionate paternalism of the officers towards Irina. A fork in Act 1 is banged by Masha to show her dominant energy: in Act 4, Natasha waves it in the air as an excuse to bully the servants. There is a washstand where Chebutykin can wash his hands of the sisters, like Pontius Pilate; there are cognac and champagne as ironic comments on the anguish and sadness. A candle symbolises both Natasha's meanness (like Zinaida Lebedev's in *Ivanov*) and her ominous perambulations. Fretwork picture-frames show Andrey's boyish creativity in Act 1; a pram demonstrates his enslavement in Act 4.

Three Sisters is a rare example of author and theatre in close contact. But the closeness was not perfect: any reading of Chekhov's letters shows that he was sceptical about Stanislavsky, who was determined to re-create reality, physical and emotional, on the stage, whereas Chekhov always knew that the stage world must be artificial. To Chekhov, Stanislavsky often seemed stupid in his failure to see comedy in the midst of tragedy, naïve in his elaborate staging and 'like a young merchant' in his full-blooded acting. What mattered to Chekhov was that Stanislavsky tried at least to subordinate the play to the text, the actors to the direction: but the results often displeased Chekhov, as his reactions to performances of *Uncle Vanya* and *The Cherry Orchard* show.

Even though much of its structure and content seems a hybrid of *The Seagull* and *Three Sisters*, *The Cherry Orchard* is a different play from Chekhov's other works in its links with his prose, particularly that of 1887. Like *The Bishop* and the other last prose pieces it has connections with the steppe stories. The panpipes that play at the close of Act 1 express the same sorrow for lost harmony as they do in *Panpipes* of 1887; the breaking string is the same broken mine-cable as in *Fortune*. The cherry-blossom flowers in the stories of 1887 and 1889, in the first section of *The Literature Teacher*, for example. The other unique quality of *The Cherry Orchard* is in its ghostly emptiness: there is no doctor, no love and no death

H

(barring the final collapse of the old servant, Firs). Without death or love there can be little tragedy or drama. The play justifies its title of 'comedy', which Stanislavsky could not comprehend, because its characters cannot or will not understand what is happening—one of the distinctions between comedy and tragedy. There are more tears than in *Three Sisters*. The heroine, Ranevskaya, returning from her lover in Paris to her estate in Russia, her daughter Anya and her ward Varya, her old woman of a brother, Gayev, their neighbour Simeonov-Pishchik—all cry: but they cry for the wrong reasons, at the wrong time. The music of the play does not harmonise with their tears: the ball in Act 3 is a series of quadrilles and waltzes of comic irrelevance.

The Cherry Orchard, according to Stanislavsky, was planned during the rehearsals of *Three Sisters*; some of the material, especially the half-German waif Charlotta, came to Chekhov while he was staying with Stanislavsky. MKhAT waited two and a half years for the play to materialise and even then could not cope with it. Stanislavsky forced Chekhov to cut from Act 2 a beautiful scene of Firs rummaging by moonlight for a lost purse, muttering nonsense, while Charlotta sings. Chekhov had to write to actors individually, explaining his conception of their parts. Much of his irritation with the production can be explained as the impatience of a dying man, but he had grounds for accusing both Nemirovich-Danchenko and Stanislavsky of 'not having read my play properly once': they refused to print 'comedy' on the posters and put 'drama'. Only the young Meyerkhol'd, who had not yet split away to form his own theatre, saw that the play had to be realised by non-realistic techniques if its symbolism and its comedy were to emerge.

The Cherry Orchard not only requires for full appreciation a knowledge of Chekhov's other plays and of the prose of 1887 which, in 1901 and 1902, he was revising for his Collected Works: it is also related to his late prose. The story of 1898, *A Visit to Friends*, prefigures the situation. Like the cherry orchard, the estate of Kuz'-minki is to be auctioned and the family that owns it can neither face up to the fact nor fight it. Instead, the mistress of the house tries to engineer a wedding between the hero Podgorin and her daughter, just as Ranevskaya tries to force a wedding between Lopakhin, who is to buy the estate at the auction, and her ward, Varya. In detail, *A Visit to Friends* anticipates the play: as in Act 3 of the play, there is a party in which the quadrille is danced and in which the distraught hostess begs her visitor to advise her. Her speech, 'I swear to you by everything holy, by the happiness of my children, I can't bear life without Kuz'minki! I was born here, it's my nest, if they take it away, I won't survive, I'll die of despair' anticipates Ranevskaya's words to Trofimov, 'I was born here, this is where my father and grandfather lived . . . I can't understand my life without the cherry orchard.' In a nocturnal scene, the hero of *A Visit to Friends* exchanges phrases that Trofimov and Anya are to use in Act 2 as the moon rises. Much of the character of the eternal student, Trofimov, was being created at the same time as that of Sasha, hero of *The Bride*. Sasha denounces the provincial household, whose luxury is based on exploitation and dirt, in the same words as Trofimov, upbraiding the inhabitants for their eating, drinking and philosophising, uses in Act 2 of the play.

The characterisation of *The Cherry Orchard* is developed from *The Seagull*. Ranevskaya, like Arkadina, is a sensual middle-aged woman, easily bored with life on her brother's estate, interfering with her ward's life as Arkadina does with Nina's. Gayev, like Sorin, is an old woman of a landowner, void of willpower, but while the disabled Sorin still has dignity, Gayev is comic: his rhetoric embarrasses his listeners, his declarations of hope are made with a boiled sweet blocking his mouth. Only under this cover of senility can Chekhov slip into Gayev's speeches the few words of sense in the play. It is Gayev who says that 'if a disease has many treatments, then it must be incurable', using almost verbatim a sentence that Chekhov had put in a postscript to a letter of seventeen years before. It is Gayev who objects to Trofimov's vision of human progress, 'All the same, you'll die', and thus takes on some of the depth of Sorin. Varya's dreams of a nunnery, Anya's vision of a new life serving mankind and reading to her mother make them comic: Chekhov said that he intended them to be respectively a 'cry-baby' and a 'silly girl'. A few phrases link Ranevskaya with Yelena of *Uncle Vanya*: both are sensual women and, bored with the men around them, they turn on them, saying, 'How grey your lives are.' Here, however, the male has abdicated even more definitely than in the earlier plays. Trofimov dispises sexual love: Lopakhin has no time for it; Gayev is too fastidious ever to have considered it. It all makes Ranevskaya's sensuality like a volcano in Iceland. In *The Cherry Orchard* only the trees arouse a response: they fill the first act with whiteness, scent and birdsong; in them Ranevskaya sees the ghost of her mother, and Trofimov hears the voices of the serfs who have worked there. Only in Act 3, while the owners dance their way to perdition, are the trees ignored : Act 4 is punctuated by the axe chopping at their trunks. Humanity is dead in *The Cherry Orchard* : the characters are ghosts in their tenuousness or sub-human in their grotesquerie. Only the trees are alive and, if there is tragedy in the play, nature is the tragic hero.

The structure of *The Cherry Orchard*, like that of *Uncle Vanya*, takes us from summer to autumn. Its imagery, however, of May blossom in Act 1 and autumn leaves and chopped trees in Act 4, is reminiscent of *Three Sisters*. As in *Three Sisters*, time is para-mount : the date of the auction, which takes place during the ball in Act 3 ; the anniversary of the death of Ranevskaya's son ; Lopa-khin's constant looking at his watch ; the counting of the minutes before the arrival and departure of the train which brings and re-moves the cast—everything drives home the passage of time. In the disposition of the characters, *The Cherry Orchard* is largely typical. As in *The Seagull* and *Uncle Vanya*, the estate is disrupted by the arrival of the heroine (Arkadina, Yelena Andreyevna or Ranevs-kaya) ; two girls, here Varya and Anya, present an opposition of active and passive, black and white in dress. The manager of the estate has become its tyrant : Yepikhodov is only a pure grotesque version of Borkin (*Ivanov*) or Shamrayev. The life of the heroine is denounced by Trofimov in terms like those of Tuzenbakh, Treplev or Astrov.

Much of the plotting, too, parallels the earlier plays. Money, the auction of the estate, is the mainspring of the action, just as in *Platonov*, or in the attempt to sell the estate in *The Wood-demon* and in *Uncle Vanya*, or Andrey's misappropriation of the three sisters' inheritance, or Arkadina's miserly treatment of her son and brother. Act 2 of *The Cherry Orchard*, set in a forgotten grave-yard as the moon rises is, despite its ghostly quality when Trofimov senses the souls speaking in the trees, the same 'restless night' as Act 2 of *Uncle Vanya*, Act 3 of *Three Sisters*, or Act 1 of *The Seagull*. As throughout Chekhov's work, the febrile moonlight releases the conflicting passions of the characters. Stanislavsky complained that the final act of *The Cherry Orchard* was reminiscent of *Uncle Vanya*, with a stage littered with luggage, and an impatient ex-pectancy of the end, all action spent. It also echoes Act 4 of *Three Sisters*. The same Russian cry of 'Au !' (cooee) echoes offstage from

Trofimov as from the minor officers, hurrying the actors away; the same bottle of champagne tries in vain to turn a wake into a party.

While many of the stage properties of *The Cherry Orchard*, such as the champagne and the cards, and many of its trivia, such as the observation of temperature and weather, remind us of the earlier plays, there are some radical differences. First of all, it is a play of intruders: Lopakhin, the peasant turned businessman, who befriends and betrays his former masters by buying their estate, is a thrusting force, quite new in Chekhov's drama. We meet him in prose, as Dolzhikov, the forceful, heavy-drinking railway engineer in *My Life*, the incarnation of a sociological force. Lopakhin is more subtle than Dolzhikov: dreaming of an idyllic new life growing out of his demolition of the orchard, unable to propose marriage to Varya, he is cut off from reality and as sexless as Trofimov or Gayev. There are other intruders: the drunken coughing beggar who passes through Act 2, and Yepikhodov, who not only mismanages the estate, but also gatecrashes the ball in Act 3 and passes in the background in Act 2, have a frightening quality as strong as that of the triumphant Lopakhin breaking the chairs and stamping on the floor at the end of Act 3.

These intruders take over the estate: Yepikhodov, the estate's office-keeper, is the only member of the household whom Lopakhin keeps on. Yepikhodov, barely in command of human language, lapsing into obscene malapropisms—'Allow me to copulate to you', crushing suitcases, burbling of revolvers, cockroaches and spiders, walking like Satan to and fro across the stage, is a spirit of evil far more horrible than Borkin or Solyony, who still have a semblance of humanity: they can communicate. *The Cherry Orchard* also has its strays: the comic neighbour, Simeonov-Pishchik, with his Gogolian name and equine appearance, and the waif Charlotta, with no real name or papers, are all that is left of good, natural human beings, flotsam in the wreckage of the estate. They have no real precedent in Chekhov's work.

The servants of *The Cherry Orchard* are even more unusual: they present a parody of their masters. Ranevskaya's manservant, Yasha, is, like her, now tied to France; the maid, Dunyasha, mimics her mistress's passionate nature; the rivalry of Yepikhodov and Yasha for Dunyasha is all that is left of love. Only Firs, senile, wise and nostalgic, continues the image of the servant begun by *Uncle*

Vanya's Marina and *Three Sisters*' Anfisa; but while Marina and Anfisa survive the catastrophe, Firs is left locked in the house to deliver the only moral indictment in late Chekhov: 'They've forgotten the man.'

The presence of evil and, thus, of a moral is striking. It is suddenly manifested in Act 4, when Ranevskaya announces that she is taking all the money left to spend on herself and her lover in France. Evil and morality are hinted at in the ominous irruptions at the ball of Act 3, in a way that was far clearer to Chekhov's contemporaries in Russia than to us. This ball is extraordinary for three reasons. Firstly it is conceived even more operatically than the last moments of *Three Sisters;* a flute, four fiddles and a double-bass play for two-thirds of the time, reducing speech to fragments uttered by pairs of dancers. This fragmentation of the dialogue and the action is not only more realistic, it also makes for surreality. The second peculiarity of the Act is the appearance of extraordinary guests— the postmaster, the stationmaster, and a figure in a top-hat and checked trousers, to which Stanislavsky added the figures of the Jewish musicians. Horrified vulgarity, *poshlost'*, makes for yet more absurdity. The third and most important aspect of Act 3 is the quotation of a poem, *The Sinning Woman*, by the late-romantic poet A. K. Tolstoy. It does not matter that the stationmaster recites only the first few lines: in Chekhov's day the poem was notorious. It is a long poem about a courtesan who boasts she can seduce anyone, even Christ: John the Baptist enters; she mistakes him for Christ and starts charming him; then the real Christ appears and the sinning woman is overcome with repentance. This is a poem that Chekhov refers to on several occasions in his work of the early 1880s; here it is a sign not only of provincial taste, but also of a guest's tactlessness toward his hostess. Most important, it is a warning of the intrusion of Lopakhin into Ranevskaya's world and of the catastrophe to come that will silence her gaiety for all time. It is the most subtle and, unfortunately, the most ephemeral of Chekhov's literary allusions.

Symbolist criticism,[4] in particular Andrey Bely's appreciation of the play in 1904, made much of the Gogolian horror—the dancing and pretences, the doom breaking through the merriment—to show that *The Cherry Orchard* was a Symbolist work. Chekhov might have been horrified to read Bely, but he is not the first Symbolist *malgré lui*. The symbols of *The Cherry Orchard* are not

so profuse as those of *Three Sisters*, but they are more dominant.
The first is the cherry trees. Outside the 'nursery' of Act 1 and
Act 4 they provoke the action within. In Act 2, they seem to look
with human eyes and speak with human voices. They are as animate
as the characters are fossilised: this reversal of animate and inanimate is one of the most common devices of Symbolist poetry.
Offstage sounds do not become irritants or intensifiers of action,
as they do in *Uncle Vanya*: they have a meaning of their own
that the characters cannot understand. The breaking string of Act 2
and Act 4 produces only ludicrous comment: Gayev thinks it is a
heron, Trofimov a screech-owl. Lopakhin identifies it as a mine-
cable snapping—as did Chekhov when he first used the effect in
Fortune (1887)—but the symbolism of death lurking underground
is lost on the cast. The music of the play (Yepikhodov's guitar, the
ball and its quadrilles, waltzes and its final cacophony) does not
orchestrate the action: it suggests a world utterly divorced from
reality. The unreality is at its greatest in Gayev's constant talk and
miming of snooker, giving his appearances, together with his sweet-
sucking, his trance-like speeches, something not comic, not grotesque,
but unearthly. The breaking string ('dying away, melancholy' Chekhov describes it) is only one of the many symbolic breakages in the
play. Dunyasha smashes a saucer, Ranevskaya spills all her coins,
Yepikhodov breaks a billiard cue and a hatbox, the thermometer
which registers the unseasonable cold of Act 1 is broken by Act 4.
A universe is disintegrating.

In Russia, as in France, Symbolism and decadence are inseparable: if decadence means a refining of the senses to the point of
hypertrophy, then Ranevskaya and Gayev are decadent. They hear
sounds which Lopakhin cannot hear. Ranevskaya sees ghosts that
Varya and Anya cannot see. Above all they can smell. *The Cherry
Orchard* is full of almost unstageable aromas: Gayev is struck by
that of patchouli in Act 1, Ranevskaya by cheap cigars in Act 2; to
Gayev, Yasha smells of chicken; in Act 3, at the moment of catastrophe, Gayev passes a package of anchovies and herring to Firs.
True decadents, they have rejected reality for a specialised dream-
world of their own. The dream-world is only enhanced by such
tricks as Charlotta's ventriloquism, echoes of sound to which one
must add the peculiar repetition of odd phrases, such as '*Yepikhodov
idyot*' (Yepikhodov is walking), by one character after another.

The Symbolist quality of *The Cherry Orchard* leads us to see its

natural successors in drama in Blok's *Neznakomka* (*The Stranger*)
or the plays of Pinter and Beckett, rather than in the psychological
drama often credited with Chekhovian qualities. Chekhov may have
been unimpressed by the achievements of Russian Symbolists—he
had read Gippius, Merezhkovsky and Solovyov—but he had every
respect for Maeterlinck and, in fact, an understanding of *The Cherry
Orchard* or *Three Sisters* would be incomplete without an assess-
ment of its similarities to such plays as *Les Aveugles*. When Trofimov
talks of the 'sense and aim of life' as being as tricky as Chekhov's
philosophers, or conjures up *schast'ye* (happiness, fortune) imminent
and elusive, as in the story *Schast'ye* of 1887, he proves to be just
as much a false prophet as the leader of Maeterlinck's blind men.
While it is wrong to classify *The Cherry Orchard* as a Symbolist
play, it is worth bearing in mind that, like Chekhov's very last prose
pieces, it is a work in which the dream of the past or the future
protects one from the ravages of a merciless reality. Chekhov's
vision of reality is not entirely foreign to the decadent's nightmare
and rejection.

The Cherry Orchard is not only Chekhov's last play: it is also
his last work. Its frail world, old and genteel, into which a nightmarish, brutal reality irrupts, full of omens of pogrom and demolition, provides us with the most extreme confrontation in Chekhov's
work between two realities—nature's and the hero's, the past and the
future, active and passive. The play takes on its full meaning when
we consider the amount of material it has in common with the rest
of Chekhov's drama: the 'closed box' setting, the musical accompaniment, the outside noises, the stage properties, the 'types' that
underlie many of the characters, the disintegration of a household,
the techniques of one dialogue interrupting another, the imagery—
all to be found in more or less embryonic form in *Platonov* twenty
years before. The material and structural unity in Chekhov's drama
and stories naturally leads us to seek a deeper unity in their philosophy and their poetics. As in the stories, the difficulty to be
encountered here is in fact the answer. We find that it is easy to
define the technique, the components and the mood of Chekhov's
plays and yet that their final import eludes us. The plays do not
build up to a message: their structure strips, rather than imposes,
ideas. We lose, as the characters lose, illusions, and, in the desolate
clarity of Chekhov's fourth acts, we know only that time cannot
be slowed or reversed, that human nature cannot be reformed or

revitalised, that to understand a predicament is not to get out of it. The plays refuse to guide or direct, and refuse more pointedly than the stories, simply because they have no narrator to recount and thus involuntarily interpret the situation. It is true that the doctors in Chekhov's plays sometimes seem to intercede with the audience for the characters, but they never take on the impersonal objectivity of an author-narrator. The drama naturally brings out the relentless passage of time more than do the stories. Not only are the speeches saturated with references to time; our foreknowledge that the curtain will fall within two hours of the beginning heightens that sense of time irrevocably trickling away which is so essential to the quandaries of Chekhov's heroes and heroines. The plays seem more objective and more ruthless than the stories, but the two must be considered together, for they are differentiated only by the formal rules of story-telling and play-acting.

Chekhov's letters and a cursory reading of the plays and stories make it obvious that they share much raw material. Chekhov did not, in fact, himself consider his drama altogether apart from his stories. At one point he proposed to rewrite *Uncle Vanya* as a story (*povest'*), and at the first failure of *The Seagull*, his deepest regret was for the waste of so much material that could have been used in stories. The situations of moral or financial bankruptcy, the characters that face them, the doctor, the professor, the predatory and the passive females, the reckless gentry, the crude new man, the dreamers and superfluous men are to be found in the stories contemporaneous with each play. Thus *The Cherry Orchard* embodies symbols from *Panpipes* of 1887 and a situation from *A Visit to Friends* of 1898 and, in Trofimov, reworks a character and ideas to be found in *The Bride* of 1903. Each successive play gathers up material accumulated by the stories : this, in part, explains the increased complexity of Chekhov's plays. *Ivanov* of 1888–9 takes up the 'radiant personality' struck by moral paraplegia that we see in *On the Road*; *Uncle Vanya* can be linked not just with the professor of *A Dreary Story*, but with the clash of strong and weak that we find in *The Duel* as well as in the speeches of Astrov and Vanya; *The Seagull* brings the figure of the artist (Trigorin) into Chekhov's drama at the same time as *The House with the Mezzanine* introduces the narrator-painter into his stories. The female atavism that is so destructive in *The Seagull* and *Three Sisters* is to be found at the same time in *Ariadna*.

Yet arguments that hardly ever arise over the stories persist over the interpretation of the plays. Reading Chekhov's stories, one can be content with an emotion, say, of pity, such as dominates *Panpipes,* or of wry scepticism towards the future, with which, for example, *The Duel* or *The Bride* concludes. But the reader of the plays is conditioned by dramatic convention to expect a triumph of good over evil, or, at the very least, a transformation of those characters who survive the action and of their world by what has happened during four acts. Hence, against all the evidence of Chekhov as a story-teller, people look for Messianism in such speeches as Sonya's 'we will rest' (in *Uncle Vanya*) or Anya's 'we will rest' (in *The Cherry Orchard*), or in the last shreds of the three sisters' dreams; they ignore the ironic cacophony of Telegin's guitar, of the intimidated Jewish orchestra, or of the departing regiment, which are as full a part of the action as the characters' speeches.

The plays, in fact, tell us what the stories tell us : that good lies in those characters whom the action bypasses. Just as we find it in Doctor Samoylenko and the deacon of *The Duel,* so we find it in the absurd old uncle (Shabel'sky) of *Ivanov,* in the old nurse in *Uncle Vanya* or *Three Sisters,* or in Firs in *The Cherry Orchard.* Tragedy is not to be found in the heroes and heroines so much as outside them, in nature, destroyed by their ignorance and self-centredness. The forests which burn in *The Wood-demon,* or which shrink in Astrov's maps; the late buds of the birches in *Three Sisters*; the doomed cherry trees of *The Cherry Orchard* are not backgrounds, but thematic elements in the plays as central as the steppe in *Panpipes* or *Steppe,* the mountains and sea in *The Duel* and *Gusev,* the rain and millpool in *On Love,* or the trees that are battered in the gale in *The Bride.* Nature claims our attention and compassion as much as, if not more than, the characters.

The later plays, like the later stories, remind us how fugitive life is and how futile a deceit, therefore, is philosophy. In the closed world of the stage there is less room than in story-telling for characters who act positively : the import of the stories is perhaps clearer because they deal with characters such as Gurov and Anna Sergeyevna, or Ol'ga in *Peasants,* or the bride and the bishop in the stories of those names, who clutch at straws when they believe that a love affair, or Christianity, or going out into the world, or meeting death will take them somewhere worth going to, to a higher reality; they thus act, even though the results of their action are imponderable. The plays are constructed to reach a climax in the third act and to show an aftermath in the fourth; they are necessarily built around characters who waste time, refuse to face the future, and spend their lyrical energy in regrets rather than anticipation. But, for all that, Chekhov's plays, like his stories, urge us to act on the moment and the impulse, before these are lost in deserts of wasted time.

Death and Transfiguration

Chekhov's last four years were a period of increasing debility and restlessness in the face of death. They were also the years of his love for and marriage with Ol'ga Knipper. His stories, above all *The Bishop* and *The Bride*, written with great difficulty, concentration and feeling, during 1901, 1902 and 1903, are saturated with a knowledge of death, and at the same time a more violent affirmation of life than ever before. They also amount to a distillation of Chekhov's entire *oeuvre*. Most of his energy, in 1900 and 1901, was used up in revising and rewriting what he had written for Suvorin and for *Severnyy Vestnik* in the later 1880s; something of the lyrical intensity and the polarity of physical joy and intellectual despair at nature and life is re-created in the last stories, transfigured by a new directness of style, rhythms alternately limpid, passionate and abrupt, the imagery unexpected, veering suddenly from static objects to vast impressions of mists, rain and light.

The time-relationship between Chekhov's life and work alters in these years. His work has little foundation in what was happening around him—except in death and illness. His marriage, his political dilemmas, his movements—from Yalta to Moscow and back again, to Europe, to the Urals, to the steppes—reflect an inner restlessness: they leave no mark on his work. Most memoirs of Chekhov date from his Yalta period: by far the most profound is Bunin's, to which the reader is referred.

Chekhov managed to endure the isolation and boredom of Yalta almost throughout 1900. The damp in November drove him to Moscow and thence to Rome, where snow forced him back to Yalta. In 1900 his relationship with Ol'ga Knipper became very close and in May 1901 he secretly married her. His attitude shows that he felt that marriage had come too late to change him, and that what he had still to write was, perhaps, more important. Most of the time Ol'ga was to work in Petersburg and Moscow, while he lay ill in Yalta. After the marriage, Chekhov wrote to his sister, promising that nothing would be changed in their domestic set-up, that he and Ol'ga could easily separate and were to be regarded as people economically independent of each other. As a marriage, it was a deep but turbulent relationship, stirred up by Chekhov's slow dying, by Ol'ga's two major illnesses, by endless separations, a vain search for a place that both Chekhov's mind and body could tolerate, a frustrated desire for a child and, last but not least, that habit of utter privacy and kindly irony which three fragmented years together could not possibly break down. Ol'ga Knipper could never understand or care for Chekhov as skilfully as did his sister, whom years of practice and a close similarity of temperament had made the person closest to him. Ol'ga found herself partly a link with life, partly an interpreter between dramatist and actors, partly a bridge to posterity, partly a nurse, partly a mistress—but not entirely a wife.

In 1901 Chekhov spent a month (his honeymoon) in the remote steppes near Ufa to try the fermented mare's-milk treatment, which was the only one that successfully held up his disease, but the area was so lifeless that, preferring to consider his mind rather than his body, he returned to Yalta. There Tolstoy had fallen ill and seemed likely to die. Chekhov's anxiety was such that the worry caused him a haemorrhage: one of his uncompleted works of 1902 (*The Letter*) opens with a paean of praise for Tolstoy[1] purely as a writer. For Chekhov now literature was dying: the new generation of both realists and decadents seemed only pathetic rhetoricians and charlatans. All winter and spring he stayed in Yalta, completing *The Bishop*. In summer 1902 he left for Moscow, sailed up the Kama to Perm'; later he stayed with Stanislavsky on the river Klyaz'ma, before being forced south again by his illness. One by one he severed his connections with the literary world. In August 1902 he resigned from the Academy—being an academician gave a writer certain valuable privileges of free speech—because the government had Gor'ky blackballed. Later he wrote to Diaghilev, who was the editor of *The World of Art*—at that time the vehicle for the new art, especially Symbolism and the new Christians—to denounce the intelligentsia for 'playing at religion'. In 1903 he was to turn down Diaghilev's offer of the editorship. For all but a month in 1903 Chekhov was confined to Yalta. Only when death was obviously

only a matter of weeks away did he leave for Moscow, whence he
was hastily sent to Badenweiler to die. Art here predicts life, for
Chekhov's last days, drinking tea and being massaged, follow the
pattern of *Arkhiyerey* (*The Bishop*).

The most remarkable feature of *The Bishop* is that all sense of
futurity has left it. The confusion and unhappiness of the present
generate a vision of the past as something joyful, peaceful and good.
The question of the 'new beautiful life' has gone, and with it the
irony; as the suffragan bishop, the Most Reverend Pyotr, comes
closer to death the past ousts the present from his mind. Once he is
dead, there is nothing, not even a memory of him.

The Bishop, Chekhov wrote, was a subject that had been sitting
in his head for about fifteen years. In fact, it takes up themes that
are dealt with in stories like *On Easter Night* of 1886 : there is the
same parallel between the artist and the priest or monk, the same
association of nature and the church, of the seasons and the
Christian calendar. *The Bishop* also reverts to the earlier style in
that its underlying structure follows the course of a fatal disease.
The bishop's typhoid controls his thoughts as surely as illness controls the hero of *Typhus* or Ragin in *Ward No. 6*. The earlier style
is there in the contrast of ecclesiastical and colloquial languages,
in the association of moonlight with death.

In many ways *The Bishop* reminds one of Turgenev's senilia, his
poems in prose : it lingers over the goodness of life in the face of
death. But none of Turgenev's poems have anything like the plethora
of images of life and death, the bundling of time past and
present, of mind and matter, that *The Bishop* exhibits. The first of
the four brief sections opens with the Palm Sunday service, which
the bishop is taking. From the start we have the dual meaning of
strast', passion and suffering, to link the coming of Easter and spring
with his agony. The close heat—*dushno, zharko*—gives the story
the same sultry oppression that opens *Uncle Vanya* and *The Bride*.
The first symptoms of as yet unsuspected illness are revealed in the
bishop's hallucination : the faces of the congregation merge into a
'mist, a sea'. Images of light, flaring and dying away, also prepare
us for what is to happen. Suddenly a premonition of death sweeps
through the church : bishop and congregation are crying. The Russian orthodox reader will recall that Palm Sunday (in Russia,
Willow Sunday) has overtones of weeping : it is also the day of
Lazarus's resurrection, a sort of epiphany to the passion of Easter.

The bishop then goes home to his suite at the monastery. As he passes the garden in the moonlight, there is the typical Chekhovian intuition of a mystery. Like the cemetery in *Ionych*, the moonlit walls of the monastery and the black shadows arouse a lyrical response, as if they are part of a life parallel to man's. In this context, the moon suggests the garden of Gethsemane, as it does in *Ward No. 6*. (Chekhov had devoted considerable time to research on the painter Levitan's behalf into whether the moon had shone in the garden of Gethsemane.) Bit by bit, the ugly real world intrudes on the bishop. In contrast to the deadly moonlight, the local millionaire's house is flickering with newly installed electricity. Then there is a smell of pine—one of the sadly evocative images of decay in Chekhov's work, and the bright reflected light of the monastery. In the monastery there is a constant counterpoint of language as rich as that of Chekhov's plays: the bishop's thoughts and the monks' language interact with the words of his mother who has brought one of her granddaughters to see him. The bishop's mother is too awed by his grandeur to talk to him freely, and her respectful phrases contrast with the simplicity of the child and with the mother's own gossip with the monk in the adjacent room. The disparity is brought out from the start with the words 'your reverence', 'your *mamasha*' and immediately curtails the joy the bishop feels.

All these incongruities of greatness and intimacy, of past and present, of life outside and life inside the monastery have to be reconciled before the bishop can die. Without once resorting to the drama of a moral crisis, Chekhov manages to bring out in less than five thousand words a whole chaos of sensations and memories, and to resolve their discord into a harmonious set of images. First of all, as the disease takes hold of the bishop's limbs and neck, childhood memories come flooding back. The alien quality of his boyhood is stressed by his change of name: the Most Reverend Pyotr was once Pavlusha; his surroundings were once woods and fields. His delirium is interrupted by the monk Sisoy, whose entry closes this and the next section. Sisoy with his greenish beard and his massaging of the bishop as though he were already a corpse is like an incarnation of death, whose presence is stressed by the references to the clock and the calling of the cricket.

The second section is full of omens: the little girl, Katya, breaks a glass, cheerfully talks about her brother, a medical student ('Nikolasha cuts up corpses'), spills water and points out Sisoy's green beard. The reminders of spring come again with the noise of the rooks and starlings. Now the bishop recalls more of his life : his theological career, his long exile abroad and the homesickness from which he suffered seem to hint at a longing to die. The language around him seems alien to his thoughts : his mother keeps using the polite form *vy*; through the wall he hears Sisoy grumbling his nonsense about the Japanese and Montenegrans being the same people, and then everything again fades into mist before Sisoy comes to massage his body.

The discontent with reality reaches its climax in the third section. The bishop blames his mood on the insipid fish he has eaten, and this repellent image remains as we see his irritation with his petitioners, his total incomprehension of the shouting millionaire who comes to talk to him. The more he is irritated by his contact with the world, the more mysterious it becomes to him. The phrases of Chekhov's last pieces, 'it seemed to him', 'in all probability', become more frequent as he tries to pin life down. The past and the church's imagery encroach more and more : phrases of Church Slavonic blot out Russian, as death draws near 'like the bridegroom in the night'. All that lies between the bishop and euphoria is a sense of something missing. As the story finishes, it dawns on us that this missing something is the estrangement between him and his humble relatives and, as he grows thinner and weaker, so his awe diminishes and his mother can see in him the child and not the ecclesiastic.

The fourth section is a death-scene very like the death of Turgenev's Bazarov : the same delirium, the same feeling that a philosophical question has been answered, the same bridge between a grief-stricken old woman and her dying superhuman son. On the eve of Easter, after the washing of feet, the bishop collapses. The weaker he is, the more triumphant is nature : we have larks in a 'bottomless, unfathomable blue sky'. But the detail is Tolstoyan, rather than Turgenevian. The symptoms of typhoid emerge : ringing in the ears, then rumbling in the belly, and finally haemorrhage from the bowels. But before he can die, the bishop has to take his last service. There is one ironic touch in the monk's reminder to him : 'The horses are ready, it's time for the passions of the Lord.' In the four-hour service, lights again flare up and die and the congregation is blurred into a sea.

Sisoy's final massage is with vodka and vinegar[2] instead of lard, to suggest the shrinking of the bishop's corporeal existence. The thinner he becomes as he bleeds to death, the happier he is, until he dies dreaming of walking across sun-lit fields. The ecstasy is as prolonged as his ordeal at the church : the same double adjective, *dlinnyy-dlinnyy*, 'extra long' is applied to it. But at the moment of death the bishop's world and the outside world are completely separate. Gone is all the intimacy. His death is announced in the archiac formula common to princes and bishops, 'He has bid you live long.' The next day the outside world comes to life. Not just the church bells, but the drunken voices and the harmonica declare the beginning of Easter. Like Turgenev's old mother losing Bazarov, the bishop's mother loses even the certainty that she had a famous son. Ordinary life goes on uncaring; the memory of the bishop is dead.

The personal note is only too clear in *The Bishop*; it echoes Chekhov's conviction that his fame would barely survive his physical life and it also expresses that desire, common to him and to the professor of *A Dreary Story*, to be loved for himself, not for his fame. The episodes of homesickness, the battle in the mother between awe and love, the impatience with the trivia of the bishop's life are as much part of the author as the poetry of death and the symmetry between nature and Christ resurrected and man perishing. Chekhov attached a great deal of importance to the story. Like all his four last works, it was written for the Petersburg monthly, *Zhurnal dlya Vsekh* (*Everybody's Magazine*); Chekhov told Mirolyubov, the editor, that if the censor touched a single word of it, it was not to be printed.

An analysis of the tone and rhythms of *The Bishop* would produce graphs of symmetry that can in themselves prove nothing. It has cadences that are sometimes cut short to show the tired, critical intelligence of the bishop, sometimes drawn out with astonishing parentheses to follow his delirium's path into the past. Its imagery reveals in the course of the story an underlying unity. The monastery doors that the bishop has to pass through turn suddenly into a Tolstoyan symbol of death. The bishop asks about the doors he can hear being opened and closed, only to be told by the child that it is the rumbling in his belly. There is a Newtonian law of action and reaction in everything. The uniqueness of the bishop at his moment of death leads to the generalisation in the penultimate paragraph : 'Everything is well, just as it was last year and will, in all probability, be next year.' The sunlight of the bishop's dream and the next Easter morning lead to the last image of the old mother bringing the cows back from pasture in the evening. Verbal rhythm plays a greater part in this prose poem than anywhere else in Chekhov's work, as, for example, in the sudden, youthful stride in the sentence that describes the bishop's last delusion of himself as a young man walking briskly through the fields, or the brief exclamations 'How good!', 'What's the time?' that punctuate the flow of reflection and liturgy.

The Bishop is, in fact, a farewell to the Russian language as Chekhov knew it. Virtually every resource, from the most colloquial expressions to Sisoy's dialect, to the language of a medical textbook, to that of a prose-poem and the Slavonic of the orthodox church, is exploited. Nothing so rich in rhythm and in sound pattern—for here too assonance and internal rhyming contribute to the rhythm —is to be found before or after, in Turgenev or Andrey Bely, comparable with *The Bishop*. Even Bunin's stories fail to equal it, and Russian prose could only step forward when it had a new vocabulary and syntax, when non-Russians, Jews from Odessa, such as Babel, could remould it. The language of every Russian prose-writer of the nineteenth century, from the Gogol' of the exhortations to youth, 'Why does it, that for ever departed, irrevocable time, why does it seem brighter, more festive and richer than it really was?' to the Turgenevian inversions and the Tolstoyan brutality of the rumbling belly, is merged with the best of Chekhov's language, in its stage-direction terseness, in its painful honesty of pairs and triads of adjectives, its parenthetic 'it now seemed', 'it must have been', and in its sensuous lyricism.

In the archives of Mirolyubov, editor of *Zhurnal dlya Vsekh* (how we do not know) were two rough copies of unfinished stories by Chekhov. One, *Rasstroystvo kompensatsii* (*Ruin of the Compensation*), was published after his death, in 1905; the other, *Pis'mo* (*The Letter*), was intended for publication in 1906, when the authorities closed down the journal. Though both drafts end after the first episode or two, they are important links with *The Bishop*. The first has death as its centre, though the meaning of the title is a mystery; the second has the clerical background of *The Bishop* and, complete in itself, takes up the discussion on the permanence of art where Chekhov's professor of medicine left it in *A Dreary Story* in 1889, and imbues it with a new desperation.

Ruin of the Compensation in fact makes new departures. Like *The Bride*, it concerns a man dying of tuberculosis, whose impending death awakens the living to the urgency of life, but, unlike *The Bride*, it appears to have a multiple viewpoint : we see reality through the eyes of two people—in the first chapter the dying man's brother-in-law, Yanshin, in the second chapter his sister, Vera. There is considerable evidence of Chekhov's having just reread his work of 1895 and 1896 : the imagery of the alley of pines with their resinous smell and slippery needles recalls *The House with the Mezzanine*, as well as *The Bishop*, and the dying man's wife, Vera, has plans to take her husband to the Mediterranean to die, so that she can meet her lover there in freedom, just like the evil 'spouse' of *His Wife* of 1895.

The dying man, Mikhail, is disagreeable in his self-pity and envy of the living. Yanshin and Vera stand by during the service held in his house. Both come to life with hatred and guilt. The yellow of the furniture matches the yellow of the dying man's face : shaven and swollen, it is already dead. The garden too, with its heliotrope that so sickened Trigorin in *The Seagull* ('a widow's colour', he says to Nina), shows death permeating even the possessions of the man. Yanshin, like the literature teacher of 1895, can only wish to 'run, run, run'. Outside, as in *The Bishop*, the singing in the fields and the ringing of church bells show life that surges with a peace and grace that contrasts with the grudging, ebbing strength of Mikhail. Yanshin finds life by going to the railway station, letting his thoughts rest on all the vulgarity of the regular visitors he sees getting off the train. He is a man who up to now has not existed, except in other people, such as his brother-in-law : only now, with his brother-in-law dying and his wife pregnant, is he beginning to find freedom, to get out of the 'hopeless quagmire' of his past. Disagreeable though he is, at least in this one chapter, he seems on the verge of the same liberation as that of Gurov in *The Lady with the Little Dog*. The imagery of 'eggshell', of being an 'oyster' suggests the lines Chekhov might have been working on; the phrases such as 'in all probability', that mark Chekhov's late subjectivity are in fact a promise of at least an attempt to find freedom.

The second chapter takes us back to Vera at the bedside, with a letter burning through her pocket : almost the entire chapter is composed of this love-letter, the most passionate in Chekhov's work, a plea from her lover to hurry, ending in a threat to come to see her. He hates the duality between his shy mistress and her pretence of cold loyalty to her husband, between the *ty* and *vy* in her nature, and is determined, as is the bishop with his mother, to break down the barrier of convention. But there the story ends : the part of the dying Mikhail, the parallels between the rebellious brother and sister, the role of Yanshin's wife can only be guessed at. The merit of the work can be gauged by the impossibility of imagining how to carry it on.

The Letter is less tantalising. Surnames link it with other work. The addressee is Maria Volchaninova, which suggests that *The House with the Mezzanine* is somewhere in Chekhov's mind. The surname Zelenin is casually mentioned, and this was the title of a fragment *U Zeleninykh (At the Zelenins)* of the mid-1890s, also in letter form. The writer of the letter, Ignatiy Bashtanov, is by nature and family a cleric. His father is a priest, now dying; one brother is a crazed monk, and he himself has deserted religion for literature, determined to find in it as deep a significance and as sure a foundation for life. The letter opens with impassioned praise for a book of sheer power : the coincidence of Ignatiy's phrases with phrases attributed to Chekhov makes it almost certain that this is a tribute to Tolstoy's style, in which the apparent repetitiveness and clumsiness are in fact signs of strength. Ignatiy draws from this the inference that nature and art have a parallel importance, that what man creates in inspiration is of the same order as God's creation. The theory turns into a debate. Ignatiy then cites the opinions of his friend Doctor Travnikov, who maintains that literature offers nothing but entertainment, something between lies and truth. Reading *Faust*, he is too carried away by Gretchen to remember that she is a murderess. Like the professor of *A Dreary Story*, whose scepticism Travnikov shares, he reads French novels, especially those of Maupassant, because they are free from any illusions about art. Ignatiy reacts to this disparaging view of art as a 'hereditary sin' with a violent illustration of Chekhov's own arguments. He compares great art to lightning : 'Lightning explains nothing; it forces us to explain it and this is what makes it hold our attention.'

These are arguments that Chekhov brought up in his letters when he tried to say what he found so repulsive in Tolstoy's polemic on art. To deny art was, for Chekhov, as idiotic as to deny food or medicine. They were all human needs. If art made life worth living, riveted the attention, shocked like lightning, then we should not expect it to solve the problems of how to live, or of the after-life. In Ignatiy's memorable phrase, to reject literature because it solves no philosophical problems is like rejecting wine 'because wine doesn't remove stains'. This affirmation of an aesthetic principle is part and parcel of the affirmation of personal morality in *The Lady with the Little Dog*, or of life in the bishop's dying dream. It makes *The Letter*, though a fragment, indispensable to a full understanding of the position at which Chekhov had arrived: living in the moment; rejecting immortality, prime movers and ultimate purpose; not sacrificing the past and the present for a problematical future.

Nevesta (The Bride) is the most affirmative of Chekhov's works. It is not—what some critics would have liked it to be—a prediction of the revolution or a tract on women's liberation, but a picture of a girl suddenly seizing on life at the instance of her dying friend. It does not matter that the dying man's speeches are as false as Trofimov's, that his beautiful vision of the future is at odds with his shabby present, or that his urgings are as much a routine as the philistine's platitudes. He 'has turned someone's life upside down' and left the future open, not closed.

Much of *The Bride* shows that it was composed together with *The Cherry Orchard*, in 1903. The dying Sasha's denunciation of the kitchens, the filthy servants' quarters and the wicked ignorance of their employers, in the rough draft of *The Bride*, uses the same material as Trofimov's speeches to Anya on the squalid history of the cherry orchard's owners. The town which Sasha urges Nadya to abandon for the wide world of the university and Petersburg is as dead and dishonest as the town of S. in *Ionych*, and as sleepless and restless as the northern town of *Three Sisters*.

The Bride[3] is a less lyrical work than *The Bishop* and its atmosphere is far less intense. It begins in May, at night, in the garden of Nadya's household. She is avoiding her family and fiancé, but is as yet not strong enough to rebel. The family friend, Sasha, pesters her to the point of annoyance: her fiancé inspires only awkwardness. But after a catastrophic, half-comic series of episodes she is ready to follow Sasha's advice. First of all, she has to give up her illusion that her mother is an extraordinary woman. Gradually she sees that her mother's pretensions are an intellectual cover for misery, that she is helplessly dependent on the benevolent despot of a grandmother who runs the household. Then her fiancé, Andrey, who looks like an artist but talks like a fool, appears in his true colours. She sees the sycophantic roguery of Andrey's father—the priest,

Father Andrey—in his behaviour, and when she is taken to look
at the house they are to live in after their marriage, she is stupe-
fied by the vulgarity of the decorations : a picture of a nude with
a vase, a photograph of Father Andrey in full regalia. Much of
the material is taken from *Three Sisters*. This Andrey, too, plays
the violin to avoid talking, and the horrid bourgeois fortress of fur-
nishings echoes the spirit of Andrey's Natasha in *Three Sisters*.
Then, as in *Uncle Vanya*, a stormy night makes sleep impossible. In
the morning, the apple trees of the orchard are all blown down—
a symbol of the break-up of the old life—and Nadya flees to Petersburg, on the pretext of seeing Sasha off at the station.

Like the plays, *The Bride* has an aftermath, an Act 4 after a year
or two have passed. Nadya makes her peace with her family : en
route she sees Sasha and in his illness and his endless talk about
'turning people's lives upside down' she now sees only pathetic
clichés. Her family is even more the prisoner of its bourgeois world :
its members dare not go out on the street in case they meet Andrey.
As soon as news of Sasha's death reaches her, she uses it as an
excuse to leave.

Sasha's visions of the future are even more ridiculous than Trofimov's, so that not even the most hopeful reader can believe in them.
He dreams of a world after the town has been swallowed up, of
'beautiful fountains and extraordinary people', in which the mob
will have become extinct and goodness and truth reign undis-
turbed. It is not the dream that awakens Nadya, but the persistent
protest, which combines with her own against the 'iron hoop' of her
fiancé's arm round her waist. The dying man has stimulated life
in her, just as the bishop seems to create the bustle of spring with
his suffering, or Mikhail Bondarev's resentful departure goads Yanshin into bursting through his spiritual 'eggshell'. It is a message
of vicarious life, but life none the less.

In *The Bride* the contrast of life and death, of fresh and stale, is
brought out in the old neglected garden that batters against the
shutters of the house. The house is an endless bustle of servants preparing food. They eat and eat : the marinaded cherries, of which
Firs reminisces in *The Cherry Orchard*, and fat roast turkey contribute to the smells that pervade the house. The outside world can
only enter through howling stoves and banging shutters. All through
the story the garden is alive, constantly changing, like nature in
The Bishop. The lilacs in May, the sleepy rooks, the dew, all con-

trast with the staleness inside. As the short northern summer ends, the autumn spattering rain urges Nadya to break free. Her return the following May again contrasts the feeling of spring with the grey fence (as in *The Lady with the Little Dog*) that confines the household. Her pacing in the garden marks her as a free person : her mother and grandmother stay inside with the dust and flies, and the last time she sees Sasha before he goes to try the fermented-milk treatment is in a sordid Moscow office, full of dead flies and cigarette ends.

Sasha, whose questions, complaints and teasing have driven Nadya out of her mother's pattern into a 'new life', 'still vague, full of secrets', which can lure her on even if it is eventually to deceive her, has achieved through her an immortality not unlike the immortality of the writer. He has given her nothing but has taken away something that held her back : 'All previous things had been ripped from her and disappeared, as if they had been burnt up and the ash scattered on the wind.'

There is some self-caricature in Chekhov's portrait of Sasha. Like his creator, he is a man to whom love and friendship do not come easily, a man full of vitality who must stagnate in the face of death, a man who can help others only by showing them the bare truth that appears when he has broken up the layers of falsehood. Shabby, pathetic, unappealing, he overcomes the provincial atmosphere that threatens to choke the bride, simply by destroying her illusions. He preaches no philosophy, imposes no rules, and neither violates nor restricts his disciple's personality. What Sasha does to the bride is analogous to what Chekhov did to his readers and to Russian literature. He is one of the first to stop posing questions that will fit his answers. He promises nothing, using art only to remove the cataract of convention and ideologies that clouds our vision. Like the bride, the reader moves on, knowing that the future may hold neither solutions nor peace, but that standing still is certain degeneration.

To bring tablets down from Mount Sinai is a task far easier than to convince the waiting multitude that there are no tablets and that they must find their own way to the promised land. Chekhov's art evolved in a direction diametrically opposite to that of, say, the creative development of Tolstoy or Dostoyevsky. Instead of building up an ethical, aesthetic and religious system as a framework within which to write fiction, Chekhov broke down the extraneous structures of thought on which his characters and scenes might so easily have been superimposed. It was, as we have seen, an uneven and difficult process of learning to discuss ideas without philosophy and to portray human beings without anthropology.

The richer and subtler Chekhov's language becomes, the simpler and more direct is his outlook. In 1887, for example, the Tolstoyan philosophy latent in many stories goes with the methodical and relatively crude narrative style of Tolstoyan analysis of character, mood and speech. With each year, experience undermines philosophy : one by one, Tolstoyan morality, the 'radiant personality', the superman, the view of society as a system, are all dispensed with. Chekhov grows more reluctant to judge his characters, and his irony allows them more leeway, just as his language becomes more and more subjective. In the late work, from about 1896, we see the world through the eye, the mind and the words of the main characters, with all the inadequacies and complexities of that eye and mind. The sea and mountains in *The Lady with the Little Dog* are glimpsed only momentarily through Gurov and Anna, but they impress us with the unknowable and eternal otherness of nature, even more than the sea and mountains described so much more objectively in *The Duel* seven years earlier.

Nature, in Chekhov's work, gradually loses its formal position : it no longer sets the scene or concludes the action, but it irrupts more and more, until in the swaying cherry trees of *The Cherry Orchard* or the windblown garden of *The Bride* it precipitates the action, prompting the heroes' flight. A doctor who had been a classmate of Chekhov in Taganrog once irritated him by writing to him of 'anthropocentrism' and 'pantheism' in his work. But he had a point. There is a moment in Chekhov's work, culminating perhaps in *Ward No. 6*, of 'anthropocentrism' : that is, the universe revolves around the question of what man is and where he is going. Up to this point, the 'pantheist' spirit of *Steppe* weakens; after it, a pantheistic sense of a spirit in nature, deeper and more god-like than the aspirations of man, becomes stronger and stronger. The last play, *The Cherry Orchard*, and the last completed story, *The Bride*, both reduce the philosopher, Trofimov or Sasha, to a half-pathetic, half-comic figure. Trofimov only teaches Anya to throw away the keys of the household (should she ever have them); Sasha teaches the bride to see that her fiancé is a sycophant and her town a hell-hole. It is nature that moves them to act and run : the voices in the cherry trees in the moonlight, the crashing of the apple trees in the garden. Chekhov evolves as an artist by withdrawing as a philosopher. He takes away the lies that are outside us and leaves us with the truth that is in us.

Notes

Where full bibliographical references are not here given, see Select Bibliography.

Chapter 2 *The Moscow Weeklies*

1 See Aleksandr Chekhov, *Pervyy pasport Antona Pavlovicha Chekhova*, Russkoye Bogatstvo, 1911, No. 3.
2 The best of Mikhail's work is to be found in selections such as *Svirel'* (*Panpipes*), Moscow, 1969. His titles, his themes and his compassionate, meticulous observation give his writing a close, if watery, resemblance to Chekhov's style of the late 1890s.
3 See Semanova, *Teatral'nyye vpechatleniya Chekhov-gimnazista* for a complete catalogue of all the plays and operas that Chekhov might have watched in Taganrog.
4 In later life Chekhov still sang church music. See Potapenko's recollections, in *A. P. Chekhov v vospominaniyakh sovremennikov*, of the early 1890s at Melikhovo: 'He loved to make up an improvised household choir. They sang *troparia*, *kontakia*, *sticheiria* and Easter *heirmoi*.'
5 The stereotype Polish villain is one of the most persistent xenophobic elements in nineteenth-century Russian fiction. It is used by Dostoyevsky as well as by the early Chekhov. Only Tolstoy and the mature Chekhov stand out for their refusal to typecast Poles, Germans and Jews as intriguers, pedants and usurers.
6 Grokhol'sky is one of a number of surnames used in the very early work which Chekhov mentions in his last works, Kardamonov is another. It is one of the signs that the material of Chekhov's juvenilia is relevant to a study of his last pieces.

Chapter 3 *From Fragments to a Novel*

1 The *skazka* is a form of story identified with political satire through the work of Saltykov-Shchedrin. Chekhov's frequent use of the term as a subtitle places such early stories immediately in the category of a radical parable. But Saltykov-Shchedrin, himself a bureaucrat, was able to get away with satire far more virulent than that of any of his followers. The links between Shchedrin and Chekhov are dealt with in Berdnikov, *A. P. Chekhov*.

2 E.g. the opening of the leaves and the timing of dawn which betray the latitude of the town in *Three Sisters*, or the meteorological and botanical precision of *The Bride*.

3 A character's reaction to Turgenev remains, for Chekhov, an index of his philistinism or his sensitivity, whether it is derogatory as in *The Double-bass and the Flute* of 1884, or adulatory. Although, on rereading Turgenev in 1893 and 1894, Chekhov began to criticise him for his heroines, the influence grew all the stronger. See Bitsilli, *Werk und Stil*, chapter 2.

4 E.g. *The Literature Teacher* (1889–94) and *The Man in a Case* (1898), the latter an especially Gogolian treatment.

5 Trapping songbirds was one of Chekhov's boyhood pursuits; Aleksandr Chekhov remained a bird fancier all his life. The bird market is reflected in *My Life* of 1896, as well as as in the ornithological expertise of all Chekhov's nature descriptions. The Moscow bird market survives to this day on Sunday mornings, off Nizhegorodskaya Street.

6 Chekhov's class at Taganrog provided four doctors, three lawyers, an actor and two singers: he was kept in touch with their careers and, towards the end of his life, renewed contact with them. Undoubtedly they gave him the feel of a new generation, a new European professional middle class. Many of Chekhov's classmates were Jews—e.g. Konovitzer, the brothers Volkenshtein—for whom the law was one of the few possible careers.

7 Here are a few. 'Peace to your ashes, honest toiler' (February 1882) is to become the professor's ironic rejoinder in *A Dreary Story*. In *The Victor's Triumph* (February 1883), a *chinovnik* forces an old man to declaim, 'Die, you traitress', just as in *Ionych* (1898) Turkin makes the servant boy declaim, 'Die, wretched woman.' The *Order of St Anne* pun of 1895 first comes up in a collection of puns, *My Ranks and Titles* of September 1883. Lopakhin's phrase to the tramp, 'Every outrage has its proper limits', is used in *The Commercial Councillor's Daughter* of October 1883. Belikov, the schoolteacher in *The Man in a Case* of 1898, lovingly utters 'Anthropos!' as idiotically as the schoolboy's father in *The Coach* of February 1884. The Greek tag *gnothi seauton*, 'know thyself', so important to the hero of *A Dreary Story*, is to be found in *Self-deception* (*a fairytale*) of May 1884. The poem, *The Sinning Woman*, by A. K. Tolstoy, so inappropriately and yet apropos recited in Act 3 of *The Cherry Orchard*, is mentioned several times, for instance in *A Liberal Soul*, when *chinovniki* are searching in vain for something safe to recite in public.

8 Chekhov's father would read Leskov's *Enchanted Wanderer* aloud to his wife while Chekhov was trying to write in 1883.

9 *Thérèse Raquin*, especially in its dramatised version, appealed to Chekhov. He recommended the play to Suvorin in 1895. Zola's preface to the second edition of the novel uses terms strikingly similar to Chekhov's to rebut the attacks of critics who demanded a wider outlook; it should be compared to Chekhov's letters of 1886 to Maria Kiseleva.

Chapter 4 *Into Literature—The* Petersburg Newspaper

1 The Kiselevs apparently ran into financial difficulties at the end of the 1890s, and the ruin of their estates has been said to be the model for those in *A Visit to Friends* (1898) and *The Cherry Orchard.*

2 Chekhov's interest in the theory of medicine seemed to weaken him in practice. He was gullible—for instance he was to believe in a new cancer cure of marsh-marigold juice, he hated surgical decisions and he never inured himself to the smells and sights of illness. Whatever may be said in his favour, he was never a wholly professional doctor.

3 'I'm reading Darwin. What delight.' (2 March 1886).

4 The dream, thanks to Dickens's *Christmas Carol* and the 'death of little Nell', was a specifically Christmas genre of social indictment and sentiment in Chekhov's day. In his mature work dreams play a very limited role indeed, compared with their importance to Tolstoy and Dostoyevsky. The only important dream is the wintry nightmare, like *A Christmas Dream* of 1884, which Lyzhin has in *On Official Business* (1899).

5 On 21 January 1900 Chekhov wrote to Dr. Rossolimo, 'I can't really write for children, I've written for them once in ten years and I don't like or recognise so-called children's literature.'

Chapter 5 *New Times*

1 Dunya Efros remained friends with Maria Chekhov. She later married a Taganrog classmate of Chekhov's, Konovitzer, whom Chekhov used to call the 'twelve tribes of Israel'. The pattern of Chekhov's relationships with women was set by Efros: it is not unlike Astrov's drunken witticism in *Uncle Vanya,* 'Woman is first an acquaintance, then a mistress and only afterwards a friend.'

2 The first major critic to open fire was N. K. Mikhaylovsky, one of the best-loved and most mediocre of radical liberal pundits. His reactions to *Agaf'ya* show the reiterated demand for signposting in literature: 'What was the meeting of Agaf'ya and her husband like? Did he kill her or beat her? . . . In reading Mr. Chekhov's stories none of these utterly natural questions arises.'

3 The New Testament phrase of the camel passing through the eye of the needle recurs in Chekhov's work. In *Murder* (1895), when Chekhov again takes up themes of social wrongs, wealth and violence, the murderer Terekhov is tormented by this phrase. As in *The Nightmare,* the phrase is the first movement in his mind towards atonement.

4 Chekhov's titles, whether one considers them inadequate or ironical, always understate the theme and can be blamed for the misunderstanding. Using clichés such as *The Radiant Personality, On the Road, The Nightmare,* they suggest the very view of progress and protest that the stories themselves contradict.

5 Cf. Leskov's *Soboryane (The Cathedral Folk)* or the lyrical, religious episodes of *The Enchanted Wanderer* and *The Sealed Angel.*

Chapter 6 *The Steppe*

1 The moonlight imagery of *Steppe* is the beginning of a series of studies in Chekhov's work. It links his work with the moonlit scenes in Levitan's paintings; it also establishes the opposition of a dead but harmonious nocturnal world to a live, discordant diurnal world. Like other aspects of the steppe stories, the moonlight imagery anticipates the nocturnes of Chekhov's last works, e.g. the narrative framework of *The Man in a Case* and *Gooseberries,* or the night scenes in *Ionych* and *The Bride.*

2 On Dymov, Chekhov wrote to Grigorovich (9 February 1888): 'Natures like the troublemaker Dymov's are created by life not for schism, not for a tramp's career, not for settled life, but solely for revolution . . . There will be no revolution in Russia and Dymov will end either by taking to drink or behind bars. He's a superfluous man.' Thus Dymov once and for all is tied up with Chekhov's belief in the impossibility of revolution, a belief he expressed again late in life.

3 A proper analysis of prose rhythm requires a specialised monograph. A sample from Chapter 7 of *Steppe* will at least show that there is a rhythm: the long paragraphs dramatising the storm, which alternate with the short exclamations of Yegorushka and the peasants, have within them rhythm, assonance and alliteration developed far beyond the norm of prose. Take the onomatopoeic 'Nebo uzhe ne gremelo, ne grokhotalo, a izdavalo sukhiye, treskuchiye, pokhozhiye na tresk sukhogo dereva, zvuki' ('The sky no longer thundered or rumbled; it made dry, crackling sounds, like the crackling of dry timber'). There is the alliterative thunder of *gr* and *kh* consonants, and in the separation of three adjectives from the final noun *zvuki* (sounds), by the simile 'like the crackling of dry timber' we have a physical representation of the gap between lightning and thunder.

Another example is 'ne spesha, sploshnoy massoy: tochno takiye zhe lokhmot'ya davya drug druga' ('unhurried, in a solid mass: exactly similar fragments, crushing each other'), with the alliteration of *sp, t* and *d* to suggest the mass of storm-cloud. Yet Chekhov's prose remains prose: never do the rhythmic effects break up the basic narrative continuity, the A to B movement that distinguishes prose from poetry.

4 In the early 1890s important work went almost entirely to *Russkaya Mysl'*; lesser work went to the Moscow newspaper *Russkiye Vedomosti.* In 1898, Chekhov began to use Petersburg media again: the magazines *Niva* and *Nedelya.* His last stories of the 1900s went to *Zhurnal dlya Vsekh* of Petersburg. Money, importunity, good or bad printing, personal favour all motivated the changes.

Chapter 7 *Into the Impasse*

1 In 1886 Chekhov wrote over a hundred pieces, about 200,000 words; in 1887, 60 pieces, 150,000 words. The change is sudden in 1888, which is

the date that many critics think of as the beginning of 'serious' Chekhov. Discounting plays, in 1888 there were nine pieces (75,000 words) and in 1889, three stories (25,000 words). Chekhov's output was to fluctuate, but never again did he even approach the profligate rate of 1884 to 1887.

2   Vsevolod Mikhaylovich Garshin (1855–88) is known to the English reader only through a few items in anthologies of the world's short stories. Two of his best stories are *Four Days* and *The Red Flower*. Garshin's simple intensity, his concentration on the extreme suffering of a sensitive hero in an insensitive world, as well as his direct style, make him a narrow but grossly undervalued writer.

3   Whether Chekhov wanted to write a novel is another question. Both Suvorin and Grigorovich urged him to take the next step to greatness with an extended work. Like some modern critics—even J. B. Priestley—Chekhov's friends thought that the short story and the tale were responsible, because of their limited scope, for restricting Chekhov's philosophy to agnosticism and equivocation. For them, the novel had to be positive.

4   The division of heroes into Don Quixotes (active monomaniacs) and Hamlets (inactive introverts), or of admixtures of the two types, is a basic device of the Russian novel. See Turgenev's lecture of 1858, *Hamlet and Don Quixote*.

Chapter 8   *The Dramatic Hero*

1   He also wrote to Gor'ky in 1898, saying that *Uncle Vanya* was written 'a long, long time ago'. There is some internal evidence for the new material that distinguishes *Uncle Vanya* from *The Wood-demon* being added after the epidemics of 1892: Astrov complains of the stench and the typhoid in terms very like Chekhov's at Melikhovo.

2   Many of the 'new dramatists' disliked the subtitle 'tragedy'. Gerhart Hauptmann's early naturalist plays, in all of which death plays a major part, scrupulously avoid the word.

3   *Ivanov* was a play of its time, of European importance. It is followed three years later by Hauptmann's *Einsame Menschen* (a play which Chekhov knew) with a very similar hero. Johannes Vockerat, like Ivanov, is paralysed by his intellectual decay, falls out of love with his simple, good wife and is attracted to a strong-minded young Russian intellectual girl. Unable to bear the conflict and the sense of his own decay, he drowns himself. In Hauptmann the old morality still has something to say for itself, but the open-minded study of the weak hero is strikingly like Chekhov's. The question of Hauptmann's debt to Chekhov has hardly been opened, let alone closed.

4   When Suvorin came to stay with Chekhov at Sumy, the Lintvarevs would refuse to call at the house. They felt that Suvorin's reactionary role was a disgrace to Chekhov and an insult to all that they stood for. Suvorin, like Serebryakov, had also recently remarried.

5   The opening of Act 3 of *The Wood-demon* is the only real use of a Tchaikovskian motif in Chekhov's work, although there are references to Tchaikovsky's operas in several stories. The death of Zhorzh Voynitsky is a parody of the death of the noble Lensky in the opera *Yevgeny Onegin*. Chekhov responded more to Tchaikovsky's fame and Tchaikovsky's high regard for his stories: all the evidence suggests that Chekhov did not respond deeply to any music but church music. The romances that were played by guests at Melikhovo served more to keep the guests occupied than to affect Chekhov.

6   Like a number of passages in Chekhov's work in the late 1880s and early 1890s, Astrov's doubts about the future loosely paraphrase *Ecclesiastes*. 'There is no remembrance of former things: neither shall there be any remembrance of things that are to come with those that shall come after', (*Ecc.* I, 11) and Astrov's 'Those that are going to live in one or two hundred years' time and for whom we are clearing a way, will they salute our memory? Nanny, they won't.' To which the old nurse replies, 'People won't, but God will.'

Chapter 9   *The Trophies of Sakhalin*

1   Vukol Lavrov was to become Chekhov's intimate, and *Russkaya Mysl'* the journal in which he was most at home. As the chief rival of the *Severnyy Vestnik, Russkaya Mysl'* had no scruples in attacking its contributors; when Chekhov returned from Sakhalin, the eclipse of the *Severnyy Vestnik* led him naturally to seek peace with *Russkaya Mysl'*. Furthermore, *Russkaya Mysl'* was a Moscow magazine and Chekhov, who attached great importance to this, was able to check his proofs and supervise publication more easily. Whether his more radical sympathies or the trends of *Russkaya Mysl'* coincided or interacted is an insoluble 'chicken and egg' question of the 1890s.

2   Przhevalsky was the greatest explorer of his day in Asia and his adventures received the same attention in the Russian press as Livingstone's and Stanley's in the West. Przhevalsky was a modern explorer, quite without missionary aims, with the scientific meticulousness of Darwin and the brutal arrogance of a conquistador. Like Livingstone, he died on the shore of a remote lake, Issyk Kul in Kirghizia, but unlike Livingstone he insisted on being buried there.

3   Gusev is one of the nicknames that Chekhov used for Aleksandr. Likewise, Aleksandr's other nicknames are used for heroes of later stories, 'Little Profit' Misail Poloznev in *My Life* being one example. Even late in life, Chekhov's work teased and outbid his elder brother's.

4   This last phrase, 'kotoromu trudno podobrat' nazvanie', a surrogate adjective, a testimony to the failure of human language faced with nature, recurs in Chekhov's work. It is a sign that the omniscient narrator has receded from his stories, as well as a refusal to express the inexpressible.

Chapter 10 *Melikhovo*

1 There is of course a physical basis too. A man with chronic enteritis, haemorrhoids and so on is hardly likely to let his love-life develop freely.

2 The question of Turgenev's influence on Chekhov is as deep as that of Gogol's on Dostoyevsky. In both cases the influence was so strong that it had to be written out of the system. It is thematic, stylistic and structural: we see not only set scenes (especially Italian or death-bed scenes), but even slight touches, even the Turgenevian spelling 'lown-tennis', passed on from Turgenev to Chekhov. There is a full discussion of some aspects in Bitsilli's work. One might also argue that Turgenev's best-known play, *A Month in the Country* (which Chekhov detested), anticipates many of Chekhov's dramatic innovations: its action is inconclusive, except for the disbandment of the household; its characters form the same uncomfortably assorted group of prisoners; the trivia of everyday life obtrude on the action.

3 Critics, especially Bitsilli, make much of the fact that Chekhov had little at all and nothing very good to say on Dostoyevsky. But there are scattered remarks in Chekhov's letters and reported talk: enough to show that he thought Dostoyevsky embodied the defects of the Russian spirit— a tendency to see extreme black and white, for example—and that he was pretentious, but good. Dostoyevsky appears as an influence only in the Melikhovo period: the first chapter of *A Woman's Kingdom*, much of *An Anonymous Story* and *Ariadna* recall episodes of *Crime and Punishment*, *The Idiot* and *The Gambler* (Polina) respectively. It may be that the portrait of 'terrible, volcanic women' naturally led Chekhov to draw on Dostoyevsky's heroines.

Chapter 11 *1896*

1 N. the painter and Trigorin the writer are virtually the sole artists—at least, secular artists—who are heroes in Chekhov's work. This suggests that 1895–6 was a period in which Chekhov was most perplexed by the function of art in society and in private life.

2 Like many contrasting pairs and trios of girls, Lida and Misyus' embody some of the features that distinguished the eldest Lintvarev, Yelena the doctor, from the youngest, Natalia. Yelena had often quarrelled with Chekhov: her views were more decidedly reactionary and progressive and she refused to meet friends of Chekhov she considered radical. Natalia, apparently a much gentler character, often stayed with the Chekhovs at Melikhovo.

3 Misail is nevertheless in the direct line of Chekhov's clerics: natural goodness, passivity, even a certain slowness on the uptake, as well as harmony with nature, align him with Father Khristofor of *Steppe*. In Chekhov's work he is a bridge between the clerics of the 1880s and the Christian peasants of the late 1890s.

I

Chapter 12 *Peasants*

1 Voltaire's quietism penetrates Chekhov as deeply as it did Pushkin. Even the phrase 'Il faut cultiver notre jardin' enters his vocabulary (*Complete Works*, vol. 18, p. 340).

2 Some of the verbal material, especially the phrases of Yakov the victim, were supplied to Chekhov by his brother Mikhail who was then working as a legal official in the northern town of Uglich. Together with *Three Sisters*, *Murder* is one of Chekhov's few northern works.

Chapter 13 *Love*

1 It is ironic that the two writers who came closest to friendship with Chekhov are so ill-assorted. Bunin's loathing of Gor'ky is so strong that it taints even his reminiscence of Chekhov. But Bunin the fastidious gentleman and stylist and Gor'ky the self-made man and stylistic bungler reflected complementary sides in Chekhov's own nature.

2 The galoshes and umbrella were also typical of Menshikov, editor of *Nedelya*.

3 Chimsha-Gimalaysky, like Simeonov-Pishchik in *The Cherry Orchard*, are unique examples of grotesque Gogolian surnames in late Chekhov. One of the features that distinguish Chekhov's late from his early work, and one which he often altered in revising his early work, was the choice of surnames. In his mature work an enormous amount of trouble was taken to choose surnames that are probable, even colourless. Only in the plays, as Bunin points out, do we have surnames—Ranevskaya, Zarechnaya—that sound like inventions.

4 In Chekhov's early work, a few quotations from Pushkin, notably the lines from *The Conversation of the Bookseller with the Poet*, 'Glory is a bright patch / On the ragged shirt of the singer', recur with obsessive frequency. In late Chekhov, quotation again plays a part; now it is Nekrasov, of whom Chekhov said that 'he could be forgiven anything'. The love of Nekrasov, whose civic poetry expresses a burning sympathy with the suffering of the people, is an index of the movement in Chekhov's thought.

5 Lidia Avilova in her reminiscences claims that *On Love* is an allegory of Chekhov's love for her and his refusal to take advantage. True or not, Avilova certainly acted on the assumption and Chekhov was too kind to disabuse her.

6 *A Visit to Friends* and its relationship to *The Cherry Orchard* are touched on in the next chapter. Like most of the works Chekhov took a dislike to, for instance *Lights*, its material was recycled. The bankruptcy, the determined woman who cannot bear the thought of life without the estate, the abnegation of love, even the quadrille are all re-used, just as the love story and the setting of *Lights* were taken up again in *The Duel*.

7 See note 4 above.

Chapter 14   *Chekhov's Last Plays*

1 A full list of similarities between Trigorin and his creator would take too long: it is enough to point to the long speech of Trigorin's to Nina in which he tells her how he notes 'a cloud the shape of a grand piano'—a simile typical of Chekhov's cloud descriptions—or 'heliotrope—a widow's colour', which is used in the fragment of the 1900s, *Ruin of the Compensation*.

2 The duality of Trigorin's naturalism and Treplev's symbolism might have something to do with Chekhov's reading of Gerhart Hauptmann. In Hauptmann's work, *Lonely People* (*Einsame Menschen*, 1891) and *Hannele's Assumption* (*Hanneles Himmelfahrt*, 1893) demonstrate that the writer can be attracted both by the task of re-creating reality naturalistically and letting a flow of imagery suggest delirious, other-worldly images. The 'death and the maiden' romantic mood of *Hannele's Assumption* is echoed by Treplev's playlet. Chekhov's letters suggest he had read both works.

3 Here we see the side of Trigorin modelled on Potapenko. Potapenko was the prisoner of the women who loved him; like Trigorin, Potapenko was facile—he was capable of producing 30,000 words of fair copy in a day. It is said that, in the Moscow Arts Theatre, Chekhov insisted on having Trigorin dressed in trousers like Potapenko's.

4 Chekhov's connections with the Symbolist movement pose a very difficult question. That Chekhov uses symbols in his stories and plays does not make him a Symbolist, any more than his preoccupations with death and decay make him a decadent. It is a fact that many of Chekhov's associates—the *Severnyy Vestnik* contributors—and some of his best critics —Merezhkovsky—were to lead to the Symbolist movement and that the early Symbolists held him in high regard. Soviet criticism has not yet sufficiently overcome its hostility to the Symbolist movement to give it its due: there is a lot to be said for Andrey Bely's critique of *The Cherry Orchard* as a 'dance of masks' in the presence of horror, or for Meyerkhol'd's proposals for a non-realistic production of the play. But even if the reader concludes that the symbols of *Three Sisters* and *The Cherry Orchard* are sufficiently independent of the action to form a plane of their own, Chekhov still remains something far wider and more normal than any Symbolist. For one thing, he is suspicious of myth; he never rejects nature; he refuses to admit to mystic experience or to let language try to become purely musical—all prerequisites of Symbolist approaches to reality.

Chapter 15   *Death and Transfiguration*

1 In his last years Chekhov transferred to Tolstoy the affection he had felt for Suvorin. He paid no attention to the aspects of Tolstoy's thought that had once annoyed him, or to Tolstoy's violent contempt for his plays. He

concluded that Tolstoy must be worthy of love, because his daughters loved him, and the fondness that Chekhov felt for Tolstoy in 1902 is purely filial, not critical.

2   The imagery of vinegar is one of a number in *The Bishop* that make an almost blasphemous analogy of the bishop, who dies to be forgotten, with Christ who dies to be resurrected.

3   *The Bride* is hard to discuss, because it exists in five versions. It is the only work by Chekhov of which we have the rough copy, the fair copy, the first and second corrected proofs and the final printed text. Valuable though this is for a minute analysis of Chekhov's processes of revision, it can obscure the final picture of his work. We shall refer to the definitive text, but draw on some of the material of the rough draft. Generally speaking, this made Sasha a far more suspect character: he drinks, he irritates more than in the final draft. Nadya, the heroine, is more pathetic: she misses her dead father, who is virtually deleted from the final version. Nadya's fiancé, whom she deserts when she leaves the town on the eve of the wedding, becomes more threatening in each version. The final version also adds far more qualification to the text. When Nadya returns for a visit home and then gets a telegram announcing Sasha's death of tuberculosis, in the fair copy she packs her bags and leaves. In the definitive version, she leaves the town, 'as she supposed', forever. The more unknowable life is, the more Chekhov treasures it.

Select Bibliography

This is a list of texts and studies, many of which I have found useful and which readers may wish to follow up. Two full and not too dated bibliographies can be recommended: one in Petr M. Bicilli, *Anton Chekhov—Werk und Stil*, the other, of memoirs, in *Literaturnoye Nasledstvo vol. 68*.

Works by Chekhov

Polnoye sobraniye sochineniy i pisem v 20i tomakh, Moscow, 1944–1951. This is the only complete edition of Chekhov's works. It contains all his fiction and journalism and lacks only a few letters, mostly published in 1960 in *Literaturnoye Nasledstvo vol. 68* and *Voprosy Literatury*, 1960, No. 5. Its critical apparatus and appendices—a mine of information on Chekhov's addressees, early drafts, reading, friends, etc.—are Soviet scholarship at its most impressive. The faults of this edition, apart from its poor paper and printing, lie in its expurgations. Prudery has caused the editors to replace Chekhov's *zhid* (Jew) and his more Rabelaisian phrases with dots; politics led them to omit a passage in praise of British rule in Hong Kong.

Sobraniye sochineniy i pisem v 12i tomakh, Moscow, 1960–1963. More generally available and better produced than the 1944 edition, this one contains all that most readers require. It omits only a few minor comic stories, much of the early journalism, the unfinished fragments and about four-fifths of Chekhov's letters. Only scatological terms are censored; the critical apparatus is condensed but still valuable.

The Oxford Chekhov, trs. by Ronald Hingley, 1961–. This, the only collection of properly translated Chekhov in English, has two defects. One is expense; the other is a regrettable decision to omit all Chekhov stories before 1888. It has useful notes and some bibliographical details.

Polnoye sobraniye sochineniy i pisem v 30i tomakh, Moscow, 1975–1982. This edition should supersede all previous editions; it may be unexpurgated and genuinely complete.

Letters of Anton Chekhov, trs. and selected by A. Yarmolinsky, Cape, London, 1974. Perhaps the best choice of Chekhov's letters currently available in English.

Works about Chekhov

Berdnikov, *Chekhov. Ideynyye i tvorcheskiye iskaniya*, Moscow, 1961. A very thorough, if run-of-the-mill survey of Chekhov's themes, and a good guide to where to look, if not what to think.

Petr M. Bicilli, *Anton P. Chekhov—Das Werk und sein Stil*, Fink, Munich, 1966. Bicilli (Bitsilli) wrote in Bulgarian and Russian, but the German edition is the most accessible compendium of his work. Pedantry often goes hand in hand with inspiration, but Bitsilli is one of very few critics with something to say about Chekhov's style. This, and his excellent bibliography, makes him indispensable.

Ivan I. Bunin, *O Chekhove*, New York, 1955. Notes for a biography and a critical study, this is Bunin's last work. It comprises his own recollections, excerpts from Chekhov's letters, from critiques and reminiscences of Chekhov by other people, as well as Bunin's own acid comments. Perhaps Bunin understood Chekhov better than anyone. Bunin's snobbery, his dislike of Chekhov's plays and Chekhov's Marxist and Symbolist acquaintances, and his chivalrous deference to Avilova's love story do not invalidate the rest of the book.

Anton Čechov 1860–1960. Essays, edited by Eekman. The best essays, e.g. Nilsson's, are too short.

Chekhov i teatr, Moscow, 1961. A compendium of letters and memoirs, invaluable for producers of Chekhov's plays.

Chekhov v vospominaniyakh sovremennikov, Moscow, 1960. A collection of memoirs, the most valuable being by Potapenko, Nemirovich-Danchenko and Chekhov's brothers.

Chudakov, *Poetika Chekhova*, Leningrad, 1971. One of the very best Soviet studies. The author is too well-trained in statistics and hammers away too loudly at narrative standpoint, but he combines scientific objectivity with artistic sensibility into an original and brilliant study.

W. Gerhardie, *Anton Chekhov—Critical Study*, McDonald, London, new edition 1974. A 'Bloomsbury' Chekhov, but a well-informed one.

R. L. Jackson, *Chekhov—A Collection of Essays: 20th Century Views*, Prentice-Hall, Englewood Cliffs, New Jersey, 1967.

Literaturnoye Nasledstvo vol. 68, Moscow, 1960. Like many post-war volumes in this series, a medley of essays, unpublished letters, early drafts and bibliographical material.

Virginia Llewellyn-Smith, *Anton Chekhov and the Lady with the Little Dog*, Oxford University Press, 1974. A study of every known fact about Chekhov's love life which correlates them with his treatment of love in fiction. Scholarly, readable and speculative.

David Magarshack, *The Real Chekhov*, Allen & Unwin, London, 1966. A vitriolic but authoritative guide to Chekhov's later plays.

Harvey Pitcher, *The Chekhov Play*, Chatto & Windus, London, 1973. A fresh interpretation.

L. Shestov, *Anton Chekhov and Other Essays*, University of Michigan Press, Ann Arbor, 1966. Shestov, in many ways an existential philosopher, plausibly fits Chekhov into his own philosophical circle.

E. J. Simmons, *Chekhov—A Biography*, Cape, London, 1966 and Chicago, 1970. The best and fullest biography in any language, lacking only a few facts that came out in 1960. (See *Literaturnoye Nasledstvo* vol. 68.)

R. Styan, *Chekhov in Performance*, Cambridge University Press, 1971. Like Magarshack, if a little more pedestrian and exhaustive.

M. J. Valency, *The Breaking String*, Oxford, 1966. Another useful mixed bag of critical essays, this time on Chekhov's drama.

Index

(Italicised page numbers indicate where the main discussion is to be found)

1. Works by Anton Chekhov

2. *General Index*